Diasporic (Dis)locations

Diasporic (Dis)locations

Indo-Caribbean Women Writers
Negotiate the *Kala Pani*

Brinda Mehta

University of the West Indies Press
Jamaica • Barbados • Trinidad and Tobago

The University of the West Indies Press
1A Aqueduct Flats   Mona
Kingston 7   Jamaica
www.uwipress.com

08 07 06 05   5 4 3 2

CATALOGUING IN PUBLICATION DATA

Mehta, Brinda
Diasporic (dis)locations: Indo-Caribbean women negotiate the Kala Pani / Brinda Mehta.
p. cm.
Includes bibliographical references.

ISBN: 976-640-157-8

1. Caribbean literature (English) – Women authors – History and criticism. 2. Women, East
Indian – Trinidad and Tobago – Intellectual life. 3. Women, East Indian – Guyana – Intellectual
life. 4. Women authors, Hindi – Trinidad and Tobago – Criticism and interpretation. 5. Women
authors, Hindi – Guyana – Criticism and interpretation. 6. Women, East Indian – Trinidad and
Tobago – Cultural assimilation. 7. Women, East Indian – Guyana – Cultural assimilation. 8.
Women, East Indian – Trinidad and Tobago – Social life and customs. 9. Women, East Indian –
Guyana – Social life and customs. 10. Feminism and literature – Caribbean, English- speaking. I.
Title.

PR9205.05.M43 2004   820.9'9287

Cover photograph courtesy of Paria Publishing Company Limited, Trinidad and Tobago.

Book and cover design by Robert Harris.
Set in Centaur 11.5/14.5 x 24

Printed in the United States of America

The following articles have been reprinted with kind permission:

"Cultural Hegemony and the Stranglehold of Brahmanic Patriarchy in an Indo-Caribbean
    Context". *Journal of Commonwealth and Postcolonial Studies* 6, no. 1. Special issue on the Caribbean
    (Spring 1999): 125–52.
"The Colonial Curriculum and the Construction of 'Coolie-ness' in Lakshmi Persaud's *Sastra* and
    Butterfly in the Wind and Jan Shinebourne's *The Last English Plantation*". *Journal of Caribbean Literatures*
    3, no. 1. Special issue, "The Caribbean That Isn't" (2001): 111–28.
"Indo-Trinidadian Fiction: Female Identity and Creative Cooking." *Alif: A Journal of Comparative
    Poetics* 19. Special issue, "Gender and Knowledge: Contribution of Gender Perspectives to
    Intellectual Formations" (Spring 1999): 151–84.

In loving memory of my father,
Dr Jagadish Manubhai Mehta,
friend, teacher, healer

Contents

Acknowledgements

Diasporic (Dis)locations is the result of a collaborative effort. A generous grant from the American Council for Learned Societies in 1999 gave me a year's sabbatical leave to do research at the University of California in Berkeley and at the University of the West Indies in Trinidad. I am grateful to Rhoda Reddock for her gracious invitation to be a visiting scholar at the Centre for Gender and Development Studies at the University of the West Indies, St Augustine, Trinidad. I benefited greatly from my daily interactions with the Centre's faculty, staff and students.

Thanks to Shane Batchasingh for providing me with a home away from home at the Caribbean Lodge in Tunapuna.

My gratitude to Paget Henry remains eternal. He is a trusted friend and beautiful spirit. I thank him for his unconditional support of my work.

Thanks to Anthony Bogues and David Scott for introducing me to the University of the West Indies Press. It has been a pleasure to work with Linda Speth, Shivaun Hearne and the excellent editorial team.

Grant Farred, Renee Larrier, Myriam Chancy, Philippe Dilo and Arturo Dàvila-Sànchez are cherished friends, provocative intellectuals and creative souls who dare to think "from the heart".

This study would not have been possible without the feedback, encouragement, and presence of the Indo-Caribbean writers and scholars themselves. Sincere thanks to Pat Mohammed, Ramabai Espinet, Rosanne Kanhai, Leelawattee (Asha) Manoo-Rahming, Shani Mootoo, Michelle Mohabeer and Frank Birbalsingh.

This book is a gift of love to my mother, Kunda Mehta. I dedicate my work to the memory of my father, Dr Jagadish Mehta, who crossed the *kala pani* into irreversible exile in 2000.

Introduction: Mapping Indo-Caribbean Women's Writing

Remember one-third quota, coolie woman.
Was your blood spilled so I might reject my history —
forget tears among the paddy leaves.

— Mahadai Das, "They Came in Ships"

Indo-Caribbean women writers from Guyana and Trinidad have been subjected to a particular literary and cultural eclipsing by their black counterparts, by the diasporic hegemony of South Asian writers from North America and Britain, by Indian men and by women writers from India. Relegated to token recognition or complete obfuscation in contemporary anthologies and critical studies, these writers' enormous contribution to our understanding of the representation of Indian women in the Caribbean diaspora has been overlooked. Their work has explored the complexities of female subjectivity or self-representation in societies undergoing sociocultural and political transition as a result of indentureship, creolization and postcolonial realities such as immigration and neocolonial regimentation. Until recently, the richness and particularities of the experiences of these writers in the field of literature and literary studies were compromised by stereotypical representations of *the* Indo-Caribbean woman, representations that were narrated from a purely masculine or an Afrocentric point of view.

V. S. Naipaul's contempt for Indian women has been well documented in novels such as *A House for Mister Biswas*, while the Jamaican writer Olive Senior's short story "The Arrival of the Snake Woman" has revealed the thinly disguised disdain for the Indian presence in the Caribbean through her title character, Miss Coolie. *Coolie,* as a racialized epithet of inferiority and alterity to designate Indo-Caribbean populations, remains, even today, a highly loaded and pejorative term that denigrates all things Indian. Hence, the reduction of Indian womanhood to its coolie status in "The Arrival of the Snake Woman" is a further indication of the subaltern position that Indo-Caribbean women have generally occupied in Caribbean fiction. Consequently, Indo-Caribbean women have been subjected to a double literary displacement that has minimized their capacity to effectively engage in crucial issues of nation building, race, difference and identity. The paucity of adequate critical scholarship on these writers has added a further level of invisibility, so that it is quite acceptable to develop courses and organize area studies in Caribbean postmodernity and postcoloniality with minimal (if any) reference to the "Indian" experience of women writers.

Indian history in the Caribbean begins with the official abolition of slavery in 1838 when a second wave of "voluntary immigration" was mobilized from India in the form of the indentured labour trade. European sugar-plantation owners still needed a cheap and industrious agricultural workforce that was familiar with the vagaries of tropical plantation cultivation. The imperiousness of empire designated rural Indian farmers from the largely agricultural provinces of Bihar and Uttar Pradesh to be best suited for this enterprise, and impoverished farm workers were lured with promises of better financial prospects in the new lands. The contracted labour trade brought thousands of Indians to the French- and British-controlled sugar plantations in the Caribbean, South Africa, Fiji and the islands of the Indian Ocean. However, the majority found themselves transported to the alien Caribbean lands of Trinidad and Guyana.

Indians have made significant contributions to the national economy of these countries for over 150 years. In recent years, official documentation of the experiences of Indian labourers has been supplemented by the postcolonial writings of the educated elite, who have fictionalized the impact of trans-migration and indentureship on Indian life. Nevertheless, apart from the writings of a few "recognized" male authors such as Sam Selvon, V. S. Naipaul, Sasenarine Persaud, David Dabydeen and Rooplall Monar, who have themselves struggled to establish claims to Caribbean authorship, the work of the vast majority of women writers remains scattered and unavailable to a more international readership as a result of publication restrictions, lack of information or interest, cultural and social inhibitions and literary chauvinism.

This omission has revealed a serious pedagogical and scholarly flaw in the field of Caribbean studies by exposing a wide theoretical and literary gap in the analysis of Indian constructions of female identity in Guyana and Trinidad and its determining impact on issues of race, class, gender and nationhood. Notable exceptions to this gap have been the pioneering work of Caribbean scholars such as Rhoda Reddock, Patricia Mohammed, Ramabai Espinet, Verene Shepherd and Bridget Brereton in the fields of social science and cultural studies, together with the recent compilation of three anthologies that either have focused exclusively on the critical and creative writings of Indo-Caribbean women or have featured them prominently among their lists of contributors. The first such publication, *Creation Fire: A CAFRA Anthology of Caribbean Women's Poetry*, edited by the Indo-Trinidadian writer Ramabai Espinet, appeared in 1990. It includes seventeen submissions by Indo-Caribbean poets: eleven from Trinidad, two from Guyana and four from Suriname. The 1998 publication *They Came in Ships: An Anthology of Indo-Guyanese Prose and Poetry*, edited by Joel Benjamin, Ian McDonald, Lakshmi Kallicharan and Lloyd Searwar, comprises nine contributions by Indo-Guyanese women poets and novelists. Rosanne Kanhai's much-anticipated critical anthology *Matikor: The Politics of Identity for Indo-Caribbean Women* makes a crucial contribution to our understanding of the simultaneous affirmations and negations that have motivated the realities of Indo-Caribbean women at home and abroad as they struggle to overcome their exclusion on local, national and regional levels. Constituting a first-time engagement (in book form) with issues of creolization, exile, personal and communal agency, identity politics and race negotiations (especially with the dominant Afro Caribbean cultures), the *Matikor* essays inaugurate an important discursive Indo-Caribbean space wherein writers, scholars and artists alike negotiate their own terms of engagement with the problematics of a gendered interrogation of Indo-Caribbeanness by imaginatively and concretely extending the boundaries of self and community through individual acts of cultural and personal reclaiming.[1]

This book, *Diasporic (Dis)locations: Indo-Caribbean Women Writers Negotiate the Kala Pani*, situates itself within this recently created corpus of Indo-Caribbean women's writing to interrogate Indianness in woman-authored texts. These questions seek to explore how cultural traditions and female modes of opposition to patriarchal control were transplanted from India and rearticulated in the Indo-Caribbean diaspora, to determine whether the idea of cultural continuity is, in fact, a postcolonial reality or a myth. Do Indian women and their diasporic counterparts share common mythologies or histories of gendered dislocation, or has the process of migration led to a reorganization of social categories to undermine the stranglehold of patriarchal and imperialist spheres of influence? If so, has this reorganization created a more favourable feminine instance with greater access to social mobility and economic self-determination for women? How has this readjustment been articulated in the work of women writers in their quest for self-expression? These questions have been formulated within the specific rubric of a diasporic dislocation, or multiple dislocations, to reinforce the idea of a series of forced evictions or primary displacements from the ancestral land. This text also aims to show why the experiences of Indo-Caribbean women cannot be reduced to a unified Indian experience: these experiences are subject to class, religious, geographical, national and political determinants that lead to multivalent subjectivities and a certain dynamism of representation.

This plurality inscribes itself within the very history of the first women immigrants, whose personal examples of courage, determination, self-reliance and sexual independence provided their literary granddaughters with the necessary role models, worthy of emulation. The Indian women who braved the treacherous waters of the Atlantic — the *kala pani* — were dissatisfied with their continued state of marginalization and oppression in India. Anxious to convert the abjection of the pariah in their capacity as single women, dependent wives, divorcees or widows into the hope of new possibilities in foreign lands, these women demonstrated the necessary initiative to create an alternative lifestyle for themselves. This breaking of new ground through the search for new channels of self-affirmation characterizes much of the contemporary Indo-Caribbean female writing that articulates a particular *kala pani* discourse as a literary grid of (self-)knowledge and creation to negotiate otherness.

The *kala pani* is a discourse of rupture that initiates transgressive boundary crossings through creative (self-)assertions in literary production.[2] *Kala pani* innovations endorse the act of naming a culturally specific woman-centred Indo-Caribbean experience through the discursive claiming of literary and cultural space. The spatial transgressions by early immigrant women provided later generations of Indo-Caribbean women writers with the necessary point of motivation to initiate their own literary transgressions through orality and the written word as powerful media of self-representation. The *kala pani* supplied them with the necessary language and framework of reference to position Indo-Caribbean female subjectivity as an autonomous self-reflecting Caribbean experience by equating writing and pre-discursive modes of communication with a public declaration of one's identity and right to claim creative agency.

According to Hindu belief, the traversing of large expanses of water was associated with contamination and cultural defilement as it led to the dispersal of tradition, family, class and caste classifications and to the general loss of a "purified" Hindu essence. *Kala pani* crossings were initially identified with the expatriation of convicts, low castes and other "undesirable" elements of society from the mainland to neighbouring territories to rid society of any visible traces of social pollution; those who braved the *kala pani* were automatically compromising their Hinduness. Disenfranchised Hindu men, who were themselves subjected to discrimination by upper-class Hindu high-mindedness, comprised the majority of the indentured populations. However, Hindu women, who represented a significant minority, had the most to gain by crossing over to different lands because their confinement within Hindu patriarchal structures in India made them victims of abusive family and communal traditions. Enduring the hardships of the *kala pani* was a worthwhile risk to take because it offered the potential for renegotiations of gendered identity within the structural dissolutions of caste, class and religion that occurred during the transatlantic displacements. Hindu women therefore seized the opportunity to transcend their marginality within the nuclear Hindu family by embracing a more expansive Indian diasporic community. Female dislocation consequently initiated a cultural reversal of roles that paved the way for female enfranchisement.

Several studies have highlighted the economic and sexual initiative displayed by Indian women on the plantation estates during the early years of indentureship. Disproportionate sex ratios created possibilities for a certain sexual "freedom" among women, a freedom to dictate their own terms of availability or inaccessibility to multiple male partners. In addition, modest (though unequal) wages for estate labour provided a semblance of financial security in the face of the increasing male control and violence that arose as a calculated response in order to curtail female self-reliance in the public sphere.

However, by 1930 gender disparities had decreased and a sustained culture of male domination had reduced female participation to the private, domestic sphere of the family and family-related duties. Nesha Haniff states that this confinement within domesticated roles and expectations led to the cultural silencing and invisibility of these women in their capacity as dependent mothers and housewives expected to accept the unchallenged authority of the patriarch and his uncontested administration of Hindu cultural law and tradition. As Haniff argues,

> What is fascinating about this demographic transition is that it motivated the transition of the Indian woman's identity from individual to family, from the measurement of her work in her own right on the plantation, . . . to her work not being measured at all. Now, in the domestic sphere, her work had essentially not changed but it was her husband that was seen as the head of the family, and even if she worked equally with him her work had now become invisible. In part it was what real accomplished women were: housewives. It was a mark of success for a wife not to work. . . . The perception that Indian women, particularly in Guyana, were "only housewives" still prevails.[3]

Domesticity conversely located Indo-Caribbean women within the confines of a certain stereotypical conformity of expression. These stereotypes tended to gloss over the important contributions made by women in the home as the transmitters of a dynamic oral cultural heritage to future generations of children, as well as their economic skills to effectively manage household finances. Women's invisible and private power remained concealed within the walls of the home, thereby providing the necessary justification for and rationalization of social projections of essentialized negativity.

Indo-Caribbean women continue to be the objects of such one-sided readings, which have been reinforced by the revival of Hindu and Islamic religious fundamentalisms and their misogynist prescriptions for women, by racialized misconceptions on the part of other ethnic groups regarding Indian women's rural backwardness and subservience to cultural dictates, by their assumed sexual proclivity (based on stories from the period of indentureship) and by the overt chauvinism of Indian men, many of whom still believe in the philosophy that "biology is destiny". As Haniff claims, "While our politicians occupy themselves with race politics, gender does not seem to be an issue. The advocacy for males always takes precedence over females, more so over Indian females. Perhaps our advocates are not Indian men. Their chauvinism expresses itself in violence and in silence. They advocate for us only in the private sphere. Thus do Indian men keep us invisible and perpetuate certain stereotypes about us."[4]

The need to move beyond the confining limits of stereotypes has been a major preoccupation for Indo-Caribbean women writers. The *kala pani* discourse has provided them with an initial script to negotiate the simultaneous ambiguities, contradictions, affirmations and contestations involved in subjective representation. By naming a culturally identifiable woman-centred experience, in the process of self-discovery, the *kala pani* discourse uncovers a literature that emerges from a nexus that has been silenced, objectified and marginalized. Coming to writing represents an act of self-assertion and recovery, giving voice as it does to a previously unarticulated Caribbean reality in which Indo-Caribbean women have had to confront a triple dislocation within the power structures of history, culture and gender inequality by inhabiting the very "margins of marginality", as indicated by Rosanne Kanhai.[5] However, within the parameters of literature, Indian women have addressed the issues of marginality and invisibility by creating imaginative works out of historical and sociocultural obscurity.

Traditional scholarship on and in the Caribbean has tended to locate the region's specificity within a black/white-dominated historical paradigm that has stressed the primacy of European and African experiences in the Caribbean. This dialectical imbalance has obscured the subtle chiaroscuro of brownness that characterizes the Indo-Caribbean presence by promoting cultural invalidation and illegitimacy. Stressing the urgency of integrating Indianness within a broader articulation of Caribbean citizenship, Espinet asserts: "I think that the experience of Indo-Caribbean people should not remain within their relatively isolated community. It is part of the general historical movement of peoples into this archipelago and as such belongs to all, impacts on all and should be known by all. That this experience is not part of our common intellectual heritage, when Indo-Caribbean people make up 20% of the region's population, is ample evidence of the way this ethnic community has been marginalized."[6] The historical invisibility of Indians has been further complicated by the impact of creolization and its immediate association with black cultural traditions. Creoleness has, to some extent, furthered the divide between blackness and Indianness by often excluding the Hindu experience as a strategy of moving away from Indianness and indigenized Indo-Caribbean customs. This exclusion has, consciously or unconsciously, affirmed the superiority of Creole culture at the expense of the "primitiveness" of "coolie", or indentured, culture.

At the same time, creolization seductively offered supposedly lower-class Hindu and Christian women the possibility of resisting rigid patterns of socialization imposed on them by Hindu patriarchy in the name of cultural integrity. The creolization of Indian women was consequently seen as an infraction likened to the Hindu taboo of crossing the *kala pani*. Moreover, the

Hindu orthodoxy labelled the creolization of Indian women as a gendered assimilation to a dominant cultural model given the absence of a distinctive Indian component in the term's configuration. Reddock indicates that, in Trinidad, the word *Creole* originally referred to three groupings:

1. a local European minority who nevertheless controlled the entire economy;
2. people of African descent; and
3. the dominant Afro-Trinidadian indigenized culture, a most notable example being Creole food.[7]

Creolization thereby produced an ambiguous tension in Indo-Caribbean female identity. While providing an enabling alternative to gender-role conformity on the one hand, it also furthered the marginal representation of Indians as a whole.

The Indian dislocation from a majority experience has been further exacerbated by the fact that Indo-Caribbean women came to writing and self-expression at a much later stage than did Afro-Caribbean women, for a variety of cultural and social reasons. As a result, it is impossible to speak either of an identifiable genre or of a canon of Indo-Caribbean women's writing: these writers are still fighting for a legitimate place and authority within the larger domain of anglophone Caribbean literature. Kanhai attributes this late start and the relative scarcity of published material to several factors, which have, ironically, also served as a major source of creative inspiration for these writers: the heritage of indentureship and plantation labour; the inhibiting impact of repressive social and familial structures; the lack of support from and the invalidation of work by family members, which has led to feelings of insecurity; self-censorship to placate family and community; the ambivalent relationship with and negotiation of dominant Afro-Caribbean culture; isolation within community; limited access to a wider support network of diasporic writers; and exile, emigration and the symptoms of cultural estrangement, experienced both at home and in the diasporic metropolis.[8] In a similar vein, Jeremy Poynting's scholarship on Indo-Caribbean women highlights the restraining effects of "economic and domestic arrangements which do not support full-time writing, inadequate publishing opportunities, and lack of self confidence". An overriding concern in these writings, Poynting continues, "is with human happiness and its denial by social injustice, religious bigotry and sexism".[9] Moreover, traditional patriarchal attitudes towards women's education, attitudes that equated higher education with a corresponding devaluing of a woman's worth in the marriage market, provided a stumbling block to the availability of equal educational opportunities for girls and boys. While these attitudes have been significantly modified over the past three decades, they still often continue to unconsciously pervade the parental psyche.

In view of these paradoxical elements of restriction and empowerment, the act of writing becomes a highly politicized enterprise: in the process of exposing systems of inequity and injustice, it gives public articulation to deep-seated anxieties and insecurities. At the risk of facing social ostracism, threats of intimidation and accusations of betrayal, these writers have made concerted efforts to overcome restrictions; they have done so by confronting in their writings social gridlocks through *kala pani* discursive transgressions that have exposed and contested fixed notions of identity and definitions of ideal womanhood, Hindu insularity, cultural chauvinism in relation to other religions and ethnicities, patriarchal strangleholds of power, limiting parameters for sexual self-assertion, homophobia and intellectual ostracism. By adopting a particular trajectory of "migrating subjectivities",[10] these women are beginning to occupy multiple subject positionings that are gradually permitting them to confront their own gender, racial and religious biases while exposing the lack of community among Hindus, Muslims and Christians for whom biology and religion have become prime signifiers of difference and exclusion, practised most particularly by the Hindu majority. This awareness has necessitated a dual movement both within and outside societal barriers to adopt an insider/outsider position of double consciousness as an effective strategy to contest and negotiate marginality both within and outside Indo-Caribbean communities.

The idea of motion on the *kala pani* has been central to the Indo-Caribbean experience in general and to the specific experience of women in particular. From the first merchant ships that brought them to the islands, to their mobilization as workers and as domestic partners in the new lands and to their eventual migration to North America or England, women have always had to negotiate their access to space through creative reconfigurations. These spatial recreations have led to the formation of a particular fissured reality for women, wherein their individual and collective histories have been lodged within the fault lines of Caribbean memory in a particular space of *kala pani* discursive in-betweenness, or intermediary affiliation. The in-between location has favoured an interstitial subject position that resists spatial enclosure in confining paradigms.

Constituting a balancing act of straddling or dancing between hyphens rather than being sandwiched by the weight of cultural constructs, in-betweenness affords a sense of mobility through the juggling and final dismantling of pre-existing structures and fixed systems of meaning that do not accommodate the finer nuances of indeterminate identities that resist epistemological fixity. The indeterminacy of in-betweenness has been instrumental in the elaboration of new spaces of articulation that have, through the politics of hybridized (self-)awareness within the parameters of the *kala pani* discourse, favoured the creation of revised woman-centred mythologies of interrelatedness and connection.

It has therefore been instructive to situate Indo-Caribbean feminist discourse within the broader perspectives of postcolonialism and transnational feminism, while recognizing and celebrating its cultural distinctiveness. The primacy of the particular within a broader spectrum of political, historical and social realities has permitted the exploration of notions such as Indianness, cultural continuity and gendered identity, as well as possible connections among writers and theorists in different parts of a postcolonial transnational diaspora, both Indian and African. The *kala pani* discourse stresses that, rather than there being a single "Indian" experience, there has been a series of displacements or dislocations (hence the title of this book) which can be identified historically and culturally — and which can be used to develop a critical methodology for reading the fiction of Indo-Caribbean women. The *kala pani* discourse thereby situates itself at the nexus of several critical perspectives and, consequently, advances our ability to interrogate the positioning of Indo-Caribbean female identity at several levels simultaneously — most notably, the relationships between patriarchal strictures in the homeland and in the diaspora, between domesticity and cultural or intellectual formation, between women's sexuality and Brahmanical moral codes or epics such as the *Ramayana*, and between Negritude, "coolie-tude", creolization and douglarization. The *kala pani* discursive methodology brings historical and economic perspectives to bear on literary analysis, as well as on a range of feminist and cultural theories (Caribbean, so-called Third World — including women of colour from the United States — transnational black traditions, national and diasporic South Asian postcolonial critics, and theorists of colonialism and nationalism in the Indian and African diasporas).

The rubric of postcolonial and transnational feminist thought can thereby provide the necessary framework to dislodge the traditional isolation that Indo-

Caribbean literary and cultural feminism has suffered in Trinidad and Guyana by inscribing it within the synchronic positioning of a multi-conscious methodology that can create "imagined communities" of "horizontal comrade-ship," to use Benedict Anderson's terminology.[11] These transnational theoretical networks are politically expedient for a number of reasons: to energize the scope of Indo-Caribbean feminist thought through synchronic dialogue with other theoretical feminist considerations, such as Gloria Anzaldua's concept of mestiza hybridity as the site of an emerging Chicana political and social consciousness; to engage in douglarized discursive practices with Afro-Caribbean women writers such as Merle Hodge, who has played a pioneering role in creating such a space in novels such as *For the Life of Laetitia*; to expose the gender inequities and religious tensions within Indo-Caribbean communities that have forced women writers, in particular, to seek international, diasporic alliances; and to promote a sense of multiple consciousness among the writers themselves, in order to transcend partisan politics and cultural parochialism.[12] Emphasizing the political nature of such "imagined" alliances, Chandra Mohanty affirms: "The idea of imagined community is useful because it leads us away from essentialist notions of Third World feminist struggles, suggesting political rather than biological or cultural bases for alliance. It is not color or sex that constructs the ground for these struggles. Rather, it is the way we think about race, class, and gender – the political links we choose to make among and between struggle."[13] These "cartographies of struggle", to use Mohanty's phrase, have been pertinent to the situation of Indo-Caribbean women writers and critics who inhabit "First World" diasporic homes in the colonial metropolis and North America as well as of those women who continue to live in their country of origin. Diasporic solidarities through politicized transnational negotiations have provided a sense of community for writers and theorists such as Ramabai Espinet, Lakshmi Persaud and Kamala Kempadoo who have been exiled from "home", and for authors such as Rajandaye Ramkissoon-Chen who have suffered a sense of exile within indigenous patriarchies and racist ideologies at "home".

The extending of the personal to a hybridized community of political awareness can be compared to Anzaldua's formulation of the "new mestiza", whom she defines in the following manner: "The new mestiza copes by developing a tolerance for contradiction, a tolerance for ambiguity. . . . She learns to juggle cultures. She has a plural personality, she operates in a pluralistic mode. . . . Not only does she sustain the contradictions, she turns the ambivalence into something else."[14] The ambiguity of hybridization thus initiates a diplomatic and ongoing process of negotiation that resists immobility by becoming the very fulcrum of transformational agency. In fact, the Indo-Guyanese critic Kempadoo aligns herself with Anzaldua's "politics of the borderland", which predicates the need for racial ambiguity in an increasingly transcultured world. Kempadoo draws strength from her own mixed-race identity by locating it within the parameters of a transnational cross-cultural dynamic facilitated by "cross-cultural fusions and international migrations".[15] The borderland as the site of racial convergence transcends the limitations of racial absolutism, whose boundaries are fixed and impermeable. Instead, the borderland, as interstitial space, favours a certain subjective claiming which "balances within and between traditional racial and ethnic discourses".[16]

The hybridized consciousness has been particularly relevant to Indo-Caribbean women writers, who have been subsumed under a blanket characterization of homogeneity as Indian women in the Caribbean or as South Asians within the larger Indian diasporic community. Espinet stresses the importance of de-homogenizing this experience to avoid the dangers of cultural misrepresentation and erasure. Referring to her situation as an Indo-Caribbean woman writer from Trinidad who has made Toronto her diasporic home, she states:

> We are people who emerged out of the South Asian diaspora and are forming another diaspora here, but we are also Caribbean people. In a definition of our identity I don't think that we can homogenize the multiple subject identities that we bring to that definition. "Indo-Caribbean" is not a homogenous group because Indo-Caribbean people are Muslim, Hindu, Christian, atheist etc. The process that we are engaged in now is describing our multiple subject identities. "Indo-Caribbean" is now a hot site of contestation. It should remain so, or else we'll have some body from on top saying we have to be this or that; and I would resist that. I don't know if "Indo-Caribbean" is the best term for us. We ought to be prepared for it to shift and change as we come up with other categorizations. At the moment it is the most useful term to describe who we are: people who come out of India and the Caribbean.[17]

Hybridity inaugurates multiple points of connection by leading to a certain globalized creation of self through identifications with varied "ports" of reference, ranging from the ports of Calcutta and Madras in India to Port of Spain in Trinidad and the old port of King George's Town in Guyana. These ports were the terminal locations of *kala pani* arrivals and departures. Davies insists on the importance of such migratory identifications, stating, "If we see Black women's subjectivity as a migratory subjectivity existing in multiple locations, then we can see how their work, their presences traverse all of the geographical/national boundaries instituted to keep our dislocation in place."[18] Migratory subjectivities initiate a certain mobility of expression by creating a space for the insertion of hybridized discourses on creolization, douglarization and other forms of mixed-race identification that are emerging as alternative discourses to dislodge the primacy of a fixed and racialized narrative of uncontested blackness in the Caribbean.

The ideological fixity of blackness has been most evident in the field of Caribbean feminism, which remained Afrocentric in its articulation and preoccupations until the mid-1980s. With some exceptions,[19] the dominant framework of reference for feminist issues until that time continued to emphasize the experiences of black women. Commenting on the late 1970s' second wave of Caribbean feminism, the Indo-Caribbean feminist Rawwida Baksh-Sooden explains:

> In general, it is true to say that there was no multicultural framework (despite a sociological theory of "cultural pluralism" developed by M. G. Smith in the 1960's) within which the specific experiences and interests of non-African women could be viewed or contextualized. In fact, this has only begun happening since the mid-1980's in Trinidad and Tobago, and interestingly, has its roots in the assertion by the Indian population of their distinct ethnic and cultural identity. I would hence define the dominant discourse within Caribbean feminism as Afro-centric, as opposed to either a Euro-centric or multicultural paradigm. . . .
>
> Women who have been "left out" in this process include the indigenous inhabitants, Indian, Chinese, and other groups such as the Indonesian, etc.
>
> Indian women like myself, who are actively involved in the movement, have generally come to an analysis of colonialism largely through the Afro-centered discourse promoted at the University of the West Indies. It is only within the last five years or so that I have personally begun to explore the specificity of Indo-Caribbean women's experience.[20]

The need to formulate a more inclusive model of feminist articulation has prompted Indo-Caribbean feminist scholars and writers such as Kanhai to take the initiative in elaborating a more hybridized vision of women's realities through, for example, Kanhai's recommendation of an inclusive dougla feminist space.[21] Although *dougla* refers specifically to the offspring of a mixed African–Indian sexual union, Kanhai's formulation of the term attempts to go beyond the narrow confines of biology to make a political statement of self-claiming for all groups that have been relegated to marginal representation. Instead of replacing one pattern of exclusion in feminist discourse with another model of separatist affirmation — in this case an exclusive script of Indo-Caribbean feminism as a counter-framework of reference — Kanhai seeks an integrative positioning of feminist experiences to promote racial understanding and mutual cooperation among different communities of women.

The term *dougla* has seemed to be slightly less polemical in its usage than the word *Creole*. By highlighting the "Indianness" inherent in the word *dougla*, Shalini Puri's influential work on dougla identity attempts to allay fears about the cultural assimilation of Indians in a predominantly creolized social fabric. Puri argues that "the figure of the dougla could provide a vocabulary for figuring disallowed Indian identities; furthermore, they could offer ways of reframing the problematics of black–Indian party politics, and race and gender relations."[22] At the same time, by identifying dougla space as being "essentially" Caribbean, this theory predicates the exclusion of non-Caribbean douglas who face a similar predicament of marginalization in other diasporic locations, such as Mauritius, Reunion, Fiji and South Africa. While douglas have often been referred to as racial half-breeds or "ethnic bastards" in national discourses on citizenship by both Indians and blacks in Trinidad and Guyana,[23] this group has also been subjected to a particular silencing in the political imaginary of these countries. Fetishized for their alterity by serving as visible reminders of a prior taboo, the mixing of black and Indian bloodstreams, dougla in-betweenness has often been a source of derision, alienation, misperception and social rejection. The influential Trinidadian soca-calypsonian David Michael Rudder calls for the humanization of the experience of douglas in his recent song "Dougla Woman": "Dougla woman, let me understand your soul." Understanding the soul as an intrinsic part of one's identity is synonymous with the effort to de-objectify a formerly devalorized human experience that has nevertheless created a "brand new style" (from Rudder's "The Ganges and the Nile, Part Two") of living.[24]

However, Kanhai's analysis of dougla feminism remains at a very preliminary stage of articulation. A more rigorous discussion of the concept is therefore unavailable for public critique. In addition, postcolonial douglas still have to negotiate the vagaries of their contested mixed-race heritage within racial orthodoxies that do not promote the flexibility of in-betweenness. The question of dougla identity in postcolonial Trinidad and Guyana remains a thorny issue in these countries. Postcoloniality has further highlighted the supposedly questionable citizenship of biological douglas while simultaneously celebrating the hybridized nature of contemporary cultural production in the form of douglarized chutney-soca music and certain Indianized aspects of Carnival. Cultural douglarization has often glossed over crucial engagements with the specificity of biological douglas, who are, ironically, still fighting for national visibility in a very multi-ethnic social milieu. The population of douglas continues to expand in the national landscape as a result of the inevitability of interracial contact, but Reddock exposes an unspoken "truth" when she characterizes douglas as an "example of a marginalized multiracial group that has not benefited from its mixed ancestry".[25] Moreover, Hindu disavowals of racial syncretism, in the form of purist notions of Indianness, have further marginalized this constituency through a systematic negation of difference.

As a complementary model of feminist engagement, the *kala pani* discourse calls for the disruption of neatly aligned, state-determined racial categorizations and hierarchies that institute and sustain various levels of discrimination by initiating a search for common ground, an initiative that has been hinted at by dougla feminism. Implicit within the parameters of *kala pani* hybridity is the recognition of two turbulent transatlantic crossings, African and Indian, that highlight a political commonality of experience (colonial exploitation through slave or indentured labour). This common ground has nevertheless provided the opening for an important dialogic relationship between the Indo-Caribbean and Afro-Caribbean experiences as the site for enabling dialogue and syncretism between the two races. At the same time, while dislodging the immediate association of the word *dougla* from the primacy of Indocentric and Afrocentric experiences, *kala pani* hybridity reveals its potential to include Chinese, Syrian, Lebanese and other "minority" constituencies that do not necessarily subscribe to the dougla aesthetic as a locus of self-identification. The limitations of dougla consciousness could be expanded through a model of hybridized feminist awareness that includes a sense of participatory ownership among all communities of women in the Caribbean, most of whom share a common heritage of *kala pani* crossings on the "black" Atlantic, in the form of Asian indenture, African slavery and Middle Eastern commercial enterprise. In this way, *kala pani* hybridity could offer a solution to the problematics of naming and to the privileging of particular ethnic experiences. The formation of such a hybridized Caribbean feminist collectivity could provide a firm foundation for transformational

Caribbean feminisms in national and international deliberations on gender.

As an example, Kempadoo reaffirms her hybridized racial and cultural identity as an Afro-Indo-dougla-Guyanese woman who has inhabited Caribbean diasporic space in England and the United States by celebrating the story of the multiple hyphen. She states, "I could see myself as a chameleon, with no fixed appearance and no sense of an essential self, yet could enjoy the multiple spaces available due to the simultaneous inhabiting of different cultures."[26] Associating hybridization with a simultaneous vertical and horizontal expansion over multiple cultural zones, Kempadoo accommodates her douglaness by converting essentialized otherness into the dynamism of relational mutuality. Kempadoo's compatriot, the Indo-Guyanese poet and film maker Michelle Mohabeer is equally committed to the dismantling of "easy quick-fix labels of identification" in her literary and artistic creations to accommodate her multiple identities as a "creolized mixed race, bi-cultural Indo-Caribbean/Canadian woman who is also gay, from a working class/trade unionist milieu and a self-professed non-conformist rebel".[27] Mohabeer's multiple identities enable her to negotiate the quadruple dislocations of race, gender, class and sexual preference through the parameters of a hybridized *kala pani* perspective that blurs distinctions by merging them into a composite whole, thereby providing a more reflective totality of representation.

Jan Shinebourne's mixed-race identity as Indian and Chinese can be integrated into the liminalities of the *kala pani* discourse by proposing new definitions of Indo-Caribbeanness that share a common legacy of disinheritance with the Chinese experience of indentureship. Living in England since 1970, Shinebourne is the daughter of a Chinese father and a mother of mixed Chinese–Indian heritage. In an interview with Frank Birbalsingh, Shinebourne reminisces about her experience of interracial harmony in Guyana during her childhood in the face of the country's present state of racial disintegration: "But I know it from experience. I moved very easily among European, Indian, Chinese and African friends and family."[28] Endowed with a hybridized consciousness to negotiate racialized space with relative ease since childhood, Shinebourne has often used her mixed-race sensibilities to enhance her narratives. She states, "I think it gave me an advantage because of the race politics in Guyana, especially the African/Indian problem. There was a tendency to nationalism that came to the fore in the 70s in the Caribbean, and race and nationalism always lead to disaster. I think it is dangerous to shape a political, social and economic culture purely on the basis of race. Look at Hitler!"[29] Hybridized space, in this instance, ruptures the centrality of nationalist agendas of predetermined, selective citizenship by proposing transcultural and intercultural citizenries.

Like dougla feminism, hybridity calls for the recognition and specificity of those individual feminisms that have heretofore been invisible in national deliberations on women's issues by underlining the need for parity among different feminisms, as mentioned earlier. In this way, while embracing a more widespread interracial agenda of articulation, *kala pani* hybridity and dougla feminism affirm the particularities of the experience of Indian women at the same time as they project the visibility of this experience on the national canvas through the principle of equitable representation. By accentuating the Indian contributions to national discourses on hybridity and creolization, these discourses demand a re-evaluation of the full import of Indianness on the Caribbean political and cultural imaginary, by positioning themselves in a relational mode of exchange with the national economy to avoid the repeated tokenism and negation that Indian culture has experienced. Making specific reference to the contempt that Indian women continue to face in the Caribbean as a result of disparaging societal attitudes toward them, Espinet asserts, "The peasant Oriental still meets the urbanized Creole culture of the West Indies as a stranger. In spite of education and the rewards of thrift and entrepreneurship, social mobility for Indians took – and is still taking – a great deal of time. When it occurs, it often means that the Indo-Caribbean must lose that which marks her as Indian, in order to 'belong' to the urbanised Creole culture which still despises her un-creolised ways."[30] *Kala pani* hybridity attempts to convert the "loss" of (un)belonging experienced by Indian women into a process of recovery by delineating the very parameters within which Indian women can begin to interrogate their rights of participatory ownership of society through their artistic and intellectual input. Espinet describes her own process of (self-)recovery in her interview with Frank Birbalsingh, in which she stresses the simultaneous importance of being culturally specific and globally conscious in order to convert patterns of marginalization elaborated within the Indian community and outside into acts of creative assertion. Commenting on her inclusion/exclusion as an Indian woman writer in Indo-Caribbean societies in Trinidad and Toronto, as well as within the broader spectrum of other Caribbean communities, she affirms:

When I first thought of writing I didn't see myself as an "Indo-Caribbean woman writer" because I was extremely young: I just saw myself as writing. Through a series of steps I began to see myself as being more and more particularized and began to describe myself as an Indo-Caribbean writer. The particularization or specificity of that position has become quite important to me. One of its key features is the scarcity of other people like myself on the landscape. There isn't a community of people that I can talk to, even through writing: I don't experience a shared investigation of my community. I experience alienation and isolation and a sense of people hardly understanding what I am trying to do. I also do not experience support from the community for my endeavour. . . . I don't think "writing" is something that the Indo-Caribbean community wants, is interested in, or has any engagement with. Therefore when I position myself as an Indo-Caribbean female writer, I dislike the terminology, and to some extent it's meaningless, but it can't be helped.

There is much more nourishment for me as a writer participating in the larger Caribbean community, and finding people (Caribbean and other) interested in what I'm doing because they know so little about the Indian community in the Caribbean.[31]

Espinet's particular situation reflects a larger image of the ambivalence, isolation and alienation experienced by Indo-Caribbean women writers in general as they struggle to grapple with their own precariousness as cultural and literary scribes in communities that are seeking to redress decades of invisibility while, at the same time, struggling to preserve their ethnic distinctiveness through the censorship of any public articulation of its particular experiences – especially by a woman writer. The Indian woman writer poses a potential threat to her community by exposing well-preserved family and communal secrets through the written word, which serves as permanent "public" documentation of "private" knowledge. As Elaine Savory explains in her interview with Espinet, "Textuality which articulates an experience previously silenced challenges the community's assumptions. For the Indian woman who constructs that textuality, there is, as Espinet points out, the fear of making the private public knowledge, of interfering in matters which are habitually a male province, of violating a sense of modesty, of betraying a cultural expectation that women will participate in work and family life but not become bold public figures."[32] Here Savory exposes the double standards maintained by Indian communities that fight for self-determination at the expense of their female populations. Caught in the impasse between cultural conformity and the right/write to free expression, Indo-Caribbean women writers have to negotiate the slipperiness of interstitiality through a careful crafting of their creative work that has to remain respectful to cultural dictates without compromising the writer's personal integrity.

The work of the Trinidadian novelist Lakshmi Persaud reflects the tenuousness of the double bind experienced by the woman writer. Their author a product of her middle-class Hindu upbringing with its strict enforcement of female codes of behaviour, Persaud's novels betray a certain caution and tentativeness of expression. *Sastra* and *Butterfly in the Wind* are set in 1950s rural Trinidad and constitute semi-autobiographical, fictionalized accounts of the author's own childhood and passage to womanhood.[33] While the author makes several veiled references in her novels to the restrictions imposed on Hindu girls by the stranglehold of Brahmanic patriarchy and its duplicitous standards of morality and social decorum, her writing betrays a self-conscious bourgeois sensibility when social commentary gets veiled beneath cultural idealizations and a lack of critical reflection as a strategy of defence against public disapproval. Even though the female protagonists in the two novels try to assert their independence within severe societal limitations, their ultimate emancipation from such inhibitions is realized when they emigrate. The author's own emigration to England was perhaps indicative of the limited choices offered to Hindu women of her generation in her native Trinidad, women who have felt the need to avoid ossification in and by tradition by means of moving beyond local boundaries. The two novels, however, represent a substantial introductory engagement with the problematics of Hindu female subjectivity and women's fight for autonomy in traditional societies. Rather than succumb to the facile expectations of victimization, Persaud's heroines pave the way for future deliberations on female empowerment within repressive social structures by opening the necessary counterspaces of affirmative action for future generations of writers who may have less imposing class- and gender-based obstacles to face.

Emigration to North America, England or another Caribbean island in the 1970s and 1980s has thus been crucial to our understanding of the Indo-Caribbean experience. The exodus of large groups of Indo-Caribbeans can be attributed to economic reasons, to feelings of alienation experienced as ethnic minorities in a predominantly Creole environment and to political insecurities in the face of repressive regimentation, as in Guyana. With the exception of Ramkissoon-Chen, who still lives in Trinidad, and of the late Mahadai Das, who made her "home" in Guyana until her death in 2003, all the writers considered in this study have taken up residence elsewhere, thereby experiencing a dual sense of diasporic estrangement. Their writings have explored the vulnerabilities and disjunctions involved in double dislocations by highlighting their experiences of exile to and assimilation in the new countries of adoption. While several writers comment on their alienation and isolation in the new diasporic locations, they nevertheless express the feeling of a certain creative permissiveness and centredness that was lacking "at home".

Espinet is very active in her Toronto Indo-Caribbean community, where she regularly contributes to a column in a community newspaper, *Indo-Caribbean World,* that deals primarily with women's issues in society, as well as fulfilling her regular teaching and writing responsibilities. Describing Toronto as an immigrant city, Espinet politicizes her commitment to writing by integrating activism into the specificities of her everyday life. Commenting on how her politicized perspective on writing, feminism, communal welfare, identity and daily living give her a new creative energy, she explains to Elaine Savory,

> As part of the immigrant mass now putting its stamp on this city, I am intensely aware of my identity as an Indo-Caribbean person and my writing cannot help but respond to this. There is a large Caribbean population in this city and within that a large Indo-Caribbean population. This provides the ground for a kind of dialogue which simultaneously is rooted in notions of home and exile and which does not happen at "home". . . .
>
> I find it interesting to note how much of a dialogue is beginning to develop here concerning identity, place, origins, cultural retention, accommodation, with a vigour that I have not seen in the Caribbean. There is a sense of space here within which this dialogue is occurring, and this may be because there are parallel communities also doing the same kind of investigation.[34]

Espinet finds her sense of place in Toronto through vibrant interpersonal and inter-diasporic communications as a community spokesperson as well as as a more international ambassador of Caribbean relations. She also extends the motto "the personal is communal" a step further by including a globalized perspective on immigrant realities and expectations while negotiating the delicate balance between personal life and public responsibilities as a writer. This multi-vantaged position has been accompanied by its own set of anxieties and tensions as Espinet faces the moral and social apathy of her community, whose pursuit of material prosperity – and relative success in this domain – has lulled them into a false sense of complacency and a refusal to be more committed to issues other than business enterprise. Indian self-centredness has been aggravated by an inability to face criticism or to be self-critical, in Espinet's estimation, which has led Indians to demonstrate a certain close-minded smugness in their dealings with other ethnicities. However, this introversion can be attributed to feelings of unarticulated insecurity experienced by Indo-Caribbeans in the face of racist and discriminating Canadian immigration policies, of rapid assimilation by the younger generation into mainstream culture, of marginalization by Indian nationals from the subcontinent who never hesitate to affirm the superiority of the mainland Indian heritage as the only "true" form of Indian culture, and other factors. As Birbalsingh states, "What is evident is that Indo-Caribbean Canadians have prospered in a materialistic sense; but this prosperity is accompanied by feelings of psychic disorientation which might justify a general description of the community as a condition of *insecure security.*"[35]

The condition of "insecure security" has also affected the position of the "immigrant" writer. If emigration has permitted a certain freedom of expression on the one hand, it has, at the same time, placed this writing outside representation by denying it its legitimate place in mainstream literature. Referring specifically to the Canadian context, Arun Mukherjee explains how the category "Canadian" has excluded First Nations and "minority" writers of colour who have not been located in the Canadian national scheme of gendered and racialized difference, precisely because of their immigrant or outsider status. Inscribed within certain racialized codes of expression, according to Mukherjee, this writing is divided into two categories: "if it deals with subject matter that alludes to where the writer came from, it is perceived as nostalgic. If, on the other hand, it has Canadian content, it is automatically considered to be about an immigrant's struggle to adjust to new realities."[36] Nostalgia, in its association with the past, and adjustment, as a process of accommodating to an as-yet-to be determined present, are both situated in time frames that elude the current moment. Similarly, immigrant writing eludes insertion in the contemporary canon of Canadian literature through its exclusion from "legitimized" literary debate and discourse.

However, some Indo-Caribbean women writers, such as Shani Mootoo from Trinidad, have been able to transform the alienation of outsiderness into a locus of assertive authority through the "coming out" of the Indo-Caribbean lesbian experience. Of mixed Indo-Caribbean/Irish descent, Mootoo affirms her hybridized identity as an Indo-Caribbean Irish Canadian lesbian living in Vancouver. Mootoo's identity is located within two sources of rupture: the disruption of "normal" definitions of Indo-Caribbeanness and the reassessment of what is perceived to be "normative" sexuality within hetero-patriarchal hegemony. Mootoo converts immigrant otherness into a certain openness of expression through her unapologetic literary articulations of lesbian sexuality, domestic violence, incest and sexual abuse. Her diasporic location offers her the possibility of exposing the well-kept family secrets of rape, incest and other forms of family violence within Indo-Caribbean communities by unveiling the shroud of sexual deviancy that has tormented this community since the early days of indentureship. Mootoo professes her inability to have candidly written about these issues in Trinidad, an inability that results from the community's subsequent loss of face through public condemnation by a woman. This public unmasking would have resulted in the possibility of social ostracism, intimidation, and threats of violence against herself and family members. In addition, her representation of Indo-Caribbean lesbians has given visibility to this formerly underground experience by affirming the sexual, sociopolitical and legal rights of lesbians as equal members of society who claim their autonomy as women through their sexual difference.

Similarly, Kanhai fights isolation as a very visible woman of colour in a fairly homogeneous white environment in Washington State through her participation in international feminist-of-colour writing and activist groups that promote more effective lines of communication between disparate constituencies of women in the form of workshops, seminars, annual conferences, reading groups and other activities.

Sustained creative activity also provides much-needed solace for Lelawattee Manoo-Rahming, who moved to the Bahamas from Trinidad after her marriage to a Bahamian. As one of a small handful of Indo-Trinidadians in the Bahamas, Manoo-Rahming laments the lack of communal affiliation and her subsequent marginalization by Bahamian writers. Writing poetry to transcend the loneliness and dispersal of exile serves as a medium to confront and accommodate the locatedness of the present by converting her innermost feelings of personal loss into creative recuperations on paper. And Mahadai Das's refusal to conform to the dictates of her Hindu Guyanese upbringing by adopting a self-defined model of Hindu womanhood has revealed itself in the power of her poetry and in her personal example of courage and independence for daring to be different, despite the ravages wrought by a debilitating illness that led to her untimely death. The poet's seclusion in a remote Guyanese village where she was branded a madwoman by local residents made her an involuntary exile in her own home. Social and political ostracism, heavy medication and psychic alienation took a heavy toll on Das's young life. Her life story illustrates the tragic consequences of searching for exemplarity within confining social and religious structures that deliberately and systematically thwart women's quest for uniqueness. Similarly, Rajandaye Ramkissoon-Chen's literary endeavours remain largely unrecognized and unappreciated in her native Trinidad, where male prejudice and literary chauvinism impede a more favourable reception of her work.

Indo-Caribbean women writers have had to assert themselves in extenuating circumstances. The fact that they continue to write undauntedly, sometimes at tremendous personal cost, testifies to their sheer grit and to their determination to carve safe spaces of self-affirmation for themselves and their sisters. This tenacity of intent places them within the parameters of a long history of survival techniques, industry and fortitude, as demonstrated by the first Indo-Caribbean female immigrants, thereby inscribing these writers within an empowering "legacy of cane". Espinet postulates a particular "female epistemology of cane" as the very foundation of Indo-Caribbean female subjectivity that unearths and resurrects the silenced voices of Indian women from historical and cultural oblivion.[37] The female cane-cutter represents the literary muse for Indo-Caribbean women writers who position her as a valuable role model that inaugurates and sustains a vital female heritage in the Caribbean. As Kanhai argues in her essay "The Masala Stone Sings", "the canecutting woman, hidden in the cane fields, pitting her will, her endurance, her ingenuity against a system that would grind her through its mills and spit her out as canetrash, is the history and psyche of the Indo-Caribbean woman who wants to write".[38] Similarly, the woman writer's private and hidden reflections are put through the millstone of racist and sexist critical commentaries before they are churned out by the wheels of production in the form of literary publications. These publications are, in turn, subjected to further scrutiny by uninitiated readers who have heretofore been unfamiliar with the literary and cultural contributions of Indo-Caribbean women.

Diasporic (Dis)locations adds another perspective to the heritage of cane through the field of literary analysis, contextualizing these writings within the grid of cultural, feminist and postcolonial studies. The majority of women writers introduced in this study evoke a Hindu point of view to highlight the preponderance of Hindu ideology in the construction of Indo-Caribbean identity. With the exception of the creolized Indo-Christian voices of Ramabai Espinet and Rosanne Kanhai and the mixed-race perspectives of Oonya

Kempadoo, Shani Mootoo and Jan Shinebourne, these writers are overwhelmingly Hindu in their scope. The Indo-Caribbean female Muslim voice remains absent in literature, especially in Trinidad, but asserts itself in the field of the social sciences through the groundbreaking scholarship of critics such as Patricia Mohammed, Aisha Khan and Rawwida Baksh-Sooden, among others. Additionally, there are several writers and critics who have not been included in this analysis but who have made important contributions to Indo-Caribbean women's writing. This study acknowledges the work of Madeline Coopsammy, Niala Maharaj, Ruth Sawh and Debra Singh-Ramlochan from Trinidad and of Shana Yardan, Seeta T. Mohammed, Rosetta Khalideen and Parvati Persaud-Edwards from Guyana.

The book is divided into six chapters, each dealing with a particular facet of Indo-Caribbean life in a colonial and postcolonial context and its impact on issues of female identity, sexuality, Caribbean feminisms, oral culture, communal affiliations, exile, intellectual colonization and the positing of a woman-friendly decolonized Indo-Caribbean historical specificity. The chapters highlight the simultaneous overlapping and interconnectedness of the social, political, cultural and religious forces that have shaped the complexities of Indo-Caribbean female subjectivity.

Chapter 1 demonstrates how Hindu women and girls have been subjected to the disempowering effects of traditional Hindu structures of Brahmanic morality and cultural conformity, colonial education and definitions of "coolie" identity. It asserts that Indo-Caribbean female identity is based on a negotiation of patriarchy and of the machinations of colonial education, wherein the search for self is predicated by an either/or paradigm of cultural assimilation or negation. This search is based on an accommodation of Hindu tradition while mediating colonial education and creolization at the same time. In Lakshmi Persaud's *Sastra* and *Butterfly in the Wind*, this accommodation results in an ultimate break with tradition, symbolized by a postcolonial *kala pani* crossing to North America in an attempt to transcend female confinement through immigration, while Jan Shinebourne's *The Last English Plantation* associates colonial schooling with a certain ambivalence of representation reflected in the socialization of Indo-Caribbean girls.

In chapter 2, the complex model of Indo-Caribbean feminism is inscribed within a broader historical framework of Caribbean citizenship as Indo-Caribbean women negotiate their subjectivity within and outside dominant Afro-Caribbean historical, cultural and literary paradigms. The feminism of

Indian and African women has known a long tradition in Trinidad and Guyana despite the traditional erasure and obfuscation that this form of activism has suffered in the historical documentation of the Caribbean. African and Indian women in the Caribbean share a common history of geographical and cultural displacement, forced labour, economic enterprise, resistance and familial dispersal. The appreciation and recognition of this commonality of experience has often been skewed by partisan politics in favour of oppositional representation, whereby African and Indian women have been pitted against each other as rivals in the fight for legitimacy and subjective autonomy. While history continues to fragment the lives of Indo- and Afro-Caribbean women through unequal representation and the imposition of normative codes of Afrocentredness, the development of a certain hybridized consciousness in the fields of literary and cultural production has undermined the primacy of binary oppositions by creating common ground for more affirming relations between these women. By embracing a transformative dougla poetics of accommodation and renewal in their writings, Afro-Caribbean writers such as Merle Hodge and Marina Maxwell and Indo-Caribbean writers such as Narmala Shewcharan and Ramabai Espinet have created new discursive paradigms for reading Caribbeanness as a site for interracial collaborations, gender negotiations and the affirmation of negated identities.

The language of cooking provides, in chapter 3, an important script to facilitate the necessary negotiations of gendered identity, advocated in chapter 2, within both traditional and interracial models of (Indo-)Caribbean subjectivity. Lakshmi Persaud's novels and Espinet's short story "Indian Cuisine" assert, by establishing close associations between culinary discourse and Indian constructions of Caribbeanness at different stages in history, that spices are the necessary grains or markers of Indo-Caribbean immigrant history. Food becomes a symbol of negotiating racialized and gendered otherness by demonstrating how "culinary belongingness" is a type of oral transmission of culture that allows an ethnically subordinated group in Trinidad to resist patterns of domination and acculturation. Persaud and Espinet promote foodways as synecdoche for attitudes towards Indianness by highlighting the relationship between gendered perceptions of food and the construction of Indian female identity in order to demonstrate how Indo-Caribbean women have had to negotiate their identity between two competing models: a specifically Hindu rural ethnic identity from the "Old World" and a more theoretically hybridized one from the "New World".

Chapter 3 establishes the importance of the kitchen as domestic space in the elaboration of Indo-Caribbean female identity; chapter 4 extends the argument on the relationship between women and space in the Indo-Caribbean household by demonstrating how women try to redefine the gendered segregation of space in Hindu culture. This chapter establishes how the houseyard becomes, in addition to the kitchen, the major locus of historical and cultural production by positioning the female characters as active feminist agents of history through their participation in various forms of yard culture and pre-discursive forms of oral communication such as story telling and an Indo-Caribbean-specific *aji*, or grandmother/wise-woman, culture. The yard represents the very site of Indo-Caribbean feminism through its enabling location of belonging, whereby women politicize the yard by transforming it into a microcosmic woman-centred representation of the nation. Control of the yard parallels an effective "sexing" or reclaiming of the nation by women, who feminize history through feminist agency and a rearticulation of nationally composed identities and gender affinities.

Spatial negotiations by women have transformed gender ideologies while simultaneously creating dissonance in terms of women's alienation and exilic dispositions within patriarchal and colonial systems of power. Chapter 5 demonstrates how the trope of exile constitutes a major theme in twentieth-century Caribbean writing by providing a valuable basis on which to comprehend the complexities of the postcolonial Caribbean exilic predicament that has been shaped by the disenfranchising forces of colonialism and mass migration, racism, sexism and class stratifications. However, reflections on exile have characterized a predominantly male-defined Indo-Caribbean literary tradition in which the experiences of women have received marginal attention. The poetry of Mahadai Das (*Bones*), Lelawattee Manoo-Rahming (*Curry Flavour*) and Rajandaye Ramkissoon-Chen (*Ancestry*), together with Ramabai Espinet's short story "Barred: Trinidad 1987", addresses the question of the suppressed exilic consciousness of women through an effective claiming of exile space in which to assert their rights of authorship. Their writings explore the complexities of exile from the vantage point of disenfranchised Indian women who have had to negotiate the physical, sociocultural and psychologically (self-)imposed levels of exile, both at home and abroad.

Sexuality has been an important marker of exile and affirmation for Indo-Caribbean women. Chapter 6 affirms that Indo-Caribbean female sexuality remains a hotly contested site of debate and controversy in Indian communities in the Caribbean and other diasporic locations. Inscribed within a particular culture of violence and shame, this sexuality has been subjected to the machinations of elitist Brahmanic prescriptions for Hindu femininity elaborated in India as well as to the colonizing impact of British imperialism and the influence of the Canadian Presbyterian Missions in Trinidad. Associated with a series of taboos imposed by male-ordered strategies of confinement and inhibition, female sexuality has constituted the ultimate fetish for male and female writers alike. At the same time, chapter 6 shows, the interrogations of female sexuality in the writings of Shani Mootoo, Ramabai Espinet and Lelawattee Manoo-Rahming have provided the very basis for active contestations of preconceived state and religiously legislated sexual mandates for Indo-Caribbean women, mandates that have mirrored the primary sexual negotiations undertaken by women under indentureship. These negotiations have located female sexuality within the dual problematics of sexual repression and control on the one hand and a dynamic, often contradictory site of self-recovery on the other.

1

Framing Indo-Caribbean Female Subjectivity

In childhood a woman must be subject to her father; in youth to her husband; when her husband is dead, to her son. A woman must never be free of subjection.
— *Laws of Manu*

Until the 1980s, the representation of Hindu women in Indo-Caribbean writing was the preserve of male writers and critics who inscribed their female characters in a mythologized past that was at odds with the dynamic and ever-changing realities of the Caribbean present. Writers such as Sam Selvon, V. S. Naipaul and Shiva Naipaul created female fictions that reduced women to what Ramabai Espinet calls "the phenomenon of invisibility" by obfuscating their presence behind a screen of shawls, saris and *ohrnis* (Indian headscarves).[1] Stereotypically essentialized depictions of Hindu women characterize the work of these authors, who perpetuated the myth of the eternal feminine, in which women are marginalized by a particular strategy of narrative petrification that negates the possibility of more wholesome and plausible representations. In other words, female characters are objects of male fantasies and projections, passive receptacles of the male writer's cultural unconscious.

As a result, female characters in male fiction often become fetishistic reproductions of the male writer's image of the ideal women, whereby he can reorganize and restructure his own prescriptions for Hindu womanhood. Espinet describes this manipulation by commenting on the male writer's "vision" of Indian women: "The Indian woman is located in a largely peasant, village culture, firmly attached to the traditional values of the home and seeking no active combat with the external non-Hindu world. Safe in the ascriptions of the female Hindu role, she lives as an extension of the dominant male figure in her environment and she transmutes all her needs into those which he can fill."[2] Existing as mere satellites or appendages of the male protagonist, female characters are of secondary importance. Their sole function is to enhance the prestige of the hero and his (self-)interests in their capacity as immature sisters, subservient wives and adoring mothers.

The need to provide more accurate, interesting and complex images of Hindu women has been a major preoccupation for Indo-Caribbean women writers such as Espinet and Lakshmi Persaud from Trinidad and Jan Shinebourne from Guyana, who have tried to resurrect women from the clutches of ritualized myth and abstraction by re-presenting them in accordance with their specific, ontological realities. Persaud's female protagonists refuse fictionalized immobilization by questioning and, at times, undermining male-prescribed cultural mandates for Hindu women. They introduce an element of rupture into the novel by attempting to crack the monolith of male readings, proposing a new model of Hindu femininity based on an alternative reading of the feminine. However, is a feminine revisioning possible in the female script given the overriding stranglehold of Hindu patriarchy as presented in *Sastra* and *Butterfly in the Wind*, or is the Indo-Caribbean woman writer herself a victim of cultural constraints whereby she is limited in her capacity to rewrite patriarchy on her own terms? Can the Draupadis, Sitas and Lakshmis of yesteryear shed their veils, both psychological and material, to be reinscribed in an active fictionalized present? The Indo-Caribbean female characters in this chapter negotiate their subjectivity within a dialectical framework of Brahmanic patriarchy and colonial education that limits the search for self to cultural assimilation and/or a negation identity. Female identity is constructed through the mediation and contestation of an indigenous and colonial patriarchy and an accommodation of Hindu tradition while adjusting to colonial education and creolization. This accommodation results in an ultimate break with tradition, symbolized by a postcolonial *kala pani* crossing to North America in search of a recuperated self that transgresses confinement through immigration.

Set in rural Trinidad in the mid-1950s, *Sastra* and *Butterfly in the Wind* are novels of female initiation into Hindu womanhood. These novels describe the trials and tribulations of growing up as Hindu girls within an exclusive Hindu community. The first-edition back cover of *Sastra* contains the following inscription: "The pundit warns Sastra's mother that her daughter's birth signs foretell two possible karmas, one of prosperous security if she keeps to the well-tried path, the other of mixed joy and misery if she should attempt to 'fly'. These are indeed Sastra's choices – between the traditional, collective Hindu society of her parents, and the world of individual destinies and responsibilities to which her generation is increasingly drawn."[3] The synopsis of the book implies that from the very beginning, the heroine will be implicated in a series of complicated negotiations between self, family and tradition before trying to achieve successful individuation or recovery of self. These negotiations place Sastra at the centre of the narrative in which she becomes the author of her own subjective reality when she is confronted with a set of choices that either accelerate or hinder her journey of personal exploration. These choices are by no means easy or self-evident, highlighting the idea that for several traditionally raised Hindu girls, the word *choice* is, in fact, a trap – it creates the illusion of opportunity or of the possibility of choice. In other words, the heroine begins her journey at a disadvantage: she is inscribed within a tradition of statutory limitations for women at birth, limitations that are justified and sustained in the name of age-old traditions and conventions.

Sastra's search, therefore, can be based not on a linear progression that marks its fruition by the successful overcoming of obstacles to achieve transcendence but, rather, on a series of regressive or backhanded confrontations with the past as a prerequisite to projecting a more favourable future for herself. The past positions itself as an invincible barrier whose frontiers are fortified and policed by the sentinels of Hindu traditions represented by priests, teachers, fathers, brothers, sons and other male members of the family, as well as by women who have been manipulated into accepting the dictates of patriarchal culture as a way of validating their own existence. Persaud's texts – *Sastra* and *Butterfly in the Wind* – imply that individual attempts to penetrate the bastion of Hindu culture are marginal within the specific cultural context described in her novels, even though sustained and systematic attacks might effectively chisel away sections of hegemonic impenetrability. The preoccupation with the past becomes a major fixation for the Hindu patriarch, whose nostalgia for all things past has major implications on the positioning of female subjectivity.

Hindu patriarchy found its legitimacy in a series of codified laws, elaborated by Manu the Lawgiver, that, while positing women's constitutional or biological inferiority, relegated women to an irreversible second-class citizenship. Prescriptive laws became normative models for female behaviour, which was constructed within the gridlock of what Anita Sheth and Amita Handa call a "Hindu-Brahmin-hetero-patriarchy", based on cultural hegemony and gender and class discrimination.[4] Women's subordination was thus constructed within the parameters of this reductive formula that sanctioned a totalitarian discourse on women, in which they were outlawed and silenced. By being placed outside discourse, women became apoliticized objects of male readings that characterized them as passive, powerless and thereby deserving of male protection. In other words, masculinity was chosen as the yardstick by which women were measured, found lacking and consequently subjected to culturally institutionalized discrimination. Gayatri Spivak evokes the Hindu woman's subaltern position of sexualized otherness, in which her inaccessibility to language leaves her outside the elaboration of a discourse of power in a silenced, aporetic space of abjection.[5]

The various Hindu scriptures reflect the aporetic spaces that inscribe women in an "extraterrestrial" reality by endowing them with a certain mythical incongruity. The Hindu epics, most notably the *Ramayana* and the *Mahabharata*, offer a plethora of examples of male-constructed mythologies of the feminine in which ideal Hindu womanhood is constructed on a "purist ideology of Hinducentric categorizations".[6] These categories have successfully compartmentalized women into a series of domesticated objects valorized for their adherence to the *pita vrata* (father worship) and *pati vrata* (husband worship) ideal. In other words, a woman's worth is measured in terms of the specific amount of "male service" she can accomplish in her lifetime in her capacity as wife, mother and daughter. Ramashraya Sharma observes that in the *Ramayana*, the self-sacrificing Hindu wife is, in fact, the very paradigm of Hindu femininity: "The *Ramayana* presents a galaxy of women who are simply exemplary in fidelity to their spouses, in rendering ungrudging service, in enduring untold hardship in the hour of trial, in being ever vigilant about the welfare of their husbands, in making sacrifices for the interest of their lords, in ready obedience, and their promptness to stand by the side of their husbands in the hour of need."[7] These texts, elaborated by male Hindu sages such as Valmiki and Tulsidasa, contained cultural specifications for Hindu women that were soon to be validated as cultural truths of the Hindu faith. Cultural fictions were incorporated into religious texts that posited a ritualized Hindu feminine mystique that deified the virtues of the Hindu woman, who was the perfect woman: chastity, fidelity, passivity, self-abnegation and purity. Women were thus victims of an elitist Brahmanic construction of gender that reflected "internalized notions of the golden age of the Hindus, and of the highminded and spiritual qualities of Vedic women", according to Uma Chakravarti.[8] The asexual glorification of women limited them to socially confined roles whose boundaries were fixed and well defined, eliminating the possibilities of transgression or cultural errancy.

The confinement of women within male-delineated space found its most graphic illustration in the medieval version of the *Ramayana* written by Tulsidasa, in which the sage advocated the imposition of spatial restrictions on women to provide for their safe keeping. Once women were immobilized within culturally sanctioned boundaries, they were impervious to the outside world or to external forces of "contamination" that could undermine their honour and integrity.[9] Mystified and mythified characterizations of Hindu women were thus "protected" from non-Hindu influences through hegemonic control and cultural and religious insularity. Woman as abstraction was satisfying to men because her conceptual attributes froze her in time and space by making her a much-cherished and timeless ideal that was worthy of attention. Referring to the limitations of male conceptual thinking, Haimanti Banerjee comments, "So long as the Indian male psyche comprehends the woman within the parameters of the well-established myths, he is able to give her a personality and physiognomy of her own. But as the reality around demands a matrix for the women's image different from the mythic, she is rendered almost faceless because the male psyche fails to comprehend her."[10] In other words, mythical thinking validates the past by situating women within the parameters of an archaic and regressive timeline. The patriarch's tenacious adherence to the past goes beyond sentimentality and nostalgic evocations, as far as women are concerned, because it sustains his uncontested powers of myth making, in which Pygmalion fashions his created object to his own liking whereby she can be "refined, reorganized, recast, regenerated".[11]

The cultural manufacturing of female imagery is a transgenerational and unfortunate transgendered activity that reinforces the stronghold of the monolith, especially when this cultural manufacturing is transplanted to diasporic locations. Cultural fixity, as it is portrayed in the two Persaud novels, inscribes the narration in a particular cultural time lag whereby archaic Vedic constructions of Hindu womanhood are still being imposed by traditional Hindu men and women in transplanted Hindu communities in Trinidad.

The preoccupation with the past becomes more than just a fixation for hegemonic cultural permanence authenticated by the rule of the patriarch who has everything to lose in the process of transition. As Keya Ganguly remarks, "The past acquires a more marked salience with subjects for whom categories of the present had been made unusually unstable or unpredictable, as a consequence of the displacement enforced by post-colonial and migrant circumstances."[12] The destabilizing forces of the *kala pani,* which led to a certain fracturing of the past, threatened to upset the male-centred (im)balance of power maintained in India by creating the possibility of alternative social structures in the new territory. Remembering the past was thus the ultimate defence mechanism for the displaced patriarch to make some sense of his present insecurity. In other words, memories of the past were associated with an ideological recovery in order to maintain a feeling of rootedness for men whereby "for many in the immigrant Indian community the past is an absolutely vital element in the negotiation of identity but it comprises a 'renovated' and selectively appropriated set of memories and discourses".[13]

The selective appropriation of the past was particularly pernicious with relation to those women who became victims of a double ancestral burial carried over from the homeland, as reflected in Persaud's novels. Patterns of disenfranchisement experienced by Hindu women in India were replicated with a vengeance in the diaspora as a means of preserving the "integrity" of Hindu culture. Thus, the immortalization of Hindu culture depended upon the renewed restriction of women who were immobilized within a particular cultural freeze, predicated, according to Espinet, on the "ownership of woman and her reproductive capacity — the only means by which the powerful male can perpetuate himself".[14]

The impact of this marginalization has been felt most thoroughly by Indo-Caribbean women, who have been made to compensate for the alienation and despondency of their menfolk by being caught in a tragic double bind of cultural and gendered dislocation. The protagonist Sastra, whose very name means "script" or "textual inscription", epitomizes the complexities of the double bind that can only be broken by a process of cultural detouring or distancing whereby physical exile becomes the only outlet that, according to Persaud, enables Hindu women to come to terms with themselves.

Sastra begins with a discussion about Sastra between her mother and the local pundit or priest, in which they programme the path of action she is expected to follow as a Hindu girl. The birth of a daughter coincides with a certain anxiety of influence to closely monitor and regiment her life: "Seventeen years had passed and care had been taken to ensure that the creeping child kept close to the ground" (15). The efforts to keep the child Sastra "grounded" despite her natural tendency to creep and explore preface the limitations that she will face during her passage to adulthood. The fear that she may fly or steer off the prescribed path is based on a collective neurosis cultivated by the pundit with his access to scriptural knowledge. He advises Sastra's mother, "Yet, at the spiritual level, I would try and prevent her from taking a path that has not been tested, or from a way that leaves tradition behind and shoots off in another direction without serious consideration for anyone" (9).

The pundit's counsel finds its justification in his personal interpretations of the scriptures through the imposition of his own narrative onto the cultural texts. In this way, he subjects Sastra to a double narrative marginalization, when superimposed interpretations from the male narrative and the culturally authenticated text lead to a particular obfuscation or misreading, as is evident in the following exchange, in which the priest tries to "interpret" Sastra's karma, or destiny:

> "It will come to pass that someone will teach her how to . . . how to . . . lift . . . to fly."
> "To fly, Pundit? You mean to fly?"
> "The exact translation is: will show her how to lift herself, raise herself above the earth."
> "What can it mean, Pundit?" "Translations are not easy."
> "Translations are not easy; interpretations are even more difficult." (8–9)

Here Persaud implies that interpretation by personal manipulation is often misleading and arbitrary due to a misrecognition of signs, which are often lost in translation. Since the translation of religious texts has always been a male prerogative, it is easy to infer that women's realities have thereby been constructed within the parameters of irretrievable loss and absence, within a non-space of non-representation. The loss of female selfhood manifests itself in the priest's pontification on the value of tradition: "Parvatee, the old ways have been tried and not found wanting, they have served us for thousands of years. . . . There is no concept of dharma that has not been thought about and explained in the *Mahabharata*, the *Ramayana*, the *Puranas*, the *Upanishads*, the *Vedas*. If Sastra keeps to the traditional path of honour, dignity, womanhood; if she keeps to the heart of her culture, her life will be secure, content like her sister's" (9).

The dangers of upsetting the prescribed order of contentment and security in which "we are connected to everything and everything to us" (9) by creating a structural imbalance will, in the pundit's estimation, lead to a tragic reversal of the chain of being and its aftermath of destruction. In other words, women's acts of self-affirmation, their desire to act as independent agents by writing their own cultural scripts, will have tragic consequences on family and group cohesion. He warns, "a period of violent upheaval would come to pass. . . . [P]ersons close to the child would be gravely inflicted by intense pain and deep sorrow. . . . [T]he faith of one and the life of another would be severely handicapped. . . . [S]uch close juxtapositions of death and life ever brought turmoil — volcanic explosions, upheavals of the earth and sea — Tsunamis" (11). The upheaval caused by the move to establish a sense of self-definition becomes a violation of Hindu prescriptions for girls and women, who are deprived of a specificity of their own by being reduced to communal property. Women are not seen as individuals but as personifications of a particular social role. In this way, Sastra becomes the daughter of her parents and, by implication, of the entire community as she is given a communal identity: "But try as she might, she could not see herself defying her parents or her village. I am my father's daughter and my mother's daughter and a daughter of this warm village" (57). The obliteration of self in the interests of family and community reflects the commodification of Hindu girl and womanhood by the imposition of culturally motivated gendered anonymity. Another passage bears witness to the stifling of self, as Sastra's sense of indebtedness to her family initially prevents her from probing alternatives: "I need the reassurance and the affection of my family; they have been like gods to me, they are older and wiser than I am; they have more experience of life. . . . My father is a good husband and father, and a worthy member of this community; why shouldn't I listen to what he has to say?" (107). Sastra's self-worth is predicated by her conformity to the expectations of her parents in their capacity as value and identity-conferring models. Her being a good Hindu daughter depends upon her ability to live up to the standards set for her by her parents, standards which remain lofty and unreasonable: "If Sastra doesn't live up to the expectations of those parents, you will never hear the end of it and every year parents are expecting more and more — an ungrateful job" (130).

The idea of self-sacrificing Hindu femalehood extends itself to the community level when women are reduced to exemplified ideals or keepers of the Hindu faith. Susie Tharu, commenting on the imaginative construction of women as symbols of the nation state, makes the following statement about women's traditional role as the purveyors of culture: "It was women, their commitment, their purity, their sacrifice, who were to ensure the moral, even spiritual power of the nation and hold it together."[15] Although women's participation in community building is actively solicited, their commensurate recognition in the form of equal citizenship and direct participation in communal policy making has been largely ignored. Located outside citizenship, female characters are concretized in glorified images of Mother India or Mother Nation, or in glorified ideals of Justice, Patience, Virtue, and so on. Because women are excluded from the process of self-definition within their community, they are reduced to a certain homogeneity, in which they are deprived of their subjective particularities. This deprivation has warranted the lower status of women and the establishment of a duplicitous standard of morality based on women's economic and social disenfranchisement.

This power over women consolidates itself through the levying of moral obligations on women that further immobilize them within the circle or noose of patriarchal protection. The strict enforcement of moral codes of conduct on women is legitimized by ambiguous and limited interpretations of sexual morality, whereby women are valorized for their asexuality when they uphold the virtues of honour and chastity.

In several patriarchal societies, family and communal honour depends upon a girl's virginity as a sign of her moral righteousness. The family's reputation is maintained first and foremost by the daughter's virginity, followed by the wife's fidelity and the mother's ultimate sexual negation. Sexual restraint for women becomes a patriarchal mandate whereby women are traditionally held responsible for maintaining communal honour through an extreme privation of their bodies, "that strong tradition of restraint for women folk brought about from the land of the Ramayana" (*Sastra*, 174). In Persaud's novels, schizophrenic demands that are made on girls and women lead to the development of a psychic splitting in which they are caught in a dialectical configuration that is propelled by externally imposed images of self (social reality) and an inner psychological reality (personal reality) that very often remains repressed.

The Indian system of arranged marriage institutionalizes the lack of fulfilment of feminine desire whereby women become tokens of exchange within the patriarchal economy that reinforces male guardianship of women. The marriage pact that is concluded between parents on behalf of their children transfers the dynamic of control from the father to the new husband, who is chosen for the daughter. The negation of personal choice maintains a structure that denies autonomy by showing how conventions are a way of preserving Brahmin "respectability". This preservation assures the smooth functioning of the system of exchange, whose terms and conditions are controlled by men or women who are willing to act as patriarchal agents, most notably mothers and older female relatives. Shakuntala and Parvatee are convinced of the suitability of their childrens' eventual union in marriage without discussing the matter with them. Shakuntala manipulates Parvatee into believing that her son Govind will be a good match for Sastra because he embodies all the qualities of pedigreed Brahminhood. Parvatee finally admits, "It would be like marrying in the family, Shakuntala. You know nothing will give me more pleasure than to see both my daughters so well married. There is Govind, a good looking, educated, Brahmin boy, from a nice respectable family" (43). The confinement of woman's movements within the parameters of the extended family makes Sastra susceptible to a dual system of control, manipulated by her parents and the newly adopted family. The preservation of the overall structure of marriage takes precedence over the rights of the individuals, who are objects of the marital contract, which, in fact, symbolizes a commercial transaction between interested parties. However, the terms of the contract are disadvantageous to young Hindu women, who lack the necessary powers of negotiation to demand equitable terms of engagement. The daughter-in-law is outlawed by a system that works against her interests, especially if those interests conflict with the requirements of the marital system and its specifications for "honorable wifely behaviour".

While both sons and daughters seem to suffer from the inequities of the marriage contract, especially when the marriage fails, it must be pointed out that Hindu culture privileges the mother–son bond, which is cemented by strong ties of love, reciprocity, complicity and (self-)gratification. This rapport is psychologically satisfying, as mother and son can provide for each other the necessary locus of comfort, protection and security to counter the father's authoritarian rule. Hindu culture favours the Oedipal configuration whereby mother–son complicity becomes a "natural" mechanism of defence in which the son seeks intra-uterine comfort against societal pressures while the mother claims self-validation through her son's presence.

The mother–son bond renders the daughter an outsider, as she is not a value-conferring referent. A closely sustained mother–daughter relationship is self-defeating, as the daughter has already been designated the property of the other. The daughter's residency at her parents' home remains short lived. Sastra's selection in the marriage market is preordained and fixed. Govind's mother states, "what a fine girl Sastra is, after comparing her with everyone else and finding she is the pick of the crop" (158). The cultural manipulation of women is thus arranged, codified and contained by totalizing ideological discourses and institutions that are geared to initiate and maintain women's participation as patriarchal stooges, pitting mother against daughter, mother-in-law against daughter-in-law, older sister against younger, and the list goes on. As Kumkum Sangari and Sudesh Vaid observe in their introductory remarks in *Women and Culture*, "What can emerge from an analysis of both contemporary and older cultural forms are not merely the suppressed or rebellious self-images of women but the extent of their necessary or voluntary collusion in dominant 'male' ideologies."[16] An insidious process of psychological conquering complements the physical and cultural conquering of women to expose the diabolic underpinnings of Hindu and other patriarchies that isolate and fragment the realities of women. Sastra confesses, "yet on the path of duty one must often walk alone, without either family or friends" (52).

The complexity of female character that Persaud tries to introduce in her novels makes her protagonists deviant in their search for a different lifestyle. Her women characters initiate a cultural de-masking in their attempts to lay claim to their own right of ownership of their culture. Sastra's relationship with Rabindranath offers an example of this deviance, whereby she refuses the conventional arranged marriage proposition from Govind's family to choose her own life partner. By breaking the traditional code of honour, resisting immobilization in tradition, Sastra tries to redefine her own karma: "To believe that is to believe in some destiny, in karma, or to believe that people and situations remain static with time. . . . Sastra will make something worthwhile of her life wherever she is . . . for she carries with her much courage and an ability to separate the substance of things from its shell" (217–18). Rabindranath compliments Sastra's ability to contextualize and re-evaluate situations according to their present-day applicability and relevance in an attempt to eliminate the social hypocrisy that is maintained in the name of communal honour. Jeopardizing her reputation and that of her parents seems to be a worthwhile risk to take in place of compromising her own integrity by marrying Govind, whom she likes out of convention. The breaking off of the engagement threatens the integrity of the social structure by disrupting the planned sequence of events that ensure social stability. This disruption has an unsettling impact on the community, as is seen in Govind's mother's reaction to the news that threatens her own sense of control over situations. The breaking of the contractual word becomes an act of betrayal in Shakuntala's mind because it fosters an amoral individualism that is at odds with the collective ethos. She proclaims, "Little does the community know the sacrifices others make on its behalf" (214).

Sastra's decision to marry Rabindranath is based on what I term a "backhanded sacrifice", which illustrates the choices – or, rather, the lack of choices – available to Hindu women. It is true that Rabindranath forces Sastra to strive for excellence by making her question her own cultural beliefs, but, in this questioning, she unwittingly follows a path engineered by him. Rabindranath provides Sastra with the illusion of an alternative lifestyle. His attraction stems from the fact that he becomes a destabilizer of convention: a Christian, and a teacher by profession. In other words, he represents the perfect foil for Hindu tradition not only by his non-Hindu and thus socially "inferior" status but also because, as a teacher, he has a feminized profession based on the traditionally woman-associated qualities of nurturing, patience and selflessness. Rabindranath is thus located within a double interdiction that violates Brahmanic expectations of class and gender-role fixity. Sastra will be more susceptible to the influence of a man who is Indian but "out of her culture" as a result of his social and religious difference. As Keya Ganguly comments, "For most people being Indian has to do with particular ideological understandings of tradition; consequently, divorce, homosexuality, interracial alliances do not figure in such discourses."[17] In other words, the Sastra–Rabindranath match, because of its trangressional boundary crossings, does not have a place in Hindu discourse and the ideological fixity of that discourse.

Sastra's father expresses his concern when he notices the growing friendship between the two of them. The father implies that his daughter's relationship with Rabindranath will warrant a necessary loss of self by making them social outcasts. His fear of excommunication overrides his concern for his daughter's happiness even though he is convinced that he intends well. His desire to intercede on behalf of his daughter, while displaying parental care, exposes his own vulnerability at being unable to control her movements; his identity as a Hindu patriarch will be suspended or called into question if she wanders beyond the imaginary circle of male protection by delineating her own space. Sastra's transgressions thus compromise the father's perceived invincibility by threatening to diminish his power within the household, a failed father who has lost face.

However, Rabindranath quickly replaces the power relinquished by Sastra's father when he becomes her mentor and husband. He wields an invisible power over her that reinforces itself by their supposedly equitable relationship. When Sastra completes her education as a teacher, the only career possibility that presents itself to her immediately is that of a substitute for Rabindranath when he gets sick. She is expected to be steered by him in the preparation of classes and other schoolwork, thereby maintaining the student–teacher dynamic that has previously been set up between them. The spatial distribution of male power between the "inside" (home) and the "outside" (the workplace) maintains its equilibrium when access to the outside does not necessarily symbolize a recourse to liberating space for women. Emancipatory ideals that may be imbibed in school are neutralized when they are brought into contact with the realities of the workplace, where women continue to be of secondary importance.

Nevertheless, Sastra's marriage to Rabindranath, in which she chooses love over convention, illustrates a paradoxical affirmation in negation. The possibility of making an alternative choice is accompanied by a joyous celebration. That celebration is short lived, however: the doctors diagnose Rabindranath's terminal cancer. An unconventional love marriage symbolizes a requited relationship with death punctuated by feelings of loss and pain because it remains unrecorded and thus invisible in the Hindu marriage registry: "A pain, at times unbearable, came upon her at the loss his absence would create" (176). The inevitable connection between love and death places the Sastra–Rabindranath pair in a star-crossed relationship that is most often sustained by the woman's martyred sense of love, based on her undying devotion to her husband.

Sastra's sense of duty is also maintained by a perverse reversal of power whereby Rabindranath's physical debilitation and consequent dependence enable her to take charge. Ironically, Rabindranath's death brings about a certain release for Sastra, who gives a new meaning to widowhood. Traditionally, widowhood has been regarded as the ultimate scourge of Hindu womanhood, whereby a woman is considered to be literally non-existent without her husband's presence. His physical death predicates her moral, spiritual and, in some cases, actual death. Widowhood is an unacceptable social category because it does not involve an active upholding of the *pati vrata* (husband-worship) ideal. As early as 1896, the noted Indian feminist Pandita Ramabai denounced Hinduism's negative prescriptions for widows, who, when allowed to live, were subjected to the worst abuses as punishment for having outlived their husbands:

> The strongholds of Hinduism and the seats of sacred learning . . . where the sublime philosophies are daily taught and devoutly followed, there are thousands of priests and men who are spiritual rulers of our people. They neglect and oppress widows, send out hundreds of emissaries to look for young widows, bring them to the sacred cities . . . and rob them of their virtue. . . . Thousands

of young widows . . . are suffering untold misery . . . but not a philosopher or Mahatma has come out boldly to champion their cause and help. . . . There are many hard and bitter facts that we have to accept and feel. All is not poetry with us.[18]

Widowhood reflected the ultimate devaluing of the Hindu woman, made the victim of several social taboos. In other words, a widow loses her resale value as she has been "contaminated" by a previous marriage that has robbed her of her virginal allure like "a nicely laundered sheet, but that was not the same as brand new" (*Sastra*, 254).

Sastra's release from her wifely duties encourages her to emigrate to Canada with her children. She attempts to create a new space for herself that is located in the outer space of exile. Her brief stay in England, as a student before her marriage, has led to a sense of liberation despite cultural displacement and marginalization in the (step)mother country (Trinidad is a former British possession), "And now in this new, colder environment, Sastra is at last at ease with herself. No longer the strain of expectations" (189). Exile in England has brought about a recovery of self through a long-distance awareness of the limitations of cultural and territorial confinement in her own country. Exile has thus facilitated a rite of passage for Sastra and the marking of a new phase in her development to neutralize the feelings of inferiority and insecurity expected "at home". She states, "There is something about travel; it widens your perspective. You see the limitations of small islands and small places, but most of all the foolhardiness of youth" (199–200).

For women who have been deprived of a sense of ownership at home, travel leads to a questioning of the true meaning of home. Eleke Boehmer, referring to women's exclusion from national and communal citizenship, states, "The dilemma is that where male nationalists have claimed, won and ruled the 'motherland', this same 'motherland' may not signify 'home' and 'source' to women."[19] The primordial rupture or dislocation from homeland as a result of several levels of discrimination makes homeland an imaginary construction for women by obfuscating a potential source of meaning. Women are thus exiled from their own land especially if they do not identify with the ideals of the motherland. Sastra experiences conflictual emotions when she returns "home" only to discover that her life at home had been characterized by its homelessness or lack of centre, whereby "the needs of self were too enmeshed with family and community, too interwoven to unpick, to separate; but she had seen another pattern" (198). In other words, the lack of home or self precipitates the need for physical distancing and cultural detouring, as the only viable options for young Hindu women to deal with the conflictual demands of tradition and sociocultural transition in which female subjectivity is achieved by a paradoxical process of errancy and a movement without to avoid ossification in and by tradition.

In Canada, Sastra finds her community among other displaced immigrants, who are all involved in the process of renegotiating culture and self. Emigration ironically establishes a sense of solidarity among the dispossessed, who shed their alienness by uncovering a new identity in Canadian naturalization. Immigration offers the only possible (re)location of self-determination by creating a multidimensional hybrid space that blurs boundaries. The self takes on a new form within the locus of a spatial formlessness, which is liberating. As demonstrated in both *Sastra* and *Butterfly in the Wind*, Hindu women, in their attempts to circumvent cultural confinement, are faced with only one option: going abroad to restructure their lives by creating a revisionist postmodern Hindu female subjectivity.

Through the complicated and contradictory explorations of her heroines, Persaud tries to envisage more holistic representations by removing women from the gilt-edged framework of mythical abstractions and reinscribing them within the complexities of the transitional present. Although her prescriptions for Indo-Caribbean female subjectivity are, at times, unwittingly and naively located within the patriarchal mould as a confirmation of the latter's presence, she nevertheless endows some of her female characters with the capacity to move beyond boundaries through the gradual development of their self-awareness. This awareness, in opposition to static male fictions, provides the scope for refreshing and much-needed counter-representations. Her heroines demonstrate the "reality" that the confrontation with patriarchy involves a serious revisioning of the past that undoubtedly provides the necessary first step towards female emancipation.

—·—

Colonial school offers a similar pathology of confinement evidenced in the commodification and subsequent devalorizing of Indo-Caribbean culture and the incompatibility of colonial education with ethnic traditions. While there has been ample scholarship on the effects of colonial education on Afro-Caribbean boys and girls in the novels of Jamaica Kincaid, Grace Nichols,

Joseph Zobel, Merle Hodge and others, the impact of colonial schools on Indo-Caribbean children, especially girls, remains a relatively underdeveloped area of literary analysis in Caribbean studies. As in the case of Afro-Caribbean children, colonial education has also been a driving force in the socialization of Indo-Caribbean girls and in the creation of Indian female subjectivity. The overriding influence of the colonial school has been located within a certain ambivalence of representation by providing a potential alternative to traditionally circumscribed gender roles within the family while, at the same time, instigating feelings of cultural alienation, insecurity, inferiority and psycho-social dependency. This section demonstrates how Indian (Hindu and Christian) female colonial subjects are informed by a formalized, visible curriculum exemplified by the British colonial school as well as by a more insidious invisible curriculum of psychological destabilization or "cooliehood" that maintains its equilibrium through a process of socioeconomic and cultural displacement.

Caught in an impasse between the overt and the covert display of colonial power and authority, the female protagonists of Persaud's and Shinebourne's novels have to negotiate the intricacies of racialized, gendered and class differences in their search for identity and cultural stability. It is important to indicate that the experiences of colonial socialization in Trinidad and Guyana cannot be conflated because of each country's specific history and engagement with the colonial curriculum. In the case of Trinidad, Ramabai Espinet highlights the unique presence of the Canadian Presbyterian Mission schools and their influential impact on the creation of an isolated Indo-Creole middle class that was considered to be a buffer class between the Creole populations and the rural, uneducated Indians.[20] Assimilated to the point of accepting Western values and norms as their own, this class was subjected to a dual colonization represented by British and Canadian points of view. As Espinet states, "This represents a double colonization, because the Canadian 'way' was largely made up of a colonized world view, and we became another colony within an existing British Caribbean colony. . . . The curriculum in schools was influenced by Canadian (colonial) ways of teaching and Canadian ways of situating oneself in the world, that is to say not as *managers* but as the *managed*."[21] Within this confining structure, Christian girls were domesticated through the imposition of a gender-determined syllabus that stressed the importance of home economics and other "woman-centred" subjects that would prepare them to be suitable partners for their upwardly mobile spouses. Education was thus a double-edged sword: access to educational opportunities conversely relegated Indo-Christian

girls to the secondary role of wife and homemaker through the development
of a middle-class domesticated sensibility that followed the model of Victorian
morality and its prescriptions for urbanized female gentility. Espinet further
indicates that the influence of the Canadian mission schools was less invasive
in Guyana, thereby exposing a crucial difference in the level of colonial
socialization experienced by religiously differentiated Indians in the two countries.
In addition, it is also important to highlight a crucial distinction between
the Presbyterian Mission schools and their Catholic counterparts. While the
Presbyterian schools were "sympathetic" towards the inclusion of Hindu hymns
and prayers in school culture as a means of authenticating ethnic difference,
the erasure of Indianness in Catholic schools was absolute. However, the guiding
principle behind the imposition of the colonial curricula agenda as a unilateral
hegemonic construction remained the control and manipulation of colonized
minds and bodies, thereby creating a certain commonality of expression in
Sastra and *Butterfly in the Wind.*

This semblance of uniformity can be explained by the fact that the colonial
school, as a symbol of sociocultural and political authority, paralleled the
workings of the plantation state and its economic hegemony. The plantation
and the colonial school symbolized the very foundation of colonial Caribbean
societies wherein colonial cultural permanence was institutionalized and
maintained through the effective collaboration between these formidable systems
of control that ensured the successful operation of the colonial machinery. As
a result, colonial-imposed socialization took place on the assembly line created
by the two hierarchies of economic and sociocultural discrimination, leading
to the commodification of both local and foreign culture.

However, the commodification of British and Hindu cultures, as reflected
in these novels, did not follow complementary channels of articulation. The
mass dissemination of *angrezi* (English) ideology and traditions as value-conferring
ideals led to a corresponding devaluing of Hindu customs. Persaud's and
Shinebourne's female characters, who are predominantly Hindu or affiliated
with Hinduism in a significant way, begin their educational trajectories within
the parameters of this cultural inversion.[22] At the same time, these comments
do not suggest that the Hindu model was a self-affirming alternative for Hindu
girls. The Hindu model, like its Christian counterpart, was itself defined by a
system of patriarchal domination that was almost as self-defeating as the colonial
paradigm in the elaboration of female subjectivity. Hindu girls had to confront
a dual system of imperialist and patriarchal control that was not, however, based

on an equitable distribution of power. The marginalization of Hindu men within the larger structure of colonial hegemony assured a more pronounced impact of the colonial model on the socialization of Hindu girls, according to the specifics of Western education. In fact, colonial education was incompatible with Hinduness because of the irreconcilability of Western modes of thought with indigenized ethnic traditions.

Traditional Hindu patriarchal perceptions of female education are best reflected in this oft-quoted passage from V. S. Naipaul's *A House for Mr Biswas*, part of a conversation between Seth and Mr Biswas regarding the educational qualifications of the latter's future bride:

> "She is a good child. A bit of reading and writing even."
>
> "A little bit of reading and writing . . . ," Mr. Biswas echoed, trying to gain time. . . .
>
> "Just a little bit. So much. Nothing to worry about. In two or three years she might even forget."[23]

Seth considers the future spouse's level of education a minor obstacle that can be effectively eliminated before it interferes with the more important wifely duties of domesticity and obedience. In this exchange, Naipaul presents the education of girls as a frivolous hobby that keeps them occupied until they reach the right age for matrimony. Minimal access to education enhances the marital qualities expected of a young Hindu bride without threatening the overall expectations of the marriage contract through an "overexposure" to education or critical inquiry.

Moreover, differing standards of educational expectations for girls and boys are a further confirmation of the relative unimportance accorded to girls' education and justification for keeping them within the confines of patriarchal dominance. Patriarchal domination colludes with a certain colonial pathology that bases its power on enclosure or confinement, represented on two levels in the novels: spatial enclosure and the closure or fixity of the colonial syllabus. Like the prison, army barracks or plantation, the physical dimensions of the school are defined by localized space, symbolized by confining classrooms and assembly halls. The movement of students remains under constant surveillance in the same way that prison inmates, plantation slaves and indentured "coolies" are subjected to strict supervision by guards, overseers and wardens.

The partitioning of enclosed space into rural versus urban, Indian versus African versus British, upper class versus lower class, guarantees spatial immobility through the unequal reconfiguration of space, as a further level of control. Spatial fragmentation hinders the formation of communal space by consolidating varying hierarchies of discrimination. Jan Shinebourne's novel *The Last English Plantation* offers several examples of spatial exclusions that maintain their (im)balance through the hegemonic technique of divide and control.[24] Hindu girls are particularly vulnerable to spatial dislocations because they encounter a dual disenfranchisement, in school as colonial subjects and at home within conservative family structures. Although both boys and girls suffer from the inequities of the colonial system, the double standard maintained by gender-determined expectations places girls at an added disadvantage.

The intersection of gender disparity and class privilege locates upper-class urban Hindu girls outside the system of colonial domination but within the parameters of parental control, in a non-space of exclusion that complements (but also complicates) the exclusion that their economically disfavoured counterparts suffer in school. In other words, schools maintain a power dynamic between the production of knowledge and the economic status of students by advocating and upholding a policy of "learning for the privileged". Rural Hindu girls find themselves at the very bottom of the pyramid of socioeconomic stratification by serving as a glaring reminder of the historical and institutionalized disenfranchisement of Indians who were brought to the islands from India as a cheap plantation workforce. Since the labourers are a disadvantaged economic underclass, with indentured women reduced to a further gendered subcaste, the presence of rural girls in school becomes a source of embarrassment for other Indians students who are anxious to forget a "shameful" history of cooliehood.[25] In this way, a rural Hindu student, Mahadai, becomes an object of ridicule in *The Last English Plantation* when her name and accent betray her origin:

> The girl directly behind June laughed and mimicked "Mahadai Gopaul" in an exaggerated country accent: "Ai gal Mahadai ah wah' y'a ah do gal, beti, Mahadai." Then she changed to her own voice and declared that the name sounded like "mad eye".
>
> Someone laughed loudly at this. . . . (71)

However, even victimization has its own lines of demarcation when ethnicity, gender and economic status do not constitute the only basis for discrimination. Religious distinctions between Hindu and Christian impose a further level of marginalization whereby "no one laughed at the Indians whose names were half Christian" (71). The names "Tina Jaikarran, Lavender Jones, Beverly Khan" (71) are awarded a certain distinction as they symbolize a primary initiation into "Christian respectability" and a rejection of cooliehood.

Christianity becomes the organizing principle of the colonial school by propagating its civilizing mission to educate and refine the natives, by preparing them to serve as cogs in the proverbial colonial wheel (of progress): "The convictions of Mother Mary Rose in the infallibility of the doctrines of the Catholic Church" (143) personifies the newly adopted credo of the colonial school when the collusion between church and state further consolidates the power of the school by legitimizing the connection between moral law and educational policy and law.

Religious impositions lead to a further constriction of space predicated by the marginalization and attempted eradication of indigenous beliefs and traditions associated with moral and spiritual backwardness and decadence. By reinforcing the religious and cultural otherness of Hindus, the Catholic way of life becomes the only prescribed route to salvation, advocating a purging of pagan systems of worship that undermine allegiance to a single master.[26] The superimposition of the authority of the Divine Master and the Colonial Master creates a system of absolute justice wherein "they seldom gave the real reasons for their own actions" (140) because "this was Catholic territory" (141).

As mentioned before, Hindu girls have to negotiate between two levels of internal (home) and external (school) religious disenfranchisement when neither model upholds female subjectivity. Each model inscribes itself within the paradigm of patriarchal exclusionary practices that provide a common barrier to self-affirmation. The female protagonists are forced to combat a dual alienation that results from the anticipated clash of cultures, both of which demonstrate varying degrees of foreignness. Commenting on the ambivalence she feels when she has to sing Christian hymns, Kamla admits, "Then we sang, 'Jesus loves me this I know, for the Bible tells me so', at the top of our voices, though none of us had opened a Bible" (153). However, she feels equally estranged during the performance of Hindu ceremonies: "Our services were conducted in Sanskrit, which I did not understand" (144). She reveals her confusion and self-doubts: "[M]y mind was restless. My former concept of God had been shaken. . . . Were non-Catholics doomed to hell?" (145).

However, the confusion she experiences is a well-calculated strategy of manipulation undertaken by the Catholic school, using an efficient system of "organisation, discipline and achievement" (144) to expose "the simple rural way of the Hinduism I knew" (144). Associated with sophistication, modernity and scientific rationality, the colonial school undermines the integrity of informal methods of worship that are "of earth", "usually small family prayers in the home" (144). The imbalance of power between organized religion, with its business-oriented, mercantile philosophy, and "small . . . modest . . . quiet" (144) community-oriented religious practices engineers a shift from traditional levels of organization to formalized capitalist hierarchies. These categorizations reveal the imperialistic tendencies of colonial schools and their strategies to impose alien economic, social and cultural structures on indigenous societies that have the least to benefit from these impositions.

The most efficient method of ensuring the distribution of colonized knowledge was through the careful structuring of the colonial syllabus. The colonial curriculum imposes two levels of alienness on Indian students, predicated by a double false reality represented by a foreign language and a set of foreign referents. The foreign language, as a unitary imposition, has the power to establish and control meaning by negating native linguistic agency. The acquisition of a new language places students in an infantilized position of dependence, whereby meaning is interpreted *for* them until they reach the required level of proficiency. This situation of linguistic dependency empowers the school with what Homi Bhabha calls a certain "governmentability"[27] in order to "protect" its subjects. The establishment of the protectorate school enforces a series of negations that lead to the development of a colonized subjectivity symbolized by a loss of history and linguistic aphasia.

The colonial language is a discourse authenticated by difference when words become signifiers of racial and class distinctions. In *The Last English Plantation*, the incommunicability of the English language when it is transposed into a local setting is demonstrated as June experiences a certain linguistic alienation when the English language creates a world that is foreign to her immediate surroundings: "The new language, English, did not only translate the books into her mind, it also translated New Dam. The more she absorbed the books, the more she became conscious that their words were not the words the people around her used about the same life, and she would listen for the differences" (33). In other words, English as a medium of expression reveals its inability to translate or interpret for June a familiar frame of reference. On the contrary, English imposes a series of mistranslations of local culture, mistranslations that are more in keeping with colonial perceptions and prejudices. The foreign language becomes a strategy to control indigenous realities by re-presenting them according to colonial specificities. As a result, the colonial syllabus seems displaced and out of context, ensuring that the colonial subject will always fail in his or her attempts to fathom this irreality or "crooked thinking" (*Sastra*, 27).

The selective processing of school culture is based on a forcible ingestion of the bourgeois Christian model exemplified by English literature, "a wonderful subject" (*The Last English Plantation*, 77), and its immediate association with Victorian morality and high-class gentility. The disjunction between reality and ideal reinforces itself when Jane Austen becomes the paradigm of Victorian femininity to be imposed on Hindu girls. The need to properly socialize and discipline Hindu girls through the imposition of Western value systems regarding "appropriate" manners, modes of dress and morality reveals the colonial attempt to (dis)place Hindu girls within the confines of a class-determined cultural imaginary that advocates acquiescence and sexual passivity, as signifiers of proper feminine demeanour. In other words, the English cold-cream culture, to effectively lighten (that is, render invisible) dark Indian skin (*Butterfly*, 167), is juxtaposed with the vulgarity displayed by "mati coolie" or Hindu female culture (*The Last English Plantation*, 127) in order to stress the need for colonial sophistication as a prerequisite for success. The adoption of Austen-prescribed whiteness, achieved through the systematic use of cold cream or vanishing cream, becomes a method for Hindu girls to eliminate the difference created by gendered otherness and an illusory attempt to identify with whiteness.

Epidermal lactification is symptomatic of a larger and more pernicious process of historical whitewashing and its attempts to establish a one-sided master narrative through linguistic domination. The "elegance" and "mystery" (*Sastra*, 24) of English camouflages an agenda of deception and distortion when words serve as an "elixir" (25) to highlight "the magical process of learning" (24). In other words, the memory of the colonized is based on a borrowed memory, a false point of reference, that leads to the introjection of an externally imposed historical ideology.

In *Writing in Limbo*, Simon Gikandi states that Caribbean selves are inscribed "within an economy of representation whose institutional and symbolic structures have been established since 'the discovery' ".[28] This statement implies that colonial history in the Caribbean is associated with a "false" start resulting from Columbus's misnavigations — or, to put it plainly, a mistake — that dislocates the primary referentiality of Caribbean colonial discourse. The ambivalence of this discourse posits the illegitimacy of false beginnings that underscore the "logic" of colonial impositions and their repercussions on colonized subjectivities. In a lesson on West Indian history, Kamla and her classmates learn about the important contributions of famous English explorers such as Sir Walter Raleigh, Sir Francis Drake and Sir John Hawkins, and Hawkins's pioneering efforts to mobilize the slave trade. Puzzled by the association of knighthood with human degradation, Kamla secretly asks her instructor, "Sir, why should the Queen of England honour with a knighthood men like Sir John Hawkins who started the slave trade to the West Indies and America?" (54). Kamla is baffled by the inverse logic inherent in the colonial system, in which genocide, exploitation and other human atrocities become the basis for public recognition and merit. The teacher's response — "The slave trade made England rich and her colonies too" (54) — provides Kamla with an unsatisfactory explanation.

The logic of colonial inversion can be attributed to English's being the language of the international money market, whose buying power imposes a unitary script of self-vindication. Words can be bought, just as histories can be manipulated by discourses of coercion and exclusion. Colonial history is thus based on the paradigm of a colonized subjectivity or, in many cases, on a negation of subjectivity. It situates itself within the thematics of violence because, as Gikandi states, colonial history "negates cultural authority", leading to "excommunication from history and isolation from genealogy".[29] Promoting a level of ideological censorship, History (with a capital *h*) is embedded with deep fissures that conceal "tales of far darker iniquity" (*Butterfly*, 18) and, as June laments, "Schoolwork had the same effect. It all erased the Hindi, the language of the coolies, the poor" (*The Last English Plantation*, 33).

Schoolteachers guaranteed this erasure in their classrooms through a process that Frantz Fanon describes as a "nationalization" of the curriculum.[30] While Fanon's use of the word *nationalization* refers to postcolonial national bourgeoisies, this study stresses the applicability of the term in a colonial environment where members of the formerly educated elite were being assiduously trained by ruling systems of power for their role as colonial intermediaries. School was the ideal location for the formation of these mimic men and women who were to be the eventual transmitters and consolidators of the colonial mindset, even after independence.[31]

As a result, teachers became colonial stooges who projected their own feelings of insecurity and lack of agency onto their students, as this passage from *The Last English Plantation* demonstrates: "Although the headmaster was Indian and Mrs Farley was African, they looked alike: Hair streaked with grey, thick spectacles, lips twisted into a pout, large front teeth. They looked down scornfully at everyone and everything around them, their look changing from disgust to anger in turn" (65–66). Mrs Farley and the Indian headmaster resemble each other in their common abjection, made visible by facial contortions, premature greying and myopic distortions of vision. The passage highlights the collusion between an African and Indian creolized intelligentsia across the lines of ethnicity and gender in the perpetuation of the colonial mindset. External signifiers of physical decrepitude mirror a more serious internalized moral decrepitude, characterized by feelings of self-loathing and disgust that are displaced onto the students through a process of transferral that reveals the teachers' inherent psychic instability.

Mr Singh, the Indian principal, ridicules his people for their social and ethnic backwardness. He plays into the colonial stereotype that characterizes all Indians as indolent and unmotivated and thus incapable of participating in their own social enhancement. After labelling his own students as inferior, he punishes them severely in the hope that whiplashes will eliminate all traces or visible manifestations of their inferiority. There is a particular psychology of self-defence at work here whereby Singh tries to conceal his personal mental scarification or inner malaise under external blows and other forms of violent behaviour that assure the guarding of a well-kept secret. Within this cycle of violence, upper-class Hindus maintain their sense of superiority at the expense of their lower-class peers, boys discriminate against girls, and "pure-blooded" upper- and lower-class Hindus vilify those of mixed racial heritage.

June's situation is particularly acute in this case because of her mixed Indian and Chinese heritage. The multiple levels of discrimination that face her, unlike other characters in the novel, are concretized in demeaning racial slurs that are thrown at her by Hindu classmates:

> Rita put her fingers to her eyes and pulled them upwards into thin slits. "Chinky Chinee!" This brought down scornful laughter on June's head. . . .
>
> She could not let it be, she turned around and declared: "I am Indian too!"
>
> . . .
>
> No, she was not Indian like them, not the country girls, or the town girls not what they called "pure" Indian. (73)

June's identity is located in a double dislocation that highlights two colonized histories in the Caribbean: Indian and Chinese indentureship. Her origins are thus located within a dual source of shame or embarrassment, especially for her mother, Lucille, who actively tries to eliminate any signs of alterity displayed by her daughter by forcing her to conform to an imaginatively constructed notion of Englishness.

The process of renaming symbolizes an initial attempt to obscure the ambivalence of one's origin. By changing their Hindu names, Lucille attempts to radically alter their identities into a more convincing model of acceptance by others. However, if the proper name establishes legitimacy and subjectivity, the changing of one's name predicates an alienating absence, leading to a certain loss of meaning through the initial loss of self. June's Hindu name, Muluk, which means "ancestral home" or "motherland", suggests a sense of rootedness or stability, while Lucille's Hindu name, Vijay, stands for "victory". The Hindu names, as signifiers of self-affirmation and authority, lose their potency in conversion. Models of agency are transformed into agents of disinheritance when both June and Lucille suffer from a primary dislocation, initiated by the process of false adoption. Like specular images that project deflective or distorted images, the new names become defective appendages that further confirm the visibility of ethnic otherness. In other words, the new names are not self-reflecting mirrors that authenticate the location of self. On the contrary, alienating images displace the centrality of self to create an existential vacuum in self-representation. In addition, Nani Dharmadai, the communal mother figure in the novel, informs June that June's father is himself the victim of a case of mistaken identity because his Chinese name, Li Hau, had been wrongly anglicized into Lehall in the official English registry, thereby falsifying his identity and making him a stranger to himself (132).

The decentralization of the alienated self is symptomatic of Lucille's behaviour when she tries to delude herself into believing that the adoption of Englishness, as a key to transcendence, is an accessible and viable option for economically and ethnically disenfranchised Indians. Her use of "proper" English becomes a strategy to distance herself from other Indians so that she can feel superior to them through linguistic distinction: "Lucille spoke her English English, rounding the vowels so that her accent changed completely and distanced her from Boysie. 'And please don't call June "Muluk". That is not her name. Her name is June' " (5). Lucille thus sets up two barriers to protect June and herself from "contamination" by other Indians, whose "difference was in their race and position" (6). Hatred and shame for one's community betray feelings of extreme inferiority and resentment for being recognizably identified with this community in any way. Denial of this reality exists on both internal and external levels, revealing the visible and invisible forms of colonial domination.

Lucille's identification with whiteness encourages the formation of a *café au lait* mentality, characterized by a rejection of Hindu customs and an open declaration of British self-identification. She claims, "This is the West Indies, not India, not China, the West Indies! We are British!" (128). Her allegiance to Britain exposes her unconscious complicity with the politics of whiteness; because whiteness in the colonial context is associated with power and prestige, as the works of Albert Memmi and Fanon have shown, the greater the identification with whiteness, the greater the lactification/assimilation it ensures.[32] In fact, Lucille imagines that she and June will come to personify the white ideal itself by using English products such as Lifebuoy soap and Yardley talcum powder (81) to ensure the effective "rubbing off" of the ideal on their skin.

Lucille's scorn for Hindu customs is based on her conviction that they exemplify an inverted image of the white Christian ideal. Similarly, her devaluing of Creole follows the logic that proper English symbolizes propriety and pedigreed upbringing while Creole, the popular language, represents an inherent bastardization or illegitimacy. She ironically associates Creole with the language of assimilation and cultural debasement that reveals an inferior status. Admonishing June for speaking Creole, she states, "You know very well how to speak proper English. Why you prefer to talk that terrible Creole?" (13).

Lucille equates propriety with a blind imitation or mimicry of colonial culture. Her attempts to speak carefully enunciated proper English do not reveal an Oxford or Cambridge accent. On the contrary, "the imitation of an English accent" (6) indicates a certain caricature-like posturing that becomes as much an object of derision as the humiliation that June faces when the overseer's children ridicule her accent.

Lucille's delusions maintain her in a self-created glass bubble of ignorance, where the body blocks its own psychic defences through a process of self-imposed amnesia or an unwillingness to remember communal history. Taking colonized history as her primary source of reference, Lucille buys into the ideology of the biologically constituted inferiority of the colonized, leading to an outburst when June informs her about her decision to quit school: "Lucille lost her composure. 'All right! Stay at home then! Turn into a coolie! You used to be a coolie and I manage to turn you into a civilised person, now you want to turn coolie again!' " (126). The inscription of cooliehood and civilization within a binary oppositional power dialectic essentializes the specificity of these signifiers by locating cooliehood as a converse dimension of civilization. As a result, Lucille's sense of personal history begins with a primary fracturing or misinterpretation of meaning that expresses itself within the problematics of cooliehood.

The term *coolie*, as an original signifier of caste and class disparity in India and China, refers to the porter class of unskilled, cheaply employed labourers, a readily exploitable mass labour force whose only value was located in its utilitarian capacities. Created by class-determined occupational necessities, coolies were situated at the very bottom of the four-tiered Hindu caste structure, within a non-space of untouchability or inhumanity. Confined to a subhuman level of existence by upper-class Hindu superiority and prejudice, the coolies were dehumanized as beasts of burden and reduced to functional body parts – strong arms, legs and necks to carry out back-breaking labour. In other words, cooliehood signified a rigid caste-determined fixity, a point of no return that permanently placed disenfranchised workers within the gridlock of their sub-altern status.

The colonial appropriation of the term to characterize Indian indentured history in the Caribbean, South Africa and the islands of the Pacific and Indian oceans added a level of racialized marginalization to an already disempowered social categorization. Colonial misappropriation inscribed cooliehood within a double displacement, characterized by the physicality of cooliehood, as demonstrated by the indentured slave trade, as well as by a more pervasive (and invasive) attitudinal or psychological cooliehood that was constructed in India as a result of three centuries of colonial domination and, later, transplanted from the ancestral land to various diasporic locations. A detailed commentary on the construction of attitudinal cooliehood informs this analysis of the psychological destabilization imposed by colonial ideology on the Indian psyche. Clem Seecharan's study, *India and the Shaping of the Indo-Guyanese Imagination, 1890s–1920s*, provides a useful, though somewhat misguiding, source of reference.[33]

If physical cooliehood – that is, subjugation by class discrimination – was the scourge of a socio-economically disenfranchised segment of society in the nineteenth century, then attitudinal cooliehood included the intellectual brainwashing in colonial school and other milieu, as represented at a later date, for example, by the Nehru dynasty and its instrumental role in shaping the post-independence Indian imaginary. Subjected to racialized and gendered second-class citizenship by the colonials, indigenous elites exposed their own lack of agency through their slavish perpetuation of colonial ideology in the name of modernity and progress (attitudes that were adopted by Indian diasporic writers such as Nirad Chaudhuri and V. S. Naipaul). In fact, Nehru inadvertently revealed his intellectual alienation: "Personally, I owe too much to England in my mental make over to feel wholly alien to her."[34] He publicly acknowledged his indebtedness to colonial England, whose "most significant" act of benevolence towards India was a legacy of physical and psychological disempowerment.

The ideal of Hinduness was thus located within a certain politics of alienation, as can be seen in comments made by Tapan Raychaudhuri in his characterization of the nineteenth-century Bengali elite: "A lack of cultural self-confidence, the continual need for assurance, preferably from reputable European quarters, was very much a part of the preoccupation with the Hindu heritage. . . . The belief that the white masters were not very distant cousins of their brown Aryan subjects, provided a much-needed salve to the wounded ego of the dependent elite."[35] Imported Aryan constructions of Hinduness were imposed as a monolithic, hegemonic reference for the entire country, displacing the heterogeneity and primacy of indigenous sociocultural models of agency that did not conform to Westernized perceptions of Hinduness (I refer to various forms of Dravidian culture that were subsequently pushed further south by Aryan conquest to be mistakenly renamed "South Indian culture", with the north retaining its primacy of control). The reductive association of Aryanism with a universalized formulation of Indianness posited a dislocated paradigm of anglicized Indianness, symbolized by the fragile links between the white masters and their not-so-distant brown cousins. The constitution of the Hindu self by an external reference inscribed Indianness within a binary power dialectic, whereby the white Aryan masters imposed their lineage through conquest and domination. The white/brown colour dynamic was reflective of this imbalance, wherein white, as a primary colour, maintained its pristine qualities, unlike the darkish hues of brown that symbolized inferiority through contamination and subjecthood. In other words, Aryan-imposed standards of perfection established Hindu Aryans as cultural half-breeds whose brownness nevertheless contained traces of white solvent as a "purifying" agent. As a result, Hindu Aryanism represented a deflective paradigm of identity that was based on exclusions and the justification of discrimination through the visibility of difference, most notably skin colouring. Varying shades of darkness were associated with different degrees of marginalization, culminating in the establishment of the caste system, which institutionalized discrimination based on class, profession and the colour bar.

The not-so-fortuitous discovery of the Indian country cousins was symptomatic of the later "discovery" of Indian culture by eighteenth-century Orientalists, who, through the "rigor and scholastic integrity of European scholarship",[36] familiarized Indians with themselves. Europeans, as master translators, interpreted Indian realities through the revival of ancient Aryan texts that, as shown earlier, located Indianness (in)difference. Ancient Hindu epics such as the *Ramayana* confirmed the north–south divide between the "enlightened" leadership of the Aryan king Rama and the "villainy" of the dark-skinned southern demon king Ravana, who was finally vanquished in the clichéd triumph of good over evil, symbolized by the proverbial return to light (the festival of Diwali). The resurrection of Hindu culture through the common, though distant, affiliation between Indo-European languages and cultures, as stressed by the German Orientalist Max Mueller,[37] reactivated (selective) racial pride in Aryanism. Aryanism, as a "heroic self-image",[38] was, once again, based on a misconception whereby European primacy was reaffirmed as the source of reference. As a result, Indian attitudinal cooliehood was constructed within a double obscuring of origin (ancient and modern) that was to suffer a third degree of erasure through its diasporic translations in the "New World".

Khal Torabully coins the term *coolitude* in the Indo-Mauritian context as a nativistic reaffirmation of Indian literary and cultural identity in the second half of this century. Associating coolitude with a kaleidoscopic identity that mirrors internal fragmentation and cultural displacement, Torabully posits it as a cultural compensation, a celebration of difference that goes beyond ethnicity to embrace creolization and a cultural *métissage* of experiences.[39] However, Torabully's attempts to create an Indianized version of Negritude by stressing a cultural positivity that distances itself from racialized positivity (unlike Negritude) negates the temporality of political agency. A depoliticized agenda of cultural affirmation reinscribes coolitude within a historical lack of agency that does not lead to the inscription of ancestral memory or give voice to the silences created by colonial history.[40] By advocating the "personal is poetical" approach, coolitude becomes a displaced imaginary construction of nostalgia and not an agent of political self-control, as promulgated by Negritude.

Similarly, the late Indo-Guyanese writer Rajkumari Singh's passionate plea to venerate the ancestors through a positive identification with "coolie" culture contains (well-intended) romanticizations that nevertheless call for a "new lease on life". Rajkumari Singh's tribute to the ancestors contains the following affirmations and recommendations:

> COOLIE is a beautiful word that conjures up poignancy, tears, defeats, achievement. The word must not be left to die out, buried and forgotten in the past. It must be given a new lease on life. All that they did and we are doing and our progeny will do, must be stamped with the name COOLIE, lest posterity accuse us of not venerating the ancestors. . . .
>
> . . . Brave, courageous, daring, exciting, industrious thrifty nation-building, humble folk — our COOLIE ancestors. . . .
>
> . . . Proclaim the word! Identify with the word! Proudly say to the world: "I AM A COOLIE".[41]

Singh's pride in her coolie identification is slightly short-sighted because it is not accompanied by the necessary decolonization of the term, as a first step to achieve political self-positioning. The fact that the word is still associated with racialized second-class citizenship in the Caribbean and elsewhere stresses the urgency of moving beyond sentimentality that has the unfortunate effect, in many cases, of reinforcing cultural stereotypes and racism against Indians. However, as each diasporic location begins to negotiate its own tryst with "coolie" culture, the necessary politicized deconstructions of meaning will give new agency to the term as a locus of postcolonial identity.

Until such revisions are actualized and sustained, this study affirms that coolitude remains a companion signifier to attitudinal cooliehood in the Indo-Caribbean context because of its lack of value neutrality. If, as Seecharan claims, the Indo-Guyanese educated elite of the 1890s and the early twentieth century imagined India through a transatlantic instinctual identification with this ancient culture, I affirm that this association was based on the misrecognition of a colonized ideal and a misreading of Hindu culture, as a source of self-deception. Seecharan writes, "Because many retained no direct contact with India, their conception of it tended to assume mythical dimensions; the heroic, ethereal, idyllic Aryan India of the Hindu epics — a Golden Age — lodged permanently in the Indo-Guyanese psyche. This inviolable, surreal India was a potent, malleable instrument of self-preservation, of racial dignity, in a society where few, if any, dared to challenge European definitions of the human condition."[42]

The identification with the Aryan ideal as a basis for self-affirmation and as an antidote to the violence of colonial repression was equally problematic in that it was these very principles of "heroic" Aryan selfhood that provided the moral justification for indentureship. Selective definitions of humanity, created by "idyllic Aryan India of the Hindu epics", imposed gendered, coloured, class-based and religiously defined human categorizations that, through metonymic representations, deemed a chosen majority as being less worthy of human consideration than others. The representation of the indentured labour force as an anonymous and amorphous collectivity deprived them of the subjective particularities that were needed to establish their selfhood. The collusion of Indo/Euro-Aryanism conversely disfigured the Indo-Guyanese imagination through intellectually composed cultural disarticulations that resulted in the cultural alienation that Indo-Caribbean communities face even today. In other words, Caribbean cooliehood was established by an immediate physical violation as well as by a more primeval idealistic/ideological infraction that established an effective chain of command between different periods of Indian colonization in different geographical locations. As a result, false frames of reference were themselves engaged in duplicitous games of posturing, manipulation and control to dispossess entire populations.

—•—

Lucille's predicament in *The Last English Plantation* reflects the consequences of false associations. Her rejection of Hinduism, as a way of protesting class and cultural biases, relocates her within another pattern of discriminatory practices as exemplified by the colonial Christian ideal. In both instances, she is placed in a disjointed space of non-representation through her lack of hegemonic authentication that reminds her, instead, of her third-class status as a former Hindu, Catholic-converted Indian woman from a racialized and economically deprived subcaste. In other words, Englishness and cooliehood posit colonized subjects as passive victims of history whose blind adherence to signifiers fabricated by internal and external systems of control negate authority and the power to negotiate alterity.

Kamla and June, however, through individual critical questioning, attempt to contest and offer a remedial cure for ideologically imposed pedagogical manipulations. Kamla develops an "inner voice" (53) as a defence mechanism to circumvent brainwashing in school. Describing her inner voice as a subversive instrument of individuality and self-control, Kamla states, "The presence of such an inner voice is not the sort of thing you would wish to speak about, and I had no way of knowing whether anyone I knew had one. So, unwillingly, I carried mine in silence" (53). The cultivation of an inner voice for questioning authoritative readings becomes an antidote to the intellectual censorship enforced in school; the protagonist secretly begins to question the prescribed order of things. She says, "As I grew taller, I began to think there was something contrary in the way my mind worked. It began innocently at first . . . to question quite simple things" (53). The inner voice attempts to make some sense of cultural disorder through a process of critical engagement that seeks to destabilize the rote learning and passive memorization of school. It is a transgressive tool that calls for change in order to overturn the inherent inequities in the curriculum, by converting classroom docility into radicalized possibility. However, even though Kamla's inner voice does not realize its full potential in the novel, its transformative capacities can be compared to bell hooks's articulation of the "engaged" voice: "The engaged voice must never be fixed and absolute but always changing, always evolving in dialogue with a world beyond itself."[43] Offering a countervoice to colonial authoritative fixity, the engaged voice encourages a two-way system of learning through a reciprocity of input that displaces absolutisms by equating education with the practice of freedom.[44] Education, as a liberating practice, reactivates collective memory from its state of imposed dormancy to initiate new beginnings. Indian histories are thus given new meaning through the politics of engagement, which creates the necessary space for alternative narratives. In other words, the erasure of parallel histories from traditionally composed narratives is counteracted by new articulations of decolonized histories that reclaim their lost origins.

Gikandi associates this return to origin with a desire to evolve a genealogy of one's origins. He affirms, "This genealogy leads to the development of a radical consciousness of history, but it also actualizes the trauma of imperialism which has overrun the ancestors."[45] Genealogical documentation displaces the primacy of colonially imposed or false points of reference for colonized histories by exposing these manipulations. As a result, voyages of return serve the dual purpose of establishing family history and of confronting and dealing with the trauma created by the shock of forcible historical lobotomies. The cathartic value of such returns facilitates the launching of multiple histories from local points of view through a creative suturing of open wounds that represent lost impressions or gaps in memory, thereby converting historical disenfranchisement into active remembrance.

Interestingly, in *The Last English Plantation*, it is the female characters, such as Nani Dharmadai and Kamla's grandmother, who initiate the necessary decolonization of Hinduness by inscribing Hindu customs and traditions within the realm of orality and pre-discursive modes of communication that attempt to rectify the distortions created by colonial and patriarchal readings, as will be developed in chapter 4 of this study. Similarly, when Kamla chronicles her family history, she simultaneously documents the collective history of indentured Indian immigrants in Trinidad. The narrator writes:

> In 1890 my grandfather, a babe in arms, was taken off the ship by his mother. It is difficult to know what these new arrivals expected to find, but after many weary, fearful months at sea. . . . [T]o disembark, to set foot on land, would have brought some comfort to these indentured labourers, many of whom had never seen the wide open ocean before. . . .
>
> Whatever harshness these labouring men and women endured, and there was much. . . .
>
> Instead, all hopes were set on what blessings tomorrow would bring. . . . [T]hey built their homes with competence and skill. . . . [W]hen a house was built, neighbours heaved shoulder to shoulder. (83–84)

In Kamla's narrative, her ancestors, despite their imposed economic disenfranchisement, are able to circumvent their psychological cooliehood by becoming active participants in history. The positing of history, like the building of community, affords a sense of participatory ownership that can be empowering. The immigrants transgress prescribed patterns of victimization that confirm an inferior status by breaking stereotypical expectations of passivity, moral lassitude and compliance to position themselves instead as active agents of transformation. Radicalized histories lift the veil from ideologically constructed obscurities through a clearing of vision that heightens one's sense of political and social consciousness. Within the scope of this heightened consciousness, journeys of origin no longer represent misdirected and regressive ideals but serious counter-excavations to resurrect lost memory that has been buried deep within the recesses created by colonial archaeology.

The politics of engagement further contribute to the raising of Kamla's consciousness when she leaves the convent school to join St Augustine Girls High School (SAGHS). The new school provides an experimental model of education, especially for girls, by providing a more holistic concept that integrates global perspectives of learning. As the narrator affirms, "We were the beneficiaries of the new concept of letting the outside come within" (158–59). The interactive, communicative approach between the inside and the outside lays the foundation for new, energized and relevant curricular initiatives that generate excitement and the desire to participate. The new school offers the hope for such excitement: "SAGHS was an important part of a quiet revolution taking place amongst the East Indian population" (161). By offering a free-spirited and light-hearted environment that promotes learning through experimentation, the new school offers a refreshing outlet for creative possibilities that had been stifled by the heavy-handed management of the colonial school. In this case, the passage from (colonial) darkness to light is a much-welcomed change from archaisms and pedantry to progressiveness.

Similarly, June creates a third space of synthesis through her access to a formal and informal education that enables her to counter the alienation she experiences in school. The lessons she learns in the company of Nani Dharmadai, the communal village mother, give her a certain sense of place in history when Nani introduces her to Hindi, the ancestral language, and to Hindu rites and rituals. Rituals provide a structuring force that maintain social stability, especially in instances of social disorder. June's sense of self is thus maintained by a holistic balance between two models of learning that develop her textbook skills as well as her skills of "worldliness". While the incompatibility of the two systems of learning are highlighted in several passages, June's sense of worldliness allows her to successfully balance the relative merits and demerits of each system. Her critical skills lead to her denunciation of institutionalized education when she uncovers its hypocritical practices and discriminatory standards: "June snapped, 'Yes! Yes! It better than New Dam children! All they go to school to do is 'buse down one another. They not interested in studying one little bit. At lessons today they didn't know anything and the teachers don't dare criticise them so we country children take all the blame! Only 'busing down, insulting and beating go on at that school!' " (126). June's outburst exposes the colonial double standard that enforces and maintains the illiteracy of students ("they didn't know anything"). This illiteracy is masked under layers of formalized colonial thinking that maintains its subjects in a state of ignorance.

Ironically, Lucille ridicules the informal education June receives with Nani ("that illiterate women who can't speak English" [127]) because it runs counter to the dictates of rational thought that exposes "native primitiveness". Lucille continues her tirade:

> Lucille hissed, "Stupid girl! You believe all that ignorance she tells you?" . . .
>
> "Is not ignorance! Nani not ignorant!"
>
> Lucille shrieked, "All right! Go! Go then! I will disown you! You go and live with your mati coolie!" (127)

June's "two mothers" represent antagonistically opposed ideological and cultural viewpoints. However, while Lucille's prescriptive model inscribes June within an imaginary Englishness that nevertheless remains elusive to her, Nani helps June to develop her survival skills by demystifying the loftiness of these misleading identifications. Her lessons are threatening in their groundedness, whereby, "although they hardly saw Nani, Lucille talked about her as if she was a threat, as if she was always interfering in their lives" (42). While Lucille associates literacy with acquired modes of knowledge, June's literacy is demonstrated by the unlearning of these very systems of processed knowledge that encourage conformity and the suppression of self: "Lucille grumbled, 'I send you to school to be educated, not to defy me' " (135).

Indo-Caribbean female characters negotiate the ambivalence of colonial education, represented as a double-edged sword that offers the illusion of transcendence at the cost of personal compromise. Demonstrating varying degrees of allegiance to or rejection of the colonial ideal, all characters in these novels are seriously involved in daily engagements with the colonial school, in the form either of nostalgic commemoration or of contestation and struggle. While the minimal agency provided by colonial education to Hindu girls cannot be denied, such an acknowledgement should not obscure the reality that all educational models that sustain totalitarian discourses are in serious need of re-evaluation. Lakshmi Persaud's *Sastra* and *Butterfly in the Wind* and Jan Shinebourne's *The Last English Plantation* offer a definite plan of action for these revisions, in two geographical locations. The girls affirm their subjectivity through intellectual and physical movement beyond boundaries and thereby provide an emerging blueprint of how to establish Indo-Caribbean female identity by dislocating Brahmanic and colonial patriarchies.

2

Engendering Indo-Caribbean and Afro-Caribbean Feminist Dialogues

The complex model of Indo-Caribbean female subjectivity and feminist identity analysed in chapter 1 is inscribed within a broader historical framework of Caribbean citizenship in this chapter as Indo-Caribbean women negotiate their subjectivity within and outside dominant Afro-Caribbean historical, cultural and literary paradigms. The feminism of Indian and African women has known a long tradition in Trinidad and Guyana despite the traditional erasure and obfuscation that this form of activism has suffered in the historical documentation of the Caribbean. Apart from token recognition awarded to figures such as Nanny of the Maroons in Jamaica, Rosetta Smith of Trinidad, Rachel Pringle of Barbados and the Indian cane-cutter Phoolbasie of Trinidad, female historical subjectivity has been largely ignored or misrepresented in "official" accounts until the recent scholarship of leading Caribbean feminists such as Rhoda Reddock, Bridget Brereton, Patricia Mohammed, Ramabai Espinet, Rawwida Baksh-Sooden and others. As Bridget Brereton states, "The exclusion of women from conventional history thus reflected systems of gender oppression and in turn reinforced them by encouraging the definition of women as 'Other', the passive, there but not there, never the makers and movers of history."[1] Presented as passive victims of history in several accounts, women were either discounted or subjected to a racialized and gendered alterity in the colonial narratives of planters, immigration officers and male historians. Stereotypical misrepresentations obscured the dynamism and complexity of women's lives under African slavery and Indian indentureship by relegating women's experiences to the "private" or domestic spheres of influence, spheres that were unworthy of public exposure. It has been the task of Caribbean feminists to resurrect women's history from the archives of oblivion by insisting that "personal life such as family relations and women's roles within the family is just as crucial and just as much part of history".[2] By reconceptualizing and deconstructing the very notion of history as a masculinist narrative, feminist scholars have posited Caribbean women as active agents in history-making through their economic, cultural and political contributions during slavery, indentureship, the post-emancipation period and present-day living.

African and Indian women in the Caribbean share a common history of geographical and cultural displacement, forced labour, economic enterprise, resistance and familial dispersal. The appreciation and recognition of this commonality of experience has often been skewed by partisan politics in favour of oppositional representation, whereby Indian and African women have been pitted against each other as rivals in the fight for legitimacy and subjective autonomy even though both groups of women were brought to the Caribbean primarily as plantation and estate workers in the eighteenth and nineteenth centuries. These foremothers of Caribbean labour were engaged in field labour before assuming domestic activities, thereby locating their productivity within the visibility of the public. As Reddock claims, "Migrant Indian women, at their point of entry into the society, were reconstructed into otherness, often in opposition to the negative values associated with working-class African women in the society."[3] Imposed alienations, in the form of gendered rivalry, mutual disregard, suspicion and cultural and religious high-mindedness on both sides, fragmented the lives of women and constituted an initial stumbling block to reciprocal engagement. The exploitation and exaggeration of the "racial divide" in colonial, patriarchal and hegemonic feminist narratives (both white and black) seriously impeded the formulation of a more reflective theory of Caribbean female agency that included the contributions of women from various ethnicities, most notably Indian women, who constituted a significant majority after the African populations. It has largely been the pioneering work of Rhoda Reddock, a prominent Afro-Caribbean feminist scholar from Trinidad, that has rectified this imbalance in representation, through her research on the specificities of the Indian female experience under indentureship. By highlighting the conjunctions in the African and Indian experiences in terms of female self-reliance, rebellion and capacity for hard work and the disjunctions created by different cultural systems and their varying degrees of patriarchal control over women, Reddock's work serves as an important bridge that spans and encompasses the dual crossings on the *kala pani* to promote a more holistic understanding of Caribbean feminisms, both past and present.

However, despite Reddock's best efforts to position Indian and African women on an equitable platform of representation through scrupulous documentation and visibility in academic discourse (a role that has recently been taken up by other feminists in the region), the experiences of the women of Indian and other ethnic groupings continue to be viewed as secondary to the dominant Afro-centred experience in terms of "Caribbean authenticity" and citizenship. This is not to naively imply that the subjective agency of Afro-Caribbean women was automatic, self-evident or easily negotiated. The pioneering struggles of African women (and their struggles for empowerment even today) serve as a springboard to establish a more complex and diverse network of gender negotiations in Trinidad and Guyana, through an operational grid that is relational rather than oppositional in its strategies. Within this framework, it would be safe to assert that Indo-Caribbean feminism emerged in the context of the dominant Afro-Caribbean feminist discourse and briefly spoke through the voice of the latter. However, within the complexities of Indo- and Afro-Caribbean feminisms, the latter imposed certain themes, objectives and discursive spaces that Indian women found confining, repressive and culturally inappropriate. This chapter exposes these affirmations and negations by showing how both African and Indian women were awarded and denied voice in their individual cultural contexts as well as in their negotiations with one another before forging new relations of inter-ethnic solidarity or renewing old ties of cooperation.

While history continues to fragment the lives of Indo- and Afro-Caribbean women through unequal representation and the imposition of normative codes of Afro-centredness, the development of a certain hybridized consciousness in the fields of literary and cultural production has undermined the primacy of binary oppositions by creating common ground for more affirming relations between Indian and African women. By embracing a transformative dougla poetics of accommodation and renewal in their writings,[4] Afro-Caribbean writers such as Merle Hodge and Marina Maxwell and Indo-Caribbean writers such as Narmala Shewcharan and Ramabai Espinet have created new discursive paradigms for reading Caribbeanness as a site for interracial collaborations, gender negotiations and the affirmation of negated identities. Hybridized discursive sensibilities/sensitivities have promoted enabling cross-cultural interrogations in the works of these writers to offer radicalized possibilities of resisting racial binaries in their writings. Espinet's engagement with Creole cooking proposes a new model of Caribbean citizenship based on equitable representations (see chapter 3) while Hodge's douglarized discursive space facilitates the relational positioning of Indian and African female subjectivity. In a similar fashion, Shewcharan's literary incursions into dougla space create the possibility of coalition building between Indian and African women as a politicized strategy of "sexing" the masculinist ethics of the new Guyanese nation.

The first part of this chapter will discuss Afro and Indo-Caribbean women's oppression and resistance through similarities and differences in representation, while the second part will discuss the process of Indo—Afro cultural fusion and dialogues in the literature of selected and selective authors such as Merle Hodge.

In the context of Afro-Caribbean feminism, Rhoda Reddock, Bridget Brereton, Verene Shepherd and others pay tribute to the founding efforts of enslaved African women who established their autonomy through their active contributions to labour production on the plantations. Feelings of selfhood, despite the dehumanizing aspects of slavery, gave these women the necessary strength to organize and participate in various slave revolts, sabotage plots, labour disputes and strikes. Their voices and their actions of protest and rebellion temporarily humanized them from their daily degradation on the plantations and dispelled any myths about their passivity and their subservience to male and colonial female dominance. Continuing their tradition of self-reliance, many women withdrew from plantation labour in the post-emancipation period to become small-scale subsistence farmers and petty traders. These activities did not imply a retreat to domesticity within the confines of the home even though they involved the cultivation of small family plots. For Afro-Caribbean women, home space was a projection of external workspace. The simultaneous overlapping of the inside and outside blurred the binary fragmentation of space by leading to the creation of neutral ground that warranted public recognition. As Brereton comments, "The peasant woman was an integral part of the household economy, combining production (crops and livestock) and marketing with child care and housework."⁵ Women's tasks were thereby transgendered and multifaceted in their dynamism, positioning women as both mothers, spouses, producers and traders. On the other hand, spatial segregation adversely affected post-indenture Indo-Caribbean women, who were confined to the privatization of the inside through the dictates of Hindu patriarchal demarcations of space. Spatial manipulations were a strategy to control Indian women within inhibiting familial paradigms by limiting their input to the functions of mother and home maker.[6]

Afro-Caribbean feminism, like its Indian counterpart, establishes itself within a tradition of work and its wage-earning potential. As Brereton states, "In the Caribbean towns after slavery, most women worked for their livelihood. They were domestics, seamstresses, washerwomen, petty traders and shopkeepers; by 1930 some were in factories; and a few women, often descended from the free coloured group, ran quite substantial urban businesses like hotels and taverns."[7] Women's participation in the paid labour force afforded them a certain degree of economic agency as compensation for backbreaking labour, long working hours and sexual harassment in the workplace. Both Brereton's and Reddock's studies maintain that domestic service was a major occupation for Afro-Caribbean women after agricultural activities; the paid caring for other's children elevated this task from the invisibility of unpaid domestic chores within one's own home to the "respectability" of remunerated work. Afro-Caribbean feminism was thereby inscribed within a tradition of women working outside the home and earning money. It was never the norm for women to just stay at home and look after the children (although this was a goal for middle-class women aspiring to colonial models of femininity). However, it must be pointed out that this access to the labour force carried its own set of restrictions; the jobs that women could actually perform were rather limited in nature, capitalizing on women's nurturing and caregiving capacities. In this respect, low-paying jobs such as teaching, nursing, secretarial services and retail sales became woman-identified occupations, leading to the devaluing of such professions.

Moreover, Brereton's study highlights the fact that women gradually began to withdraw from the paid labour force between the late nineteenth century and the 1940s because of male migration and economic depression. This withdrawal had its most dramatic impact on poor rural families, in which the absence of men led to the formation of female-headed households with shifting familial structures and unreliable sources of income based on subsistence farming. The onus of child rearing and providing for the family became the sole responsibility of the women at home who had to single-handedly function as caretakers and providers even in the presence of informal communal networks of childcare. The hardships of reality-based experiences were a far cry from the idealized images of African matriarchs, who were represented as superwomen in male fictions.

The gendered imbalance in task performance has been attributed to the lower social, economic and political value ascribed to women's responsibilities over the centuries. Reddock attributes this discrepancy to what she calls the "naturalization of women's work, insofar as it is reduced to the level of instinct or 'second nature' ".[8] The feminization of the labour force has been based on gender-determined essentialisms that have characterized certain jobs as inherently feminine (read, inferior) in nature. As a result of gender-based typecasting, these jobs have been viewed as unskilled, non-technical labour with a lower market value, whereby "the range of low-paid occupations usually held by women outside the home are extensions of their responsibilities as housewives".[9] Their productivity has been undermined through the association of their work with a long-standing, supposed female tradition of sacrifice and service to family and community. Reddock states, "The reality of women working in the domestic/household economy, usually unpaid and certainly underpaid, is that they provide a flexible body of potential wage-workers available for temporary, insecure employment, to be dismissed when this is no longer economically viable."[10] The perception of women as a dispensable workforce has justified varying levels of discrimination against them, ranging from poor wages for unreasonable working hours to job insecurity. These inequities have mirrored the previous divisions of plantation labour into "heavy" and "light" work, which justified lower wages for women through the immediate identification of light work with undocumented (read, invisible) household chores.[11] Moreover, the economic devaluation of women's work has also accounted for women's larger historical and political marginalization in the collective psyche despite women's best efforts to convert passive victimhood into active empowerment through their politicization of space and through the development of a strong sense of feminist consciousness with which to contest the status quo.

This feminist consciousness has been strengthened by the emphasis placed on education as a vehicle for social uplift and career enhancement for both girls and boys. However, the more rapid advancement of girls in secondary and higher education has initiated a backlash, supported by "men at risk" who have accused the educational system of reverse discrimination. This alleged undermining of Caribbean masculinity has further instigated the unequal treatment of women in the workplace as a means to guarantee men their "rightfully designated" place in society.

According to Christine Barrow, it was not until the formation of the regional Women in the Caribbean Project (WICP) in 1979 that women and gender were considered of importance in Caribbean scholarly discourse. The main objective of the project was to make gender issues an integral part of these theoretical discourses through a process of structural revisioning aimed at a truly indigenous comprehension of Caribbean women's lives. As Barrow states, "The project was designed to fill a knowledge gap in the social realities of Caribbean women's lives; to devise a theoretical framework for the analysis of women's roles; to develop guidelines for a cohesive social policy for women; to identify appropriate mechanisms for the dissemination of research results and to train a cadre of women in self-confidence and 'female-centered' research skills to make a meaningful contribution to Caribbean development."[12] Despite WICP's best intentions to redefine the notion of women's work and the traditional conception of women's place in society and at home, several Caribbean feminists have criticized the project's inability to realize its theoretical and practical goals on a long-term basis. For example, despite the increased visibility of women in the labour market as a result of economic insecurities, structural adjustment programmes and "equal opportunity" schemes, women's overall progress and advancement has been hindered by systematic discrimination against women at work, both in their professional status and in their salaries, as suggested by Barrow. Barrow also highlights the ways in which women themselves have participated in their own victimization by internalizing gender stereotypes of inferiority, of lack of management skills and of the inability to engage in high-level decision making. Men have capitalized on these insecurities, as a result of which women "are bypassed in critical contract negotiations, deprived of resources and training, and what influence they have had has been confined to routine matters of office management, social welfare and support services. . . . And yet, without women, the Caribbean labour movement would have come to a halt years ago."[13] Caribbean feminists have reason to take umbrage with the WICP's failure to redefine the very "nature" of women's contributions to labour, a supposed nature that has resulted in sustained lack of recognition and unequal remuneration.

Rhoda Reddock's attempts to resurrect a strong Afro-Caribbean tradition of feminist consciousness are concretized in her homage to Elma François, a founding member of the Negro Welfare Cultural and Social Association

(NWCSA) and a twentieth-century activist who dedicated her life to the uplift of women and the working class. Paying tribute to women such as François who paved the way for contemporary feminist struggles in the Caribbean, Reddock affirms, "Elma François as well as her other colleagues give lie to the myths about the acceptance of colonial and racial domination among the working classes and to the lack of political consciousness and action among women. They illustrate clearly the ways in which people, who could hardly afford to, were willing to and in fact dared to defy the racist colonial authorities in defense of the rights of poor people."[14] A native of St Vincent, François's proletarian-inspired politics laid the groundwork for the participation of women in radical politics through her hands-on, people-oriented approach that was more effective in its outcome than was boardroom diplomacy. Stressing the urgency of sensitizing young, middle-class black youth to their African roots, and advocating the importance of political resistance in the face of colonial domination, the NWCSA also encouraged the formation of solidarity alliances with other oppressed groups, most notably Indians, who, at that time, shared a common history of economic and political disenfranchisement with the Africans. As Reddock suggests,

> the definition of this organization in racial terms was not done in opposition to the predominantly poor, peasant, working-class or unemployed Indians of that period. . . . In fact, this study would go further to suggest that in rural areas, during the pre-1940s period, solidarity between the working classes of both major ethnic groups, African and Indian, were in some ways more cordial than at present. It is the increasing power of the middle-strata members of both races which, then as now, seeks to use the politics of race and religion in order to justify their control over the masses of people.[15]

In François's philosophy, inter-ethnic, class-based solidarity alliances would serve as a vital tool to dismantle the exploitative colonial machinery.

The worldwide economic depression of 1919–39 had widespread repercussions on Trinidad and Tobago's rural and urban working class in the form of serious unemployment, destitution of both African and Indian workers and the increased abjection of women, according to Reddock. In 1934, a series of hunger strikes and protest marches were organized by the unemployed under the direction of the National Unemployed Movement (NUM) in collaboration with the sugar workers of central Trinidad, who were protesting unjust working and living conditions on the plantations. Reddock indicates that the degradation suffered by the Indian workers was reported to the NUM by an Indian woman, Phoolbasie, who was also a strong advocate for the rights of women workers. Anxious to expose the daily humiliations suffered by young Indian female workers in particular, Phoolbasie assumed the role of an informant and thereby brought the grievances of Indian workers to a public forum. As Reddock's analysis indicates, "So impressed were NUM members with the militancy of Phoolbasie that they dubbed her 'Naidoo' after the Indian Congress Party activist Sarojini Naidoo whose speeches, reported in the pamphlets of the Indian Communists, had greatly impressed them."[16] Phoolbasie's identification with a prominent feminist and political activist from the ancestral land established a legacy and, more importantly, a continuum of Indian female activism within the core of Afro-Caribbean self-determination. In fact, Phoolbasie's actions were supported by Elma François and were indicative of François's determination to solicit and sustain the participation of women of different ethnicities at all levels in regional and national politics. Reddock mentions that under François's leadership, every effort was made by NCWSA members to actively recruit female members. For this purpose, the words *cultural* and *social* were added to the title of the association: it was argued that these were two domains that were managed by women and that could therefore serve as a point of identification for them. The NCWSA stressed the need to integrate women into the very fabric of its functioning by encouraging healthy working relationships between its male and female members: "The organization took the position that women and men should cooperate in the development of their collective political consciousness. It rejected the separation of women into 'women's arms' or 'women's auxiliaries'. Within the organization itself executive positions changed regularly so that these responsibilities were shared among members."[17] By espousing the notion that women's rights are human rights, the NWCSA avoided the token representation and participation of Afro-Caribbean women in the political and social scene, advocating equitable agency for them. This foray into politics by women, together with the collaboration between the sexes, could possibly explain the later involvement of working-class African women in the predominantly male-centred nationalist struggles and the Black Power movement of the 1970s, when they fought alongside men for self-governance and citizenship.

However, by the end of Elma François's career, a life's worth of activism was being undermined by a lack of public recognition of her outstanding achievements in the domain of early labour unionism and feminist consciousness-raising. Her work was being challenged by

> new, less radical, nationalists [who] sought to keep their distance from the radical workers movement which had championed the cause of the working class and independence for many years. The cause of labour and socialism to which Elma François and her comrades had dedicated their lives had now been overtaken by forces with clearly different political and social objectives, and the historic contribution of Elma François and her comrades to change in Trinidad and Tobago remained virtually forgotten until now. . . . On September 25, 1987, the day on which Trinidad and Tobago celebrates Republic Day, Elma François was declared a National Heroine of Trinidad and Tobago.[18]

This late acknowledgement of a national heroine is symptomatic of the slow process to retrieve women's forgotten histories from the national archives, where they are very often condemned to oblivion or solitary confinement in an attempt to suppress complex and dynamic women-centred narratives that could (and would) alter and challenge the traditional course of history in a significant way. The history of Indian women in the Caribbean has suffered a similar misrepresentation through cultural stereotyping and gender bias. Presented as the very antithesis of African female resilience and self-sufficiency, Indian women have been confined to inhibiting paradigms of docility, passivity and subservience even though their individual and collective experiences during indentureship present a different picture. Indian women came to the Caribbean primarily as independent field workers in the hope of securing a better life for themselves away from the gender strictures imposed by patriarchal structures in India. To locate these women solely within the limitations of victimhood and subjugation would constitute one of the gravest distortions in Caribbean history and would undermine the contributions of these women to active and independent estate labour production during the indentureship years from 1848 to 1917. While the research on Trinidad and Guyana's Indo-Caribbean female population continues to remain at an "emergent" level in comparison with studies on Afro-Caribbean women, a more serious problem lies in the perception that Indians in the Caribbean are just not Caribbean enough to warrant equitable representation. Viewed as immigrants rather than Caribbean citizens, Indians symbolized the very enigma of arrival that justified marginal representation. Kusha Haraksingh summarizes the "Indian predicament" when he states, "Indians feel powerless in the exercise of definition. Trinidad culture – whatever that was – came to have a special meaning which seemed not to incorporate but to be a counterpoint to Indian culture. . . . As for Caribbean culture, that was considered even more insidious – a device by which the national community could leap-frog the Indian presence in Trinidad in the name of some greater entity. In a word, if a calaloo was cooking, Indians seemed neither chefs nor even kitchen assistants."[19] The "othering" of Indians located them outside representation within patterns of "oblivion and selectivity" that situated them at the periphery as disenfranchised immigrants and strangers in a hostile land.[20] Indian women were to encounter a further level of alterity through their exotic strangeness, their spirit of independence, which flew in the face of expected patterns of Indian female obsequiousness, their ability to do hard labour and their scarcity in numbers. Intimidating to African, colonial and Indian men alike, these women had to endure the added burden of gender discrimination in their struggles for survival both during and after the *kala pani* crossings. As Reddock states, "For single indentured Indian women, emigration presented the possibility of a new life, and escape from a situation in which prostitution or starvation were their only alternatives. Thus these were women whom circumstances had forced to become independent . . . and take some control over their own lives and were prepared to do so in their new lives."[21] It must be emphasized that the majority of Indian women who came to the Caribbean were single, dispelling any myths about their dependence on fathers, brothers or spouses, though there were a few married women. The female population was composed of single mothers, widows, divorcees, pregnant women, sex workers and other women escaping from unfavourable familial and marital situations in India. They were employed as a fully contributing labour force that worked with the men in agricultural labour in exacting working conditions even though they were always given low-paying menial jobs that subjected them to economic discrimination.

The impact of the disproportionate sex ratio gave Indian women greater sexual autonomy in the selection and number of partners they could have, thereby affording them a sense of sexual mobility that was unknown to their counterparts in India. However, this sexual freedom was achieved at a costly price in the face of male frustration and violence as Indian men attempted to protect their own egos by curtailing the movements of the women. Reddock exposes this situation when she argues, "The relative independence of Indian women was perceived as a source of shame by Indian men and, in addition, their inability to have one woman on whom to exercise power and authority in this colonial situation, only added to their frustration."[22] Despite male attempts at control and domination, these women made their mark on the rural landscape of Trinidad and Guyana through their undaunted acts of courage that laid the foundation for future generations of Indian feminist activists.

Several Indo-Caribbean female scholars, writers and artists position the Indo-Caribbean female cane-cutter as a source of their inspiration and as a worthy role model to emulate. Indo-Guyanese feminist Nesha Haniff acknowledges her personal debt to these foremothers of Indian labour in the creation of her own sense of self-reliance and womanhood.[23] Criticizing the feminist movement in the Caribbean for ignoring the contributions of these women while at the same time failing to support and advocate for them, Haniff describes her own scholarship as seeking to make the Indo-Caribbean woman real: "How she shapes her community and landscape must be seen and valued. She has done it differently and this difference must be celebrated."[24] The positioning of Indo-Caribbean women as equal partners in history-making with their Afro-Caribbean sisters predicates the need to remove the blinders of cultural prejudice that have obscured more accurate and affirming images of Indian women. Haniff emphatically states, "The history of Indo-Caribbean women is one of work, and to cast them as housewives whose main role is to have and raise children is an absolute misunderstanding of their place in the economic and social fabric of their countries. Ours is a heritage of important work, of community work, work in the field, work in the home. This legacy deserves honour and tribute, it deserves more than honorable mention."[25] Haniff stresses the urgency of dispelling falsehoods about Indian women that have, in fact, contributed to existing misunderstandings about their secondary role in society. The services provided by these women to family and society have charted a course of action for contemporary grass-roots feminist movements that associate the cultivation of the land with the development of a strong sense of selfhood.

In a similar fashion, Theresa Ann Rajack-Talley's scholarship seeks to dispel myths about Indian women by focusing on their contributions to the growth of the sugar industry in Trinidad in a more contemporary context.[26] Paying tribute to these women for their resilience and courage and for strengthening the tradition of activism inaugurated by their ancestors, Rajack-Talley highlights their subversive role in labour disputes and estate unrest, where they often took the lead in organizing such active forms of protest to resist exploitation. Women such as Clara Panchoo, Carmen Singh and others at Barrackpore, Hindustan and Bonneventure made front-page news for their "audacity" and determination.

Rajack-Talley quotes a *Trinidad Express* article January 27, 1975, headlined "Women Play Militant Role in Cane Belt Row": "One of the many features of the cane farmers' struggles in 1974 and this year, has been the militancy of the women taking part, and several women of Barrackpore have given good examples of this. . . . In many ways the more militant people are the women, and it is an indication of their belief in what they are doing."[27] This description contrasted vividly with patterns of behavioural conformity usually expected of Indian women.

However, their valour should not obscure the hardships endured by women on the plantations during indentureship and afterwards, when the post-indenture consolidation of Hindu culture led to a return of patriarchal restrictions brought over from India in the form of restraining the movement of women. These restrictions inscribed women within familial codes of conduct and denied them access to their previous wage-producing activities. Haniff states that Hindu cultural traditions and values, together with colonial Christian morality, constituted strong anti-woman forces that seriously thwarted the autonomy of the indentured women: "Combined, the ideological forces of Christianity and Indian culture, the increasing number of Indian women and the large number of children which these women bore and reared, reflected the story of these women's marginalization everywhere. It was a classic combination of female biology and male ideology and violence that defined women's roles and kept them in it."[28] The return to home and family rendered women and their work invisible within the walls of home space and reinstated their traditional dependence on male partners in the absence of paid work. A woman's identity was reduced to a familial identity, a wife and mother whose service to her husband and children was instinctive, inherently feminine and, therefore, taken for granted. Referring to the association between the Indian woman and her family as a marker of female identity, Haniff comments, "It is this arena that women came to dominate and it is here that all their work, both economic and social, was subsumed. They became housewives, they became mothers, they became invisible, they became silent, they became again the carriers of Indian culture and tradition. This was so profoundly different from the early indentured women who were workers on the plantations, had fewer children and often more than one partner."[29]

However, women's invisibility within the home did not necessarily mean that they were entirely without agency. Indian women have had a long tradition of reconstituting confining space to their advantage by politicizing this space through their control of household activities such as the home budget, education of children, management of relations within the family and outside, and religion (as will be developed in chapter 4). Power was reconceptualized in cultural terms by these women, such that their silence in a particular situation was not necessarily a sign of passive acquiescence but, rather, a latent form of resistance to show displeasure or disagreement. It is this form of interstitial resistance demonstrated by Indian women that has been misunderstood by Caribbean men and women alike, misconstrued as docility and passivity. Indo-Caribbean feminists have accused their men of complicity in the perpetuation of these stereotypes by refusing to speak out or even recognize their own role in the marginalization of Indian women. As Haniff confirms, "They themselves refuse to acknowledge the identity of women as separate from their families, and, even knowing their mothers' leadership skills and accomplishments, can only value women's individuality within the family."[30]

Indian male collusion with women's subjugation is also evident in the various labour unions, where men have not considered it their responsibility to create dynamic leadership roles for women despite women's demonstrated leadership during periods of labour unrest. As indicated by Rajack-Talley, women continue to occupy marginal roles in national political parties such as the Democratic Labour Party and the United Labour Front. Prior to the establishment of formal trade unions, women usually spoke up in their own defence to protest any form of discrimination or exploitation that they experienced on the estates. Self-expression later gave way to representation by an elected union official who did not necessarily have the women's best interests at heart: "Today, if there are any grievances, the women depend on their union representative(s), usually male, to speak on their behalf. This does not mean that the women are silent, but that they tend to use non-formal avenues to vent their disagreement. They assured me that 'when water more than flour . . . we speak.' "[31] Rajack-Talley's interviews with women clearly demonstrate that even though women may not have a public voice in labour representation, they have always resorted to informally organizing in the absence of lobbying or a political platform to make their voices heard. The Ghandi-inspired passive resistance strategy has proved to be an effective means of communicating dissent and confronting victimization. Indian women have employed a similar technique to contest their marginal representation in Caribbean politics through the recent activism of three Indo-Trinidadian women: Occah Seepaul, speaker of the House of Representatives; Hulsie Bhaggan, member of Parliament and trade union activist;

and Kamla Persad-Bissesar, minister of education. Despite opposition to their election and severe obstacles placed in their way to undermine their best efforts, these women have nevertheless come to occupy their rightful space in the national imaginary, where "their presence should communicate powerfully that East Indian women do have minds of their own. Instead, measures have been taken to cut these women down so that the stereotype can remain intact."[32]

The need to challenge stereotypes has also made its presence felt in religious spheres, where the virulent forces of recent Hindu and Islamic fundamentalisms are constituting an effective (and violent) method of silencing both men and women. The call to return to a purist Brahmanic notion of ideal Hindu womanhood, together with a blind adherence to anti-woman prescriptions legislated elsewhere in the Islamic world, has been advocated by both Hindu and Muslim nationalists in an attempt to recover an elusive "ancestral" ideal that has been ratified by a strict adherence to the sacred scriptures of these religions, as demonstrated in chapter 1. As Haniff asserts, "Recently, there has evolved a pursuit of a pure form of Hinduism which values caste, imposes Hindi as the language of ancestry and describes the past of Hindus as monolithic, homogenous Indianness. It advocates separatism from other elements of Trinidadian and Guyanese culture and would keep women tied to a Hinduism that isolates and alienates them. This fundamentalist force in Hinduism is anti-female and casts on the woman the expectations of service, diffidence and place. Although not practiced by many, its presence is troubling to the community at large and particularly to Indian women."[33] A similar form of silencing is taking place in certain Muslims communities, which are advocating a symbolic and literal return to the veil to contain women within ordered forms of respectability.

At a conference on Indians in the diaspora, hosted in Trinidad in March 2000, the silencing of discourses on creolization and other forms of interethnic syncretism by a small group of Hindu nationalists and academics was followed by the intimidation of Indian female participants through verbal aggression. The very mention of the word *creolization* provoked a knee-jerk reaction in these men, who proceeded to argue that the virtues of Hindu purity were being undermined by the "contaminating" forces of racial interaction. The stunned silence of the conference participants and the general audience, consisting primarily of international academics (mostly of Indian origin), was followed by only three voices of protest against these nationalists. While the Indo-Trinidadian men and women in the audience did not feel comfortable enough to voice their own opinion (in some cases, understandably so), the silence of women of other Caribbean ethnicities identified the "problem" as pertaining to Indian women alone and not to Caribbean women in general. The absence of an interracial women-centred coalition against male domination represented a missed opportunity to demonstrate a united female front against the cultural and religious silencing of women in a contemporary setting. Demonstrated solidarity between African and Indian women would have minimized the impact of verbal assaults while undermining the presence of these men and the impact of their outmoded anti-Caribbean discourses on cultural inviolability in modern-day Trinidad and Guyana.

However, this situation should not unilaterally suggest that Hinduism or Islam did not provide women with some space for self-affirmation. Groups such as the Hindu Women's Organization have contributed to the establishment of safe spaces for Hindu women but have, at the same time, colluded with the prevailing patriarchal discourses of a purist notion of Hindu womanhood and woman's role as wife and mother within Hindu society. This has meant that Hindu and Muslim women alike have had to look beyond their individual families and communities for their sense of self, often choosing emigration as a way to circumvent confinement. At the same time, Hindu women such as Pandita Indrani Rampersad have assumed leadership roles within Hinduism by contesting the sole authority of men. Indrani Rampersad was given the title of pandita, or learned scholar, on September 14, 1993 by the Arya Pratinidhi Sabha of Trinidad. Since the title is traditionally reserved for male scholars, Rampersad's appointment was greeted simultaneously with enthusiasm and ambivalence. As the pandita states, "My status as pandita drew much publicity since the Sanatan Dharma Maha Sabha, the largest Puranic-Hindu body, responded to my appointment by openly objecting to women in the role of pandits. The controversy served a positive purpose, for it led to many women asking 'why not a woman?' "[34] Commenting on the loneliness that she sometimes feels in the absence of male collegiality and in the face of opposition by traditional Hindu women, Rampersad questions the cultural brainwashing experienced by Hindu women who accept some of the gender-biased dictates of the Hindu scriptures without critiquing the pertinence of those dictates to the changing circumstances of women and men in Trinidad. She is equally critical of Hindu Trinidadian men who refuse to relinquish their control over women by adapting to sociocultural and gender transformation. While claiming that "Indian, particularly Hindu, men are having great difficulties in coping with their ambivalent feelings towards women",[35] Rampersad also blames women for perpetuating this ambivalence. She retorts, "I perceive a conflict in women who fight for gender and race equality in society, but who never seriously consider the question of their own equality in religion and spiritual matters. Some have admitted that they are so fully under the control of their religious ideology that they cannot think of becoming pandits although they accept my right to be a pandit."[36] Although Rampersad herself has been accused of succumbing to male pressure by inadvertently becoming a mouthpiece for conservative male pandits, her efforts to secure equal footing with men in religious matters should not be overlooked.

It would seem plausible to state that Afro-Caribbean women were afforded a greater sense of religious agency, judging by their active role as spiritual leaders and grass-roots community organizers in the various Afro-Christian churches; in the Spiritual Baptist and Shouter Baptist faiths, which are receiving an increasingly large number of women followers in their congregations; in the Orisha-based forms of worship from Africa, such as the Shango religion, in which women have always played a crucial role as priestesses and mediums; and other African-based forms of worship. Referring to the important presence of the Mother in the Spiritual Baptist faith, Reverend Patricia Stephens comments,

> The work of the Mother is of paramount importance. A Spiritual Baptist Church traditionally must function with a Mother and a Father. The Father could be a Leader, Pastor or Shepherd. But most Spiritual Baptists will tell you there is an essence in the Mother that is not in the Father. In some churches a Mother could have more authority in the spiritual world than the Father, because God is not likened unto the flesh. Being a Mother doesn't imply that the woman is in a subservient role while the Father has the dominant role. . . . Since the Spiritual Baptist Church is likened to a family unit, the Mother and Father are the heads.[37]

Since most of the African-based religions were woman-centred in their origin or based on gender complementarity, women were either invested with superior powers or positioned at a level of complementarity with male leadership, a phenomenon that was not common to Hinduism, Islam or the Judaeo-Christian traditions. The presence of interfaith and inter-ethnic coalitions among women, which would establish a broad-based platform to fight for increased female participation across religions at the grass-roots and institutional levels, could possibly clear the ground for greater inclusion and validation. However, it is much easier to propose or impose utopian prescriptions as expected goals in an academic essay than to engineer the actual elimination of the social, cultural and religious boundaries and barriers that undermine the creation of such collaborations in daily life.

A similar situation of silence around issues of race in the Caribbean was evident at the Seventh International Conference of Caribbean Women Writers and Scholars in Mayagüez, Puerto Rico, in April 2000. At a concluding panel discussion on the specificities of Caribbean women's writing, various diasporic writers from Cuba, the Dominican Republic, Jamaica, Trinidad and Grenada discussed the importance of dissolving geographical and linguistic boundaries in their writing. While there were heated discussions on how women writers could collaborate along the linguistic divide by familiarizing themselves with other Caribbean languages, not once did the conversation focus on issues of race or of the creation of understanding along racial lines, despite the token presence of a single Indo-Trinidadian writer at the conference, a writer whose voice became representative of the Indo-Caribbean female experience in general. The omission of crucial dialogues on race that would have provided these writers with the opportunity to comprehend and inhabit several culturally defined ethnic spaces would have added a vital perspective to these conversations by taking them a step beyond the conventional adherence to the Afro/Euro-determined Caribbean model. For example, a discussion centred on the search for a common in-between space for African and Indian writers would have definitely set the stage for a newly emerging and much-needed dialogue on race relations between Afro- and Indo-Caribbean women (writers) in an attempt to initiate sustaining multilingual and multi-ethnic collaborations in the fields of literature, cultural and feminist studies.

—•—

Before beginning such a dialogue, however, it would be instructive to examine the factors that have both facilitated and hindered the coming to voice of Afro-Caribbean and Indo-Caribbean women writers. Afro-Caribbean women's writing has come into its own only within the past decade and a half as a result of the inhibiting influence of white colonial literature and of the literary chauvinism of male writers. Moreover, even though Afro-Caribbean women's literature constitutes an identifiable genre today, it must be pointed out that writers such as Merle Collins from Grenada, Grace Nichols from Guyana and Valerie Belgrave from Trinidad have themselves been overshadowed in a larger diasporic context by African American women writers and by South Asian and continental African writers from England. Black feminist scholarship, according to Carole Boyce Davies, has suffered a similar eclipsing that has minimized its truly transformational potential precisely because of a lack of diasporic solidarity among black writers and the paternalism of the black male literary establishment. Boyce Davies predicts the further marginalization of this literature despite the diversity and virtual explosion of contemporary women writers who continue to challenge "the boundaries of the acceptable".[38] She also attributes this potential invisibility to narrow definitions of blackness that have promoted racialized and geographical hierarchies of acceptability and non-acceptability through confining and highly territorialized discourses and their inability to affect a wider audience. Consequently, "for this reason, the kind of interventions that have been made by women writers and theorists seem to have no impact or little recognition beyond the academy in terms of affecting conceptually how people see things".[39] In fact, this limited scope of influence provides a sharp contrast to the actual expansiveness of black women's writing, which embraces a certain migratory boundary crossing in its expression. Boyce Davies claims, "Black women's writing . . . should be read as a series of boundary crossings and not as a fixed, geographical, ethnically or nationally bound category of writing. In cross-cultural, transnational, translocal, diasporic perspectives, this reworking of the grounds of "Black Women's Writing" redefines identity away from exclusion and marginality. . . . It is with this consciousness of expansiveness and the dialogics of movement and community that I pursue Black women's writing."[40] Boyce Davies inscribes this writing within the politics of renaming and reclaiming as the key to establishing a foundational identity politics based on contestation, negotiation and the eventual transformation of outdated literary and theoretical paradigms of representation.

Echoing Boyce Davies's refusal to be labelled or confined into restrictive categories of blackness, the Grenada-born Merle Collins bemoans "the constant need to explain myself before audiences in the role of 'Black writer from the Caribbean' or 'Afro-Caribbean writer' or 'Black woman writer' or 'Caribbean writer' or, heaven help us, an 'ethnic minority writer' ".[41] If writing, as Collins argues, constitutes a politics/poetics of existence,[42] then it should be reflective of the complexities, disjunctions and affirmations of "migratory subjectivities"[43] moulded by the intricacies of race, class, nationhood and gender. It should embrace a particular strategy of transformational discursive transgression to refashion the world from multiple perspectives that deconstruct colonial and patriarchal world views. This strategy has been the guiding force behind the impetus to write for several black women writers from the Caribbean (and elsewhere) for whom the written and spoken word represents a discursive explosion of intent through the creation of literary space that promotes the inscription of the self in history.

Joan Anim-Addo associates this writing with a particular audacity of expression, stating that it is black women's audacity to write that has promoted unprecedented literary production in order to counter decades of silence and invisibility: "For many black women, the creative (literary) act, though seemingly natural in the context of a literate world, is an audacious, daring one because of who she is, the black woman as sign simultaneously of gender, race and class oppression."[44] The "audacity" to write is motivated by the desire to dislodge the centrality of dominant narratives through a creative self-positioning in literary space that destabilizes the traditional power structure in the Caribbean, a structure that awards women writers unequal literary representation.

The problem of literary representation has been even more complicated for Indo-Caribbean women writers, who have, until very recently, shied away from this audacity of expression. This tentativeness could be explained by the fact that, unlike their Indian counterparts, black women have never had to justify their identity as Caribbean citizens. Perceived as identifiably Caribbean, African women are identified as native-born Caribbeans and not naturalized immigrants even though both groups share a common experience of enforced migration. Located as Indo-Caribbean women writers are outside representation and, consequently, outside citizenship, the coming to voice has been particularly arduous for these women, as will be discussed later.

However, "identifiable" Caribbeanness has also imposed its limitations on Afro-Caribbean writers in the field of literary publication. Anim-Addo identifies a situation of triple jeopardy that confronts these writers in their negotiation of contracts and in their search for suitable publishers: "difficulties in the search for access to a published voice; in acquiring an audience; and in debating the material of their work, even changing location from island home to metropolitan center".[45] Anim-Addo's comments reveal a certain censorship that is imposed on this writing, either by societal pressure or by the writer herself in her anxiety to be published. As publishing continues to be a white-dominated enterprise, several writers have been forced to conform to orientalized images of the Caribbean outlined by white editors and publishers who, very often, have a definite idea of what kind of Caribbean (literary) exoticism will find an international market. These "easily identifiable" Caribbean texts are vampirized by mainstream presses, which take great pride in their ethnic sensitivity and multicultural expertise, in order to promote "authentic" Caribbean literature.

In an attempt to move away from First World orientalist publishing, independent presses such as Sister Vision in Toronto, Aunt Lute Books in San Francisco and Peepal Tree in Leeds, England, are taking the initiative to provide alternative channels of publication for Caribbean writers. As Anim-Addo affirms,

> In the 1990s . . . an examination of patterns of publication reveals a gradual movement away from publication by monopoly mainstream presses with an educational interest to a broader range of smaller publishing houses. . . . Feminist publishing houses (Women's Press) have played a key role in making available a wider range of Caribbean women's voices and among them a good many black voices (Merle Collins, Velma Pollard, Joan Riley etc.). Yet the demand for publication has been such that when publishing houses, from feminist to mainstream, have been slow to publish works and project an uncertainty of the market for that work, Caribbean women writers have become involved in the publishing and marketing process. The work of black women's presses such as Sister Vision in Canada is indicative of this movement in the mid 1990s.[46]

The initiative taken by black women writers to promote their own work and the work of their sisters has revealed their powers of organization, their activism and their determination to move their literature beyond the confines of racial and literary stereotypes. It is to be hoped that their future collaboration with Indo-Caribbean women writers, in the form of co-editorship, collaborative writing projects and workshops, will provide a united Caribbean front to contest underrepresentation and discrimination. Sister Vision has already taken the lead in publishing the creative and theoretical work of Indo-Caribbean women writers, in publications such as *Creation Fire* and *The Other Woman: Women of Colour in Contemporary Canadian Society.*[47]

As mentioned earlier, douglarized engagements with literary production have enabled certain Indian and African writers to transcend racialized stereotypes in their writing by creating more wholesome representations. The Trinidadian writer Merle Hodge uses a douglarized literary perspective to make a first-time effort at positioning the specificities of Afro-Caribbean and Indo-Caribbean female subjectivity in a relational mode through the prism of secondary school education in her novel *For the Life of Laetitia*. The story, narrated by a twelve-year-old Afro-Caribbean female protagonist, Laetitia Johnson, describes the growing friendship between Laetitia and her Indian companion, Anjanee Jugmohansingh. While the novel indicates how both girls have to face the triple discrimination of race, class and gender in school, Anjanee's situation is even more acute because she does not have access to the same safe spaces of affirmation as does her African friend, even though the latter is unaware of her relatively privileged status, which she presumably takes for granted. The novel is a reflection of the disproportionate access to economic and social advancement between Indian and African girls in the field of education, where Indianness becomes a marker of ethnic difference and inferiority. In other words, the novel exposes the levels of accessibility or inaccessibility afforded to Indian and African girls in their search for self within the dictates of class and culture while highlighting the need for inter-ethnic cooperation as a necessary step for personal growth and mutual understanding.

The novel begins with a communal celebration of Laetitia's acceptance to secondary school. Her achievement receives the support of her entire family because she is the first family member to attend secondary school. The novel describes the family's sense of joy and pride: "Pappy made speech after speech about the new and blessed day that was dawning in the land. The celebration went on until Uncle Jamesie realized that darkness would catch them walking out the Trace if they didn't leave in a hurry. By then even Ma was tipsy, dancing with us one by one. Two days later my father appeared, out of the blue. He, too, was bursting with pride."[48] The emotions displayed by Laetitia's family in response to her position of distinction contrast sharply with the lack of support Anjanee receives at home. Anjanee describes her family's reaction to her decision to go to school: "They don't even want me to come out of the house! They want me to stay in the house! . . . My big brothers and my father . . . they saying that I go to school enough already, that I know how to read and write, and cook and wash, so what I harassing them for with booklist and uniform and taxi fare" (57). The father and brothers' desire to control Anjanee by confining her movements to the home demonstrates the greater spatial mobility afforded to African girls between the home and the outside.

However, this mobility is sometimes achieved at a price. Laetitia's relocation from the rural warmth of her extended family to her father's urban home dispels the aura of security that she has experienced in her village. While the move from the rural to the urban sphere is normally a sign of upward mobility, Laetitia experiences feelings of confinement and discomfort in her new environment. The novel exposes her malaise: "I was sitting in the drawing room, reading. This drawing room still made me feel very uncomfortable and out of place. It was crammed. . . . There were crowds of ornaments. . . . This drawing room was like the store windows you saw in town, not a place where you would go and sit in your home clothes" (33). Feelings of being an unwelcome outsider punctuate Laetitia's sense of alienation in her new surroundings. However, these feelings initially seem to be rather reactionary given that she is provided with every opportunity to study uninterruptedly in her new "home". In Laetitia's case, the familial emphasis on education makes household chores secondary to doing schoolwork. In fact, Laetitia's stepmother, Miss Velma, does not want her stepdaughter to mix housework with homework: "There was still a mountain of clothes on the bed to be sorted out before the hours of ironing began. . . . I made a move to help her, but she waved me away: 'No, child. That is my work. You take your book and study your lesson. And study is good' " (87). Understanding the limitations that have been imposed on women through the invisibility and unaccountability of domestic work, Miss Velma refuses to subject the girl to social restrictions that she herself had to confront when economic pressures obliged her to sacrifice her schooling and the possibilities of a professional life in favour of marriage and domesticity. Domesticity renders Miss Velma homeless through the denial of her rights as an equal partner in the marriage and through her narrowly defined functions as wife and mother. In this way, *For the Life of Laetitia* highlights the intergenerational sacrifices made by women to provide a better life for the next generation.

Laetitia's sense of existential homelessness differs greatly from the physical disenfranchisement that Anjanee encounters at home, where domestic duties take precedence over school. For Laetitia, nostalgic memories of her rural home, together with the possibility of returning there during the holidays, provide her with a sense of groundedness that is lacking in Anjanee's life. A long and difficult commute, physical exhaustion and unreasonable demands at home are stumbling blocks to Anjanee's sense of self. However, despite her designated role within the family, Anjanee refuses to remain in a place that has been allotted to her, thereby revealing the greater risks that Indian girls have had to take in their transgressive boundary crossings that were inevitably met with severe punishment by family members. Anjanee's situation is also reflective of the hardships that Indian women continue to endure in their daily negotiations of Caribbean life and in the face of the dual marginalization experienced at home and in society. Ameena Gafoor questions the validity of locating Indian female experiences within a mainstream Afrocentric grid, since "the African Caribbean woman forms the mainstream of Caribbean culture and the Indo-Caribbean woman is on the fringe as a minority and therefore further marginalized and doubly considered Other. In addition, because of cultural osmosis, the Indo-Caribbean experience is multifaceted. Unlike the African Caribbean woman, her Indo-Caribbean counterpart labors under a multiple indentureship, including race and ethnicity".[49] As indicated by Gafoor, locating Indo-Caribbean female subjectivity within the majority model serves only to promote markers of otherness that have been identified with cultural inferiority and have justified discrimination against Indians.

Anjanee's refusal to eat her lunch in the school yard in front of the other students demonstrates the feelings of shame that she associates with her poor rural Indian background. Food as a marker of ethnic difference is also an indicator of class distinctions; the simple fare of roti and talkarie (vegetables) exposes the girl's origins. While Laetitia considers this food to be delicious and exotic in its seasoning, compared with her own bland luncheon-meat sandwich, Anjanee is humiliated by its ordinary appearance and by the powerful flavouring of the spices that are a visible indication of her ethnic difference: "I was quite hungry by now, and I started to eat, but Anjanee hesitated to open her brown-paper parcel. With a little half smile she said: "Don't laugh at my lunch, you hear? It is not like what you have. Is only roti and talkarie' " (44). The act of hiding the roti in a brown paper bag is indicative of the diffidence and lack of self-confidence that Indian girls exhibit when they are compared with black girls and then disparaged in terms of their appearance. In the novel, Laetitia's "polished" appearance for school – "Miss Velma made my skirts and I tried on the whole uniform. It looked so smart!" (37) – outshines Anjanee's solitary school uniform, on which "every day I saw the same pattern of ink dots on her sleeve" (62). The abject poverty of rural Indians has often been a cause for ridicule among schoolchildren and teachers alike, who have often used economic disenfranchisement as a justification for racial discrimination. The novel initially sets up a binary structure between the good, intelligent African student and the irresponsible, backward Indian student as a model to expose the cultural stereotypes that have pitted Indians and Africans against each other and that have deemed

Africans to be suitable for teaching jobs and the civil service while relegating Indians to agricultural labour.

The desire to protect her daughter from the burden of Indian domestic life prompts Anjanee's mother to help her daughter in her educational endeavours. While the girl's brothers use physical intimidation and threats of violence to prevent Anjanee from going to school, the mother is determined to disrupt the female legacy of martyred service to home and family by supporting her daughter. She encourages her daughter by "squeezing money out of what they gave her every week to go to the shop, and giving it to Anjanee to pay the taxi to Caigual" (63). Conscious of the hopelessness of her own situation, whereby her lack of education forces her to accept a life of serfdom, Anjanee's mother is determined to see that her daughter leads a better life. This determination is shared by the daughter, who refuses to blindly succumb to her male-ordained destiny. The novel illustrates Anjanee's seriousness of intent when the girl remonstrates, "I don't want to end up like my mother! . . . I not going to end up like my mother, I rather dead. If you see how much work my mother does have to do when the day come!" (64). The mother becomes an invisible presence that ensures the functioning of the family through her unrecognized household labour, which reduces her to a mere function or utility service. Protesting her mother's misery, Anjanee exclaims, "And they don't even see her, you know that? They don't even know how much work she doing. And she working day and night for them — she don't get to do one thing for herself" (65). The mother's inability to leave and start a new life for herself is based on a lack of choice: the absence of schooling thwarts the possibility of making a fresh start. She describes her situation realistically: "Where I will leave them and go, beti? I ain't have schooling. You want me go by the side of the road and beg?" (65). The impasses confronting the mother do not, however, prevent her from collaborating with her daughter in economic enterprise; using her market-gardening skills, the mother is able to cultivate a small vegetable patch whose produce could then be sold in the village by the daughter.

The vegetable patch has constituted an autonomous space for women; successful cultivation, as another domestic skill, has enabled them to earn some financial profit. Mother and daughter set up a secret partnership that is nevertheless short lived, as Anjanee suffers from heatstroke on the third day: "When her father and one brother set out for the garden, and the two other brothers went to work, Anjanee and her mother picked some vegetables from her mother's kitchen garden, and Anjanee went round the village with a tray on her head selling what she could. She did this for two days, and on the third day was flat in bed with fever and a headache" (64). Despite this setback, both mother and daughter demonstrate their discursive insurrections by defying patriarchal authority and acting independently in the face of the consequences. The resilience of Indian women and girls lies within these subversive transgressions, which highlight their "private" revolutions within the confines of home space. The mother's abjection conversely becomes the very force to fight victimization. While these forms of quiet resistance are often unacknowledged by more overt forms of activism, they make an important statement about the need to valorize culturally available channels of protest that may not necessarily conform to an identifiable norm. Consequently, to read Anjanee's story as a classic case of Indian victimhood would be to misunderstand the very nature of Indian female subjectivity in the Caribbean, a subjectivity that has had to assert itself amid extenuating circumstances.

Anjanee's loss of girlhood occurs when she assumes woman-identified duties at a very young age. Her premature womanhood is marked by her early menstruation, which sets her apart from her schoolfriend Laetitia. This separation is revealed in a conversation between the two girls, when the narrator admits, "I felt a blow of sadness, as though Anjanee had taken one big step away from me" (134). The "evidence" of monthly bleeding destroys any charges of child abuse because Anjanee the girl-child has already been transformed into a woman. The math teacher sarcastically refers to her as "Miss Jugmohansingh" (89), as a way of addressing a young woman, only to berate her later for her mental retardation: "Mrs. Lopez wrote all over Anjanee's exercise books with her hurtful red-ink pen: 'Hopeless.' 'You will never learn.' 'This is disgraceful. You haven't a clue and you never will' " (90). Learning is presented as a form of hard labour for Anjanee, equalling the performance of time-consuming and exhausting household chores. Anjanee's refusal to be weighed down by domestic duties despite daily fatigue and sleep deprivation mirrors her tenacity of purpose in school in spite of her failing grades and the lack of school supplies. The novel describes her resoluteness: "But Anjanee tried, and worried, and put out every ounce of effort she could squeeze from her tired body. . . . On some days she simply had to put her head down on the desk for a few seconds at a time. But always she would rouse herself and bravely tackle whatever work we were given in class" (89).

The school becomes a symbol of society at large, which would like to see Indian women in particular in a secondary position by denying them some of the benefits enjoyed by African women. While Laetitia can look forward to the Christmas holidays as a time of celebration, family reunion and relaxation, Anjanee spends her break doing work. The childlike expectations of Christmas experienced by Laetitia elude Anjanee, who must earn enough money to attend school in the new year. She confesses, "I went and sell in the market every day in the holidays to get money to come to school" (167). While Anjanee must earn her way into school, Laetitia's access to education seems almost inevitable. Her godmother, Ma Zelline, reminds her of her good fortune: "Look how hard your mammy have to work to get a little education and you get it right in your hand. Don't throw away that!" (110) . Ma Zelline urges Laetitia not to squander this opportunity at self-determination.

However, Laetitia's experiences at school are themselves couched in ambivalence. Her success in school becomes her father's raison d'être; the daughter's accomplishments vicariously confer a mantle of respectability on the father himself: " 'That's the little scholar,' he was saying in a jaunty voice. 'See? Head in a book, oui! How you like that? This girl will be more scholar than the Prime Minister!' " (34). The father's facade of superiority camouflages his own insecurities for having chosen a nouveau riche lifestyle over adequate education. Laetitia becomes a mirror that reflects back to him his perceived educational success, giving him the vicarious satisfaction of being a learned man himself. The father's sense of self is ironically located in his daughter's continued success in school. For this reason, paternal solicitude gradually gives way to an obsessive control over the daughter's movements and study habits. The novel describes the father's surveillance of his daughter: "Mr. Cephas also took a great deal of interest in my schoolwork, a little too much for my liking. When he saw me at the table with my books, he would hover over me, looking, as my mother would say, like the cat that got the canary" (68). Laetitia becomes her father's prey and an object of his control so that he can carefully monitor her activities. Unwilling to relinquish his hold on her, he begins his regime by forbidding her to return to her rural home on weekends. By carefully marking spatial boundaries, the father tries to curtail his daughter's access to spaces that do not include school and his home so that he can continue to maintain his influence over her. The father's actions betray a ruthlessness similar to the patriarchal control exercised in Anjanee's home.

Rather than submit to her father's will, Laetitia will use her education as the very tool to engage in a series of discursive insurrections aimed at minimizing her father's authority over her. In an attempt to destabilize her father, she makes a determined effort to get failing grades in school by not doing her assignments and refusing to attend classes: "The following week I made sure to get every maths assignment wrong. I wrote neatly, drew tidy margins, and followed the method obediently up to a point when I thought it was time to spoil things. The Circus-horse was driven to despair" (119). Additionally, she makes every attempt to move away from her father, so that "Mr. Cephas could check up on me all he wanted to. Soon I would be out of his reach forever" (128). Her poor performance symbolizes her resistance to parental authority and her attempts to establish her autonomy. Moreover, her failing grades represent a form of punishment for her father, whose acceptance in society depends on his daughter's scholarship.

However, unlike Anjanee, Laetitia can choose not to attend classes; she does not have to make the same sacrifices as her Indian friend. Education as survival takes on a different meaning for the two girls given their different situations. Despite her humble background, Laetitia depends on the financial support of her bourgeois father. While financial control leads to a less than favourable father–daughter relationship, it also provides Laetitia with the necessary luxury of finding her self-affirming spaces because she does not have to worry about her next meal or transportation to school. She can enjoy the benefits of a peaceful night's sleep, unlike Anjanee, who has "so much work to do home that every night I going to sleep tired and in the morning I waking up more tired" (169). Moreover, Laetitia also has the option of choosing between the bourgeois material comfort of her father's home, despite her displeasure at being there, and the emotional comfort of her modest rural living. The possibility of refuge offers itself to Laetitia; she can continue to nourish pleasant memories of eventually returning to her real home in the country, unlike Anjanee, for whom home represents a living hell and a point of no return.

The possibility of choice and her own comfort level often make Laetitia insensitive to her friend's situation despite her best efforts to help Anjanee in school. Cultural differences between the two girls lead to differing modes of communication between them; Anjanee's silence and non-verbal forms of expression are often misunderstood by her more extroverted friend. Anjanee's inability to articulate her inner pain is often met by Laetitia's frustration at having to interpret Anjanee's silence. In one scene, Laetitia asks Anjanee to explain her three-day absence from school: "I was questioning her, trying to find out what had happened, and she stubbornly refused to talk. I lost my patience and got up from the log. 'Well, we can't be friends,' I reproached her, 'if we going to keep secrets from one another.' Anjanee dropped her face into her hands and began to cry. I sat down again and tried to eat my words" (62–63). However, Laetitia bemoans her own insensitivity when she realizes that words are not the only form of self-expression. The eloquence of silence can sometimes be more effective as a form of language than empty words: "Anjanee lifted her head and without speaking showed so much sympathy for me that I felt guilty" (167).

Cultural differences notwithstanding, it is Laetitia who provides the guiding force behind Anjanee's education by constantly helping and motivating her friend to study. Under Laetitia's tutelage, Anjanee's poor grades begin to improve to the point where "[o]ne day in geography class the teacher handed back our exercise books, and when Anjanee opened hers, her whole face lit up. She passed the book over to me with a broad, grateful smile: She had got six marks out of ten!" (120–21). Anjanee's improved grades testify to the depth of the girls' friendship, which commences on the very first day of school when they are paired as form partners: "I was placed in Form 1H and my partner was a girl named Anjanee Jugmohansingh. She came towards me smiling and looking straight into my face, as though she knew me and was glad to see me again" (41). Oblivious to their ethnic differences, the two girls merge into an emotional twinship of mutual trust and caring, despite the admonitions of Laetitia's father: "And out of all the children it have in that big school, the only thing you could find to friend with is a coolie?" (124–25). Disregarding the racial divide between "coolies" and "niggers", the girls' friendship is blind to the social machinations of race. Their partnership in school is indicative of an integrative dougla and *kala pani* hybrid space of mutual cooperation among women along the lines of race, class and gender, as described in the introduction to this book. As Grant Stoddard and Eve Cornwall argue, "The 'douglarization' of Trinidadian culture can be read as a form of creolization, but as a form of creolization in its most general and inclusive sense which decentres the African origins of Creole culture and foregrounds the ongoing syncretic process of cultural formation. It also highlights the power struggles inherent in those processes. It makes clear the intense relationships which cut across cultural mixing, relationships of exclusivity, identification, openness to change, social mobility, multicultural nationhood, cultural preservation and more."[50]

The positioning of hybridized space enables the characters Laetitia and Anjanee to meet on common ground in their fight against patriarchy, racism and social discrimination. Their struggle for an education that will enable them to achieve their personal subjectivities leads to the symbolic signing of a contract: each girl promises to help the other in her efforts to succeed. Each girl absorbs the other's strengths and weaknesses to constitute an alter ego or double who is sustained by the presence of her twin. Their friendship is a reflection of the Haitian Voudun trope of spiritual twinning, whereby two soulmates or *marassas* are joined in bonds of empathy, solidarity and intimacy that integrate them within a cosmic totality of representation. Their bond is also indicative of a political "marassahood" as a symbol of an integral feminist consciousness that finds its articulation within the specificities of dougla space. It is therefore not surprising to read that Anjanee's suicide through the ingestion of poison leads to Laetitia's nervous breakdown. The physical death of one twin leads to the psychic death of the other in the absence of common ties of sustenance. The novel describes the void in Laetitia's life: "But Anjanee wasn't there! Anjanee was not there for me to tell her anything, in my whole life, every again! I put my hands to my ears and squeezed them tight against my head: 'No! Not true!' I shouted" (204). Laetitia's feelings of loss are projected onto her body, which loses its will to live when it is deprived of its life support. In this fashion, both suicide and mental breakdown can be interpreted as forms of protest against and resistance to an unjust social system that sustains hierarchies of discrimination in its functioning. Although poison-induced death has been perceived as a typically Indian form of suicide – as is reflected in Miss Velma's statement, "these Indian girls so quick to take poison" (202) – Anjanee uses this cultural stereotype to make a political statement about the lack of opportunities available to Indian girls in their search for selfhood. In turn, Laetitia's collapse is a testimonial to her friend's action to establish her autonomy. Her breakdown is a form of resistance to cultural and social injustices and an unconscious act of solidarity with her Indian sister. Consequently, the two girls remain united even in Anjanee's death: "I thought about Anjanee a great deal. I wasn't afraid to think about her now. Sometimes I still dreamed that the two of us were on a bus together going somewhere, and talking, talking to each other" (213). At the end of the novel, Laetitia seems to merge into Anjanee's identity and spiritual being by giving form to her invisibility and voice to her silence. Anjanee's memory remains intact after Laetitia's recovery: "As the reopening of school drew closer, I felt as though I was taking up her life. For just like her I would now have to set out early, early in the morning and travel miles to school" (213). This merging of personalities provides the necessary cure for Laetitia's recovery and the motivation to continue her studies as an obligation to herself, her Indian friend and her family.

—•—

Narmala Shewcharan's novel *Tomorrow Is Another Day* describes the growing friendship between an Indian woman, Chandi, and a black marketwomen, Aunt Adee. This friendship flies in the face of the established racial divide between the Indo- and Afro-Guyanese populations. Ralph Premdas describes the ethnic divisions in Guyana, by stating: "The context of intergroup rivalry defines the tightness of ethnic claims and boundaries. . . . In Guyana, where a highly polarized ethnically bifurcated system emerged in the wake of zero-sum competitive elections and ethnic repression, a social context of intense tension is normal. . . . Residential, occupational, customary and racial cleavages together established a deeply divided state. Each group feared the other; each disparaged the other through a complex set of stereotypes . . . . [T]he socialist government never succeeded in re-aligning the ethnic vertical cleavages of race, religion, culture etc."[51]

Given the atmosphere of racial tension that was exacerbated during the PNC regime,[52] ethnic phobia should have separated Chandi and Aunt Adee. The novel describes Chandi's initial reaction of apprehension when she meets Adee: "Chandi thought she'd never seen a stranger person than Aunt Adee . . . . Chandi was almost afraid to go and talk to her, but Aunt Adee had a kindly smile and soon she summoned the courage to approach."[53] However, recognizing their common displacement as economically underprivileged women, the two embark on an informal economic partnership, collaboratively joining forces. The novel describes the beginning of this friendship, which is initiated by Adee's generosity of spirit: "Aunt Adee had a cheerful, philosophical way of talking: problems were an unknown species to be eradicated for their obscurity. Chandi soon found she was telling Aunt Adee her whole story. Aunt Adee told her not to worry. There was a cookshop inside the market which was hiring people" (43).

Adee's gestures of friendship promote Chandi's economic initiatives through the former's connections in the marketplace. The novel highlights this initiative: "Chandi Panday stood awkwardly at the side of one of the roads leading to the marketplace. She had left the cookshop job. As Aunt Adee had advised, she had got together enough capital to start a little selling business. This had been earned through the work she and her children had done the previous Saturday, hiring themselves out to the foodlines" (66). Chandi's skills to effectively engage in a profitable economic entrepreneurship serve as the necessary tools to subvert her subaltern status of social and sexual exploitation, by providing an outlet for female self-reliance. Filomena Steady remarks that by playing a pivotal role in economic production, women redress the imbalance inherent in the sexual division of labour.[54] Women are able to repossess themselves through the economics that offer an alternative option to confinement. Chandi's economic success ensures a certain inner stability that results from her ability to be self-sufficient and provide for her family. Her profits, though minimal, provide some relief from prolonged economic deprivation: "Chandi was glad that the profit she made from the oranges enabled her to afford the new shoes" (67–68) for her daughter. In this case, the self promotes its recovery through the dynamics of an economic body politic that necessitates a control of one's resources. The body affirms its subjectivity by negotiating its own system of exchange through the lines of production and distribution rather than being commodified as an object of exchange within the machinations of the male-propelled economic system.

Through the elaboration of interracial and class-based associations, collectively sharing responsibilities, women can create their own lines of production. Adee's crucial role as a racial peacemaker, through her market activism, sustains such collaborations: "She felt responsible for Chandi and worried about her, although she now seemed less vulnerable to the wear and tear of the marketplace. Still, Aunt Adee felt that she should keep an eye on her" (201). Her civic-minded responsibilities extend beyond her own ethnic community when her son's untimely death at the hands of government soldiers enlightens her about the tragic consequences of divided loyalties within a specific ethnicity. Adee realizes that membership within one's own ethnic community is selective and cannot be "naturally" assumed, thereby exploding the myth of racially based ethnic solidarities. Premdas punctuates the ambivalence attached to what he calls "the ethnic phenomenon" by describing it as "a hydra-headed creature alive with sociological form, psychological consciousness, political claims and religio-symbolic mysticism. . . . It is derived from the innate need of the human creature for community expressed dialectically in contradistinction to rival claims or other similar communities. It is at once relational and conflictual. . . . It bears its own internal logic, compelled by its own internal needs."[55]

Premdas's description exposes the arbitrary logic that underlines the construction of ethnic identity which can be manipulated or re-created to serve "internal needs" through mystical fabulations of conformity and allegiance. Adee's son's efforts to resist arrest for trumped-up charges of sedition against the ethnic state serve as the necessary justification for the state to eliminate any form of opposition to its mandates. His social position as an economically disadvantaged black man whose fight for a better tomorrow involves the destruction of the status quo of ethnic absolutism locates him as an outsider in the hierarchy of ethnic affiliation. Adee's own position of otherness within the state places her outside the realm of state protection that is reserved for its selective/selected membership. The character of Aunt Adee exposes the well-maintained illusion of equal citizenship within her own ethnic community while highlighting the state's insidious strategy to maintain its power by alienating the people through cross-ethnic rivalries. The character Jagru comments, referring to Adee, "It was people like her who gave the lie to stories of racial unrest, which were always being promoted with deadly effect by unscrupulous politicians looking after their own interests" (202).

—·—

As mentioned earlier, the question of invisibility and lack of voice has characterized the Indo-Caribbean female quest for subjectivity. Critical of the dominant stance adopted by Afro-Caribbean feminists who have contributed to the marginalization of Indian women through the imposition of culturally monolithic feminist discourses, Indian women have recently begun to contest their exclusion as Caribbean feminists. Indo-Caribbean feminists such as Nesha Haniff, Ramabai Espinet, Rosanne Kanhai, Rawwida Baksh-Sooden and Patricia Mohammed have been openly critical of the imposed feminist ideologies of mainstream (that is, black) Caribbean feminisms that have been predicated by the systematic exclusion of Indian women. As Haniff argues, "The biggest failure of the feminist movement in the Caribbean has been its inability to advocate for, and support Indian women. Indian women have derived limited benefits from policy changes that affect all women-like maternity benefits, the Domestic Violence Act, and equal rights guaranteed constitutionally."[56] While Haniff partially attributes this inequity to the lack of strong leadership among Indian women, she is equally critical of the ways in which dominant academic discourses continue to overlook the Indo-Caribbean female experience. Similarly, Rosanne Kanhai is critical of the Caribbean Association of Feminist Research and Action (CAFRA) and its inability to create a space for Indo-Caribbean women. The association has been dominated by African women through their sheer numbers, and these women have not taken up the cause of Indian women on a sustained basis; nor have they made any significant attempts to attract Indians into their membership, according to Kanhai, who documented her protest after a CAFRA meeting in Guyana in 1993. In a letter to *CAFRA News*, Kanhai states, "It was obvious to me that there was, for the most part, a marginal presence of Indo-Caribbean women at the meeting. Guyana has an Indian population of about 50 percent, yet there were few Indian women at the meeting and no expressions of Indian culture at the Cultural Evening."[57] This invisibility can possibly be explained by the fact that, until recently and with the notable exception of the work of Rhoda Reddock and Verene Shepherd, Indo-Caribbean feminism has been framed, in terms of the mainstream experience, as an interesting appendix or a subject to be ignored. Commenting on how she came to an understanding of feminism through the dominant Afro-Caribbean discourse espoused by the University of the West Indies in Trinidad, Rawwida Baksh-Sooden admits to the feelings of alienation that she experienced when the language of the dominant discourse was unable to translate the cultural specifics of her particular Indo-Caribbean experience.[58] While the mainstream Afro-Caribbean discourse was itself modelled after European and Euro-/Afro-American frames of reference, three levels of imposed cultural alterity proved to be confining in their scope and an inappropriate form in which to express Indianness without falling into the trap of objectifying this experience through tokenism or exoticism. The lack of multicultural channels of expression has led to a particular linguistic confinement, whereby the absence of culturally diverse heteroglossic vocabularies has limited the parameters of self-expression, as will be discussed in the chapter on exile.

Ramabai Espinet's short story "Barred: Trinidad 1987" exposes the tentativeness of expression demonstrated by Indians in their inability to articulate their experiences in an alien land amid a foreign culture that was not very receptive to Indian traditions. The story illustrates the strangeness of the Indian situation: "We are lost here, have not found the words to utter our newness, our strangeness, our unfound being. Our clothes are strange, our food is strange, our names are strange. And it not possible for anyone to coax or help us. Our utterance can only come roaring out of our mouths when it is ready, set, and can go."[59] Espinet's narrative underlines the urgency of creating an indigenized language capable of reflecting the complexities of the Indo-Caribbean experience. The immediacy of voice provides the only outlet to document this experience and to promote cultural understanding while avoiding imposed representations and stereotyping. The audibility of experience will establish the necessary Indian subjectivity that is crucial to insertion in national history.

As several critics argue, self-expression equals self-inscription in history. What sources of inspiration can the Indo-Caribbean female writer and scholar turn to in her struggle to convert silence into creative agency? How can a lack of self-confidence be converted into the audacity of self-representation that is impervious to cultural and patriarchal censorship? Many Indo-Caribbean women writers are looking into their own cultural heritage for female models of affirmation. As mentioned earlier, the female cane-cutter, as a literary muse and the mother of Indo-Caribbean feminism, has provided a primary source of inspiration. Like the historical and cultural figures of grandmothers, Nanny of the Maroons, female griots, spiritual healers and priestesses have fired the literary imagination of Afro-Caribbean women writers, so the presence of *ajis* and *nanis* (grandmothers), *bhowjees* (sisters-in-law) and mothers has provided similar creative stimuli for Indian women. The presence of strong woman-centred, culturally specific references has created original points of identification as a source of cultural stability and authority.

Indo-Caribbean feminists such as Espinet and Kanhai have identified several culturally determined spaces, such as matikor space, as particular sites of healing and reclaiming for Indian women. *Matikor* refers to a woman-centred and woman-dominated ceremony of sexual ribaldry on the eve of a Hindu wedding ceremony. During this celebration of female sexuality, which initiates the bride-to-be into the politics of the female erotic, rural women repossess their bodies through sexual parody, openly satirizing the sanctity of patriarchal codes of social and sexual conduct for women. Both Espinet and Kanhai position matikor space as a locus of cultural and sexual resistance where Hindu women can protest discrimination and sexual degradation. As Kanhai argues, "Matikor exists today, its endurance and transformative capacity providing a lens through which the identity of Indo-Caribbean women can be explored. Against a backdrop of Afro-Caribbean majority, matikor remains a closed ethnic space where Indian women do not carry the burden of minority status. As Indian women enter into Caribbean and global mainstreams, matikor acts as a reminder of the spiritual strength found in community and tradition."[60] Inscribing matikor within the parameters of the sexual, spiritual and the creative as a locus of identity formation, Kanhai and Espinet broaden its scope by simultaneously opening a metaphoric space of inspiration for Indo-Caribbean women writers. Consequently, even though the actual practice of matikor remains confined to a rural locale, where it is now being performed less frequently than before, the symbolic extension of matikor space into the realm of the creative and the political offers a certain permanence of expression through orality and the written word. As Kanhai confirms, "For Indo-Caribbean women, activism and creativity develop together since living in the margins of marginality, so to speak, does not afford the luxury of creative expression devoid of social awareness and political intent."[61] In this way, Indian women create localized, indigenous spaces where, by presenting "their understandings, affirmations and liberatory practices, they develop an open matikor space" that resists erasure and exclusion.[62]

Indian women are also reclaiming their space through the phenomenon of chutney, which makes a political statement about working-class Indian women, particularly in Trinidad. Rhoda Reddock states that " 'chutney' is the term used locally to refer to a folk form of Indo-Trinidadian music and dance. Most sources suggest that it derives its tradition from Indian folk practices of the non-Brahmanical castes and rural folk as well as the ritual sensuous and suggestive dances of Hindu women at women's ceremonies on the eve of weddings."[63] The political dimensions of chutney are located in women's contestations of class distinctions and Brahmanical notions of female purity. Located at the grass-roots, rural, folk level, chutney dancing and singing celebrate the female body in its sensual expansiveness. Pelvic gyrations that are locally called "wining" imitate the contractions of the lower pelvis during labour and symbolize the ultimate orgasmic expression of the body as it breaks free from itself and releases new life. The final outburst of life highlights the uncontrollable and uncontrolled power of the female body to negotiate its own terms of sexual agency through autonomous action. The suggestive movements of chutney dancing are a public demonstration of women's efforts to defy normative codes of Hindu patriarchal morality and its prescriptions for women's private and domesticated sexuality that should be relegated to the confines of the bedroom. By flaunting their bodies before an audience, Indian women show their disregard for the patriarchal dictates of their culture and class that associate open displays of female sexualized behaviour with vulgarity and cultural impropriety. Like matikor, chutney remains an all-inclusive female space; the majority of participants and viewers are women. Chutney represents the power of the female body in motion. Rawwida Baksh-Sooden sees the phenomenon as a positive sign of affirmation for and by Indian women and their fight for cultural inclusion in the national imaginary: "My point of view is that chutney is a very positive development. I think that it points to the growing emancipation of Indian women in this country, and is linked partly to their advancement through education and the inroads they have made in the work place, both of which have led to their economic independence. It is also related to the strength of the women's movement in this country."[64]

The resilience demonstrated by Indian women to vindicate the indigenization of Trinidadian culture through the recognition of their contributions has been met by stiff opposition by upper- and middle-class Hindu men, who have always positioned themselves as the moral guardians of female sexuality. Baksh-Sooden refers to the hysteria demonstrated by traditional Hindu men and women as a reaction to chutney and urges these women not to support the misogynist views upheld by Hindu males in terms of the control and domination of women. She sees chutney as an agent of transformation and personal freedom for all Indian women through its woman-centred strategies of subversive insurrections:

> What is also notable is that this hysteria is coming from the middle and upper classes of the Hindu community who see themselves as the preservers of the so-called authentic Hindu culture in this country. As has taken place throughout history, it is always the lower classes which lead the struggle for meaningful social change. For if it is Hindu women's growing independence which has led to this revolutionary phenomenon . . . then this expression can in turn only lead to greater autonomy and power of Indian women, both in their relationships with Indian men as well as in the wider society.[65]

Baksh-Sooden and others acknowledge the revolutionary politics of Drupatee Ramgoonai, an Indian classical singer of humble origin and the reigning queen of chutney, who was the first Hindu woman to break racial and gender barriers by singing calypso. While calypso has traditionally been defined as a black working-class male phenomenon, with lyrics that were openly derogatory to women and to Indian women in particular, Ramgoonai was able to revolutionize this art form by occupying centre stage as an Indian woman and deflecting attention away from the Afrocentric sexism of Trinidadian males. Kanhai describes Ramgoonai's presence in the calypso tent as a "celebration of the woman claiming freedom, her body itself becoming an expression of art, an act of creativity".[66] By personifying the very moment of female creativity in action, through her personal example of non-conformity and her daily struggles against racism, sexism and classism, Ramgoonai represents an icon of resistance for a younger generation of Indian women. In fact, her courage mirrors the tenacity of the indentured mothers in their fight to break new ground for women.

The Indo-Trinidadian poet Rajandaye Ramkissoon-Chen immortalizes Ramgoonai in a poem entitled "When the Hindu Woman Sings Calypso".[67] The poem spotlights the Hindu woman who redefines a "national" art form that has, until recently, excluded the participation of Indians. The singer's attempts to indigenize calypso into a more inclusive form of musical performance are reflected in her dougla appearance, where she claims agency for both Indians and Africans in the national/cultural imaginary:

> Strings of rhinestone now
> *Purdah* her forehead.
> Her hair is frizzled
> To a *buss-up-shot.*

Combining the traditional Indian *purdah*, or head veil, with the frizzles of African tresses that resemble the multiple layers of buss-up-shot, a local form of crumpled Indian bread, the singer emphasizes the centrality of her performance in creating new and transformed cultural models of expression that are more reflective of the ethnic diversity of her country. She subverts the binary exclusions of cultural nationalisms by advocating a douglarized calypso beat based on the fusion of the sweet sounds of steel pan and the pulsating rhythms of the Indian tassa drums:

> Night insects, they too
> stop their chirrings
> as she sings and *winds*
> to calypso and *pan*
> with a *tassa* blending.

By energizing calypso through an infusion of new life and relocating her art from the "backyard" to the "glare of stage-lights", the singer takes the initiative to advance the cause of minority women in their fight for inclusion in the national landscape. This fight is dramatized by the power of the female body to affirm itself through "her body sinuous with the dance of muscle". The voluptuously soft curves of the Indian female body are transformed into the tautness of muscles of steel that command an attentive audience through female assertion and self-confidence, concretized in fiery lyrics that are inscribed on "leaves of flame". The invisibility of the family backyard is displaced by the centrality of the calypso stage as an open forum where the singer can bring invisible issues such as domestic violence and female abuse to public attention. The politicizing of the stage enables the Hindu calypso woman to claim subjectivity for her Hindu sisters through a certain freedom of expression found in the openness of the calypso lyrics, where "her voice vibrates past stage to audience". Moreover, spatial transgressions into the calypso tent provide the singer with the necessary freedom of movement to break away from familial and communal restrictions imposed on Hindu women and to claim her body as a locus of autonomy where "hips gyrate, knees bend". In other words, the douglarization of ethnically defined national space created by Hindu infractions and self-insertions becomes a liberating space for Hindu women, who can create an enduring tradition of activism by searing the long bonds of unfavourable traditions "in the electricity of the mike's cord length".

Indo-Caribbean women writers have also sought to break new ground by looking for creative channels of inspiration in Afro-Trinidadian folklore. Figures of the seductive she-devil La Diablesse, the life-sucking *soucouyant*, and the water spirit Mama Glo ("mammy water") animate the poetry of Niala Maharaj, Lelawattee Manoo-Rahming and Ramabai Espinet to create a truly Caribbean poetic sensibility. However, Kanhai asks an all-important question in her essay "The Masala Stone Sings": "The Indo-Caribbean woman poet is subverting ethnic and gender taboos that alienate her from her Afro-Caribbean sister with whom she shares history, landscape and gender. The question which must be asked is to what extent are her efforts being reciprocated and valued? Is there evidence that Afro-Caribbean women are receptive to the Indian elements of Caribbean culture?"[68] These questions underline the importance of creating a certain cultural commonality of creative expression through a reciprocity of influence that will undermine the future negative stereotyping of the "Miss Coolies" or "Miss Blackies" of Caribbean fiction as a strategy to overcome racial alienations.

The feminist movement in the anglophone Caribbean has, in fact, been punctuated by alienations that have divided women along the lines of race and class. Bourgeois and academic feminists have found it difficult to make common cause with grass-roots feminists because of different agendas and gender ideologies. While grass-roots movements have emphasized the urgency of providing women with survival skills and with basic resources such as food and shelter, bourgeois feminists seem to have focused more on the theoretical underpinnings of gender by creating a gap between theory and praxis. The lack of common goals, objectives and strategies of implementation has provided stumbling blocks that have hindered a certain unity of organization. These differences were exposed by Cecilia Babb, a self-defined economically disenfranchised Rastafari woman from Dominica who has now made Barbados her home. Speaking at a CAFRA meeting in 1990, Babb stated that the basic issue for grass-roots women is to put food on the table for their children, especially in cases where the women are the sole income earners: "Until this survival is managed it is very difficult for grass roots women to engage in theoretical debate, mobilization, lobbying and group demonstrations, on issues which impact on the very survival we are trying so hard to ensure."[69] Class divisions have been further affected by a lack of resources and by the consequent inability to resolve an issue quickly. Moreover, Sandra Chouthi has described the feminist movement in Trinidad and Tobago as being more reactionary than proactive.[70] This ambivalence can be attributed to the absence of a wider network of support systems and to the piecemeal commitment of the women themselves. Chouthi quotes Jacquie Burgess, the convener of Women Working for Social Progress, who states that the entire burden of addressing women's issues has fallen on the shoulders of two groups, CAFRA and Working Women: "I say so without reservation. The others do respond but piecemeal, and without consistency. . . . The Network of Non-Governmental Organisations for Advancement of Women is vocal too, but it is an umbrella organisation. I don't see individual groups, I don't see the strength of the others coming forth. I have a problem with that."[71] Burgess's dissatisfaction is echoed in the words of Brenda Gopeesingh, the public relations officer of the Hindu Women's Organisation (HWO), who criticizes the movement for not growing fast enough despite great advances made, with governmental aid, in tackling issues of violence against women. While Gopeesingh is very critical of the Trinidadian media and its negative coverage of the HWO, she is equally frustrated by the "apathy" demonstrated by some members of her organization. However, she is also quick to recognize the fact that Indian women may not feel comfortable enough to speak out because of their feelings of inferiority and exclusion: "They don't have the gumption to come forward. It's partly cultural. The other groups have been trying to draw us out, but we don't feel comfortable coming out. We want to be part of the national mosaic, but we feel marginalised."[72]

The issues raised by Burgess, Chouthi and Gopeesingh testify to the complexities and complications involved in feminist organizing in the Caribbean, dispelling any myths about the universality of sisterhood and inherent bonds of communion. As several feminist studies have shown, these ties have been severed by patterns of internalized racism, insecurity and self-hatred ingested by individual women themselves and then projected onto other groups. As Virginia Harris and Trinity Ordona argue, "Internalized racism, cross-racial hostility, internalized sexism, homophobia and heterosexism are the particular dynamics which keep us from resolving these antagonisms and forming lasting coalitions and relationships. These conflicts are part of interactions between women of the same racial group, between women of different racial groups and between heterosexual women of color and lesbians of color."[73] The internal and external divisions that have fragmented the lives of women should not, however, obscure the important strides that women from Trinidad and Guyana have made to overcome the hurdles of race, class and gender in their individual and collective situations in order to develop solidarity associations. The story of the Red Thread cooperative from Guyana provides an affirming example of one such association.

Established in October 1986, Red Thread is a grass-roots women's non-govermental organization designed to help Guyanese women earn some form of sustainable income through income-generating projects that are independent of state and govern-mental control. One of the main objectives of Red Thread was to initiate dialogue and mutual cooperation between urban Afro-Guyanese and rural Indo-Guyanese women by demonstrating that race was not a barrier to inter-ethnic collaboration. As the author Andaiye argues, "In these circumstances, an income generating project became a springboard from which working class Afro- and Indo-Guyanese women, together with middle-class women of several races, began in a small way to work together to organize against the 'narrow interests of the broader political struggle'."[74] Using embroidery as a powerful instrument of coalition weaving, Red Thread was able to give value to women's invisible household work by politicizing the needle and the thread: "Starting with the needle and thread was therefore an attempt to emancipate and reinstate an area of women's work relegated to the status of unpaid and/or undervalued labour and to use it to transform the lives and consciousness of women within their communities, by opening up opportunities to begin the process of their economic independence."[75] Believing that a recognition of women's labour through wage earning would bring about a corresponding valorization of a woman's sense of self-worth, Red Thread used embroidery "to document and celebrate women's work, women's culture and the natural environment".[76] Women with improved self-esteem resulting from monetary appreciation of their work were more inclined to be open to women of other ethnicities and to enter into working relationships with them. Building on the commonality of experience between Indo- and Afro-Guyanese women, Red Thread was seriously committed to multiracial organizing despite cultural differences, independence from ideological blocs and a willingness to hear and respond to the needs of grass-roots groups.[77] This openness provided Indian and African women with the necessary space to learn about each other while dispelling previous antagonisms and misconceptions. By encouraging women to believe in themselves, Red Thread was able to promote its main motto, which was the rights of all women. Consequently, "relationships were built; perceptions and prejudices challenged; a gender consciousness, which recognized similarities without requiring sameness, began to evolve".[78] As feelings of mutual trust and regard began to grow among the Indian and African women because of their shared work, many women began to engage in ethnic boundary crossings as a result of their new consciousness. As Danuta Radzik, a Red Thread member from Georgetown, explains, "I remember that some [Indo-Guyanese] women said that they had never gone into a black community and they would have been scared to go were it not for Red Thread. Normally they're just frightened, don't know what to expect, but knowing each other from Red Thread, they go and feel safe."[79] Women's newly found mobility to negotiate ethnically defined space was reflective of a larger economic mobility in the form of personal choice and remunerated service.

However, African women were still able to take better advantage of whatever opportunities Red Thread provided them because of cultural differences and differences in household organization: "Fewer Indo-Guyanese members were involved in activities such as workshops, which required them to be out for long hours or overnight outside their villages. Reasons given were security; the need to supervise their girl children and households; that these activities reduced time for earning; and that they felt unable to do workshops because they had less education."[80] In spite of these restrictions, the Indian women were unanimous in their belief that because Red Thread had helped them to develop their income-earning skills, they were now able to question familial inhibitions, postpone marriage or children, contest male violence and acquire a renewed sense of self. Serving as an agent of transformational change for Indo- and Afro-Guyanese women alike, Red Thread was able to bridge the gap between gender alienations based on race, class and the urban/rural divide.

Caribbean feminism from Trinidad and Guyana has a complex and complicated history. While partisan politics continue to fragment the lives of women through ethnic and class divisions, women have always initiated change by refusing to conform to socially and culturally dictated mandates. Their (self-) inscription in history has deconstructed myths about their marginality and non-productivity in the national imaginary. As active agents of history, women have claimed their subjectivity as Caribbean citizens. While the struggles of Indo-Caribbean women for self-determination have been more difficult than those of their African counterparts, Indian women have nevertheless made their mark on the Caribbean landscape in a determined fashion. A recognition of the commonality of struggle and the relative similarity of experience between African and Indian women should provide a firm foundation for future dialogue and collaboration. As yet, there are many rivers to cross before Caribbean feminism finally provides a safe home for Indian and African women in Trinidad and Guyana.

3

Creativity, Identity and Culinary Agency

We carry
our spices
each time
we enter
new spaces
the feel
of newness
is ginger
between teeth.
– Lakshmi Gill, "Immigrant Always"

The language of cooking provides an important script to facilitate the necessary negotiations of gendered identity advocated in chapter 2, within both traditional and interracial models of (Indo)-Caribbean identity. Indian cuisine in the Caribbean offers a colourful variety of artfully seasoned dishes, ranging from everyday staples such as dhal (curried lentils) and *philouri* (savoury deep-fried split-pea balls) to the more elaborately prepared wedding and ceremonial feasts of sacrificial curried goat with saffron rice (*pelau*) and *achar* (tropical fruit pickles), followed by the customary desserts of *kheer* (rice pudding), *sewain* (vermicelli pudding) and *gulab jamun* (fried dough balls in a cardomom-flavoured sugary syrup). Inspired by the traditional regionally defined cuisines of India, Indo-Caribbean cuisine has reflected a similar culinary diversity while, at the same time, creatively adapting itself to new and unfamiliar ingredients in the countries of adoption.

The masses of indentured Indians carried supplies of whole cumin, coriander seeds, blackened peppercorns and other spices as personal mementos of home to withstand the brutalizing forces of exile and enforced separation. The carefully prepared pouches of spices became packets of memory that preserved the now-tenuous links with the motherland by providing a fragrant reminder of home. Moreover, pungent aromas disguised, minimally, the overpowering odour of human degradation that characterized the conditions of the Indian Middle Passage by offering temporary medicinal comfort from nausea, dizzy spells and other symptoms of transatlantic crossings. For those who survived the trauma of the *kala pani*, spices represented the security of continuity and self-preservation through their reassuring presence, which supplied a sense of intactness and rootedness in the face of cultural alienation and social displacement. In this way, spices became the necessary grains or markers of Indo-Caribbean immigrant history, establishing close associations between culinary discourse and Indian constructions of Caribbeanness at different stages in history. Food became a symbol of negotiating racialized and gendered otherness by showing how culinary belongingness was a type of oral transmission of culture that allowed an ethnically subordinate culture in Trinidad to resist patterns of domination and acculturation.

Lakshmi Persaud's *Sastra* and *Butterfly in the Wind* and Ramabai Espinet's "Indian Cuisine" offer two very different models of Indo-Trinidadian female identity as reflected by the multiple symbolic variants of food discourse that inscribe themselves in their writings. Although Persaud's texts are located within a specific Hindu rural frame of reference of 1950s Trinidad while Espinet's short story is situated in a contemporary context, both writers promote foodways as synecdoche for attitudes towards Indianness by highlighting the relationship between gendered perceptions of food and the construction of Indian female identity. The two writers draw our attention to women's access to kitchen space as a means of achieving culinary agency that provides women with a basis for cultural authority. However, Persaud and Espinet employ divergent modes of cultural reclaiming in their politicization of the inner dynamics of the kitchen as domesticated space by demonstrating how Indian woman have had to negotiate their identity between two competing models: a specifically Hindu rural ethnic identity from the "Old World" and a more theoretically hybridized one from the "New World". Persaud's female characters ironically find their sense of place through the conventional assuming of kitchen-related duties that benefit the entire community. Espinet's narrator, on the other hand, is

endowed with a certain culinary dynamism that is more reflective of Indo-
Caribbean realities today. In other words, a community's tenacious adherence
to its culinary traditions in times of displacement and insecurity accounts for
its equally tenacious resistance to culinary transformations or re-creations.
However, the *kala pani* crossings obliged Indians to adapt their food preferences
to unfamiliar local ingredients. These *kala pani* crossovers allowed women, as
the chief preparers of food, to indulge in subversive culinary makeovers, within
both traditional food ideologies and postmodern culinary experimentations,
in order to accommodate Indian food to the specifications of a more regionalized
structure of hybridized Caribbean cuisine over several decades.

In her book on the food patterns of various Caribbean communities, Christine
Mackie provides a brief synopsis of Indian cuisine history in the Caribbean.
She claims that since the rations handed out to indentured servants were meagre,
not nutritious and of poor quality, flour and water to make rotis or chapattis
became primary staples of the Indian diet: "Roti was eaten by the very poor
with an uncooked bird pepper or with a West Indian variety of spinach called
bhaji."[1] The Indian diet was initially based at subsistence level, eliminating the
subtle flavourings and complex seasonings of Indian cuisine. The widespread
use of chappati, or unleavened bread, was functional, as chapattis could be
made easily and cheaply and a small amount of dough could be creatively
stretched to feed several people. Chapattis were both physically and
psychologically satisfying: the sharing of communal bread created a sense of
belonging among the displaced immigrants. Indian food habits were thus
characterized by a certain adaptability to an unfamiliar environment and a
new lifestyle, whereby traditionally used food items and spices had to be
substituted for whatever was available and easily affordable. Mackie stipulates
that a new tradition of Indian food was started in the Caribbean "born of
poverty and skilful seasoning".[2]

The economic hardships faced by Indian communities continued well into
the twentieth century. As conditions improved, cooking styles became more
formalized, especially with the introduction of rice cultivation, which had
known a long tradition in the fertile delta of the Indo-Gangetic plain since
2000 BC. Small market gardens were also cultivated together with the rice paddies,
thereby broadening the scope and variety of the Indian diet. As the majority
of the indentured labourers were Hindu, a strict vegetarianism was practised;
meat, fish and eggs were considered to be "contaminated", or flesh food.
(However, not all Hindus were necessarily vegetarian.)

Mackie states that vegetable farming followed the rules of a rigid economy, in which nothing was wasted, as resources were either scarce or expensive. The successful cultivation techniques of the early Indians were attributed to divine benevolence, thereby explaining the sacred or sacrificial aspect of Hindu cooking. While food in its natural state was considered to be a gift from the gods, the cooking of these foods became a reciprocal gift of thanks offered to the gods as sacrifice, or *prasadam.*

Sastra and *Butterfly in the Wind* are illustrations of Hindu attitudes towards food as well as of women's efforts to contribute to community development through their control of the kitchen. Women's access to kitchen space is also reflective of the problematic position they occupy in Indian communities that are caught between the tenacious forces of assimilation and the desire to maintain cultural purity as a strategy of self-preservation. The in-between position maintained by women tipped the balance in favour of cultural closed-mindedness through women's control of the kitchen. Kitchen space was thus located within a paradox of positionality, whereby women displayed complete autonomy in the kitchen on one hand while being enlisted to ensure cultural permanence as a means of safeguarding the interests of their group on the other. From these two novels, the reader gets the impression that the careful preparation of certain foods and the meticulous selection of spices by the women reveal the desire to recreate the flavours and aromas of an imagined India in order to ensure cultural stability.[3] In other words, the ingestion of the ideal assures the digestion of the daily routine, in which the kneading of traditions facilitates a particular women's weave, as reflected in this passage from *Sastra*: "In this larger circle the women's fingers moved nimbly on, taking pieces of fresh dough, smooth and elastic, filling them with dhal – ground dhal with onions and garlic, dhal with turmeric and jeera – until, burnished bright and orange-yellow, it floods the house with its essence, overflows into the yard, evoking a near spiritual warmth, entrancing the imagination, lifting it higher than soaring heights."[4]

The physical appeal of the food is surpassed by its capacity to provide spiritual sustenance; intoxicating aromas, like ceremonial incense sticks, create a certain headiness of spirit. The combination of burnished cumin (jeera) and turmeric, mixed in with the pungent odours of fresh garlic and onion, creates a sensory extravaganza that culminates in a celebratory lifting of spirits. *Butterfly in the Wind* offers an example of this ceremony in a passage in which Kamla makes her way home from school:

> [W]omen cooked outside. It was a sensory delight to walk slowly in the dusk on the main Pasea road when evening meals were being prepared. The women busily darting in and out of their kitchens were probably oblivious to the pleasures I received of the rich warm aroma of wood smoke, roties lifting themselves from hot iron tarwas, vegetables in massala . . . and the intoxicating smell of warm roasted spices. . . . These flavours comforted and energized me, as one aroma mingled with another, so that by the time I arrived home I was in a more than ready state for my evening meal.[5]

Kamla experiences a sensual warmth as she is enveloped by the fragrance of the spices that remind her of the protective warmth of the mother's body. The traditional cooking and sharing of food provides a vital link between mother and daughter, while the restorative effect of food, as reflected in the above quotation, has a positive impact on the child's development. This recuperation is a symptom of a cultural rootedness that establishes a particular sense of belonging. Kamla identifies with the aromatic whiffs of mouth-watering masalas and butter-moistened rotis that assail her senses. She thinks of all the ties that attach her to the women of Pasea village during their daily preparation of food. As Anne Goldman states, "The culinary metaphor is distinctly feminine. . . . The reproductive model of cultural development and identity is specifically maternal. . . . Such a recuperation of a female legacy enables self-assertion at the same time it celebrates the lives of women family members as role models."[6] Goldman establishes a correlation between food, identity and cultural development by identifying these factors as a primary signifiers of female subjectivity. If you are what you eat, then the various spices used in Indian cuisine become cultural signifiers or hieroglyphics whose successful decoding unravels a woman's story. The blending of spices resembles a polyphony of harmonious female voices that narrate their stories in the theatre of the kitchen. Goldman further associates the reproduction of a recipe with the art of story telling that guarantees women a place in cultural production: "Yet reproducing a recipe, like retelling a story, may be at once cultural practice and autobiographical assertion. If it provides an apt metaphor for the reproduction of culture from generation to generation, the act of passing down recipes from mother to daughter works as well to figure a familial space within which self-articulation can take place."[7]

The intergenerational sharing of recipes establishes a particular female legacy of culinary cultural permanence through the documentation of individual family recipes in personalized cookbooks. Oral accounts of grandmothers, mothers and other older female relatives are preserved for posterity by the younger generation through the effective chronicling of age-old techniques of spice usage, ingredient combination and methods of preparation. Each recipe serves as an intimate journal entry in which older women are able to concretize their innermost thoughts and feelings on a sheet of paper by working collaboratively with the younger women to articulate these feelings, under the guise of recipe sharing. The level of trust and intimacy promoted by intergenerational communication encourages mother–daughter understanding by providing a safe space of mutuality and a sharing of experiences. The language of cooking offers a certain point of commonality between generations by demonstrating how "seasoned" ingredients such as dried red chillies and turmeric can be successfully combined with freshly cut tomatoes to produce a good curry base. In other words, cooking provides a common language that displaces insecurities while, at the same time, representing and validating different points of view. In this way, the kitchen becomes a sanctuary of female self-affirmation by guaranteeing the sacrosanctness of woman-centred experiences and relationships.

In a brilliant essay entitled "The Making of a Writer: From the Poets in the Kitchen", the Afro-Barbadian writer Paule Marshall transforms the dynamics of the kitchen from a site of daily drudgery into a creative poetry workshop, in which she becomes the apprentice of the kitchen table poets, represented by her mother and her mother's friends. Using the kitchen table as a creative drawing board, these women reconfigure their triple marginalization as foreign-born black working-class immigrant women in the United States into patterns of creative assertiveness, through everyday colloquialisms that give meaning to their immigrant existence: "And their talk was a refuge. They never really ceased being baffled and overwhelmed by America – its vastness, complexity and power."[8] In other words, kitchen talk involves the therapeutic exchange of daily experiences that include feelings of disappointment, frustration and humiliation in an alien land by providing functional healing space for the articulation of these emotions.[9] Inner despair is countered by the collective catharsis offered by other women in the form of nostalgic reminiscences sustained by home-grown foods and brews. Just as shared recollections in the form of "homegirl talk" ("the insight, irony, wit and humor . . . their poet's inventiveness and daring with language")[10] create a sense of community among the women to transcend feelings of immigrant powerlessness, so also food provides sustenance for the soul, to infuse it with a new poetry that transforms the alienness of immigration into the hope for new beginnings. The kitchen offers the necessary supportive space to facilitate these beginnings by enabling the women to perform everyday magic as a means of controlling their circumstances.

In other words, if the cooking of food relegates women to the confines of the kitchen, it is also important to consider how Indo-Caribbean women, in turn, politicize the kitchen by converting it into a site of creativity, as demonstrated by the women in Marshall's narrative. The power they wield in the kitchen is based on their mastery of the use of spices that transforms them into veritable "mistresses of spices".[11] These culinary artists exercise a power "in-formation" that situates the kitchen as a paradoxical location of agency and tireless industry. *Sastra* describes the kitchen as a source of creative energy: "A kitchen is where many a divine thought first reveals itself; it was when the creator was in his kitchen, listening to the throb of creamy kheer, that the idea of the universe came to him" (98). If women were responsible for the making of this creamy *kheer*, does this quotation suggest that the creator's inspiration was, in fact, motivated by the hands of a woman?

In *Sastra* and *Butterfly in the Wind*, the women are the primary preparers of food and makers of spices. The careful mixing of spices involves the skill of an alchemist because the faulty combination of the wrong spices can have an adverse impact on physical well-being. Like the chemical potions of the alchemist, spices need to be ground, mixed and then roasted with a certain expertise to avoid the dangers of overcooking or burning that will either inhibit the complete expression of their flavouring or significantly alter their taste. Spices also need to be measured and used in perfect proportion to create a tasteful curry composed of a delicately balanced assortment of spices. Any imbalance in measurement can lead to the overpowering effect of particular spices, thereby minimizing the pleasure of eating.

Indian vegetarian cuisine is based on a holistic balance between various foods in combination, structured by a system of binary classifications: spicy and sweet, raw and cooked, hot and cold. Food patterns are regulated by "syntactic rules that govern the combination of foods to create a 'grammatical' meal".[12] Women become the chief enforcers of the grammatology of food habits in the community by providing balanced meals that maintain their society's equilibrium. Consequently, their preparation of food involves the same deliberation as the making of a decision for communal welfare. In *Butterfly in the Wind*, the grandmother's decision to make soup assumes the same importance as the act of choosing qualified guards to defend national security: "A decision to make a soup was not taken lightly. A soup would only be decided upon if she noticed there was a supply of good quality vegetables. Then Daya would be told which coconut to grate from the dozen or so dry ones kept in the old shed. . . . She chose all her ingredients with the eye of an old warrior choosing young men to defend a crucial gate" (20).

The relationship to food expresses a society's cultural ethos. The women play the role of ensuring the preservation of this ethos through their participation in highly ritualized food patterns. The formalizing of food preparation is reflective of a corresponding formalizing of the social, whereby the kitchen becomes the stage on which daily interactions are played out. Food offers a microcosmic glance into a society's inner workings wherein, as Claude Lévi-Strauss affirms, "we can hope to discover for each special case how the cooking of a society is a language in which it unconsciously translates its structure or else resigns itself to revealing its contradictions".[13] This "language" of food provides a document of cultural history in which women provide the necessary script for the effective writing out of this text.

Within the system of societal exchange, it is the women who provide a sense of social cohesion. The communal partaking of a meal establishes community among the Indians for whom cultural purity is maintained by Brahmin cuisine. Food chauvinism parallels the cultural chauvinism demonstrated in the novels, where the preservation of culture becomes an excuse for cultural insularity and racism.

The Hindu sense of superiority in relation to their cuisine stems from the belief in the cultural sanctity of cooking. A vegetarian diet symbolized cultural purity as well as the preferred food of the god Krishna, whose meal plan consisted primarily of fruits, vegetables and an overabundance of milk, ghee (clarified butter) and yogurt. The incorporation of these foods testified to their holiness, converting them into the divine *prasadam*, or offering to the gods. Eliot Singer points out that the consumption of these foods ensured physical and spiritual well-being by controlling the senses through a balanced diet and the avoidance of meat: "Each type of food is believed to have an effect on bodily and psychological functioning, and it is necessary not to overdo the consumption of any kind of food. Hot foods are associated with bodily passions and awaken the senses. Sweet foods on the other hand, are filling and lead to lethargy. It is therefore regarded as crucial to maintain a relative balance between foods in the two categories."[14] Food choice was thus normative. Meat was forbidden as it was "demonic food", associated with heathen and culturally inferior (that is, non-Hindu) modes of food production. According to Singer, Hindus believed that meat was an aphrodisiac that lead to moral and physical degeneration as the result of a sensory imbalance.

The female characters participate in this "food parochialism"[15] in their preparation of *katha*, or communal food, as illustrated in *Butterfly in the Wind*: "Then from the kitchen came the teasing excitement of spiced, savoury food: *Paratha*, pumpkin, *khir*, curried potatoes with *channa*, *karhi*, *bhajee*, *chataigne*, curried mango and boiling hot rice with *kachourie* served separately and the mouth-watering pickles – *achar* or *kuchala*" (132). The *katha* offerings are a way of humanizing the gods by a collective feeding of the deities. The informality of *katha* sessions is meant to create spiritual kinship among the people as well as to seduce the gods with the enticing aroma of spices. Interestingly, the women initiate a mild flirtation with the gods through the seductive appeal of the spices. The sanctity of the food is ironically interconnected with a sensuality of expression, reminiscent of the tales of the *Geeta Govinda* that narrated the sexual exploits of Krishna and his numerous *gopikas*, or milkmaids. There are several references to Krishna consciousness in *Butterfly in the Wind*, illustrated by the choice of milk-based sacrificial offerings such as *panchamirit*, "a sweet liquid of milk and honey and ghee", and *prasad*, "rich and crumbly, made of ghee and butter and sugar and flour and raisins" (132).

Food-based Krishna consciousness offers a creative outlet for women's sexual energies by permitting women to indulge in fantasies of sexual initiative that temporarily mitigate the traditional expectations of sexual passivity required by their menfolk at home. *Katha* food ironically supplies the discourse for the articulation of the female body erotic under the (sublimated) cover of religious fulfilment. In other words, food becomes a catalyst to facilitate the complementarity of sexual and religious ecstasy through the oral ingestion of creamy *panchamirit*, the nectar of the gods, whose honey-flavoured aftertaste guarantees physical satisfaction. In this fashion, the women can control the dynamics of their sexual foreplay with the gods by choosing the appropriate foods that will ensure the desired level of satisfaction. Contrary to the commonly held belief of Hindu women's religiously prescribed asexuality as the very paradigm of Hindu femaleness, the women in Persaud's novels dramatize their powers of seduction in the kitchen, under the guise of religious devotion, by using the spices as aphrodisiacs to create a sexually charged atmosphere that ranges from teasing excitement to boiling passion, depending upon the intensity of the spices. Each spice symbolizes a particular erogenous sensation, which reaches its most climactic expression in the fiery culinary implosion of hot *achar* and its stomach-titillating combinations of preserved mango and lemon slices that have been simmering in their savoury juices.

Krishna worship also symbolizes an unconscious celebration of female oral sexuality, as represented by the promotion of milk culture. While the *Geeta Govinda* contains graphic descriptions of Krishna's predilection for women's breasts, the stories simultaneously hint at the potential for the multiplicity of female *jouissance* or pleasure that no longer limits itself to procreation. This study infers that Krishna food divination provides the impetus for female sexual experimentation by enabling women to rewrite their own scripts of sexual affirmation. Although these experimentations are situated at a symbolic level, they are an important acknowledgement of women's invisible attempts to control space through the culinary reimaginings of their personal situations.

In other words, the women's sexualizing of kitchen space as an unlikely ground of resistance valorizes the idea of women's invisible powers and of their capacity to engage in underground rearticulations. Margot Badran and Miriam Cooke question the Western feminist assumption that locates power within visible or manifest levels of activism by distinguishing between visible and invisible feminisms. Badran states, "This distinction rescues feminism from being understood as an exclusively public and explicit phenomenon, and thus provides an analytic framework within which to locate and explain the more comprehensive feminist historical experiences."[16] Badran's use of the term "discrete feminisms"[17] confirms the suggestion that the association of power with the visible or the concrete is based on a misconception that undermines the integrity of invisible or latent forms of control. As an illustration of Badran's argument, female power in the kitchen lies in its invisibility, that is, in its ability to transform an unfavourable situation to the advantage of women through strategies of subversive affirmation that guarantee the inclusiveness of a variety of experiences.

The principle of inclusion is further demonstrated by the collective nature of the *kathas,* which leads to a temporary transcending of Hindu caste distinctions when all members of Hindu society are encouraged to join the communal feasting. Kamla's mother, in *Butterfly,* plays a key role in assuring the transitory creation of a classless welfare state by inviting "all our neighbours, as well as anyone who was around my father's rum shop and any of the wandering poor who slept in the open at nights. I have seen her stop men, ragged and foul smelling, as they walked slowly past our shop, and invite them in to have some katha food" (129). The inclusion of the poor and needy to "warm their stomachs with good wholesome food" (129) is part of a larger scheme of natural inclusion. Celebrating the gods involves the simultaneous celebration of nature, whereby the appeasing of nature leads to bountiful harvests that are crucial to the survival of agrarian communities. The rural-based economies of the Indian communities in these novels are dependent upon the successful fruition of nature's cycles. Natural elements in Hindu cosmology either become personifications of divinities or are placed under the protection of a particular divinity, such as Surya, the sun god, or Vayu, the god of wind. The feeding of nature is thus a form of worshipping the gods as well as a means of replenishing nature's resources through a reciprocal system of give and take. Offerings of *katha* food made by Kamla's mother to the river illustrate this principle: "If at the end of the day there was still some food left over, the remainder would be taken to a river and placed on its bed so that the fishes too could rejoice" (133).

However, the Hindu principle of inclusiveness is limited in its scope as it does not extend itself to include non-Hindu communities. Persaud's novels illustrate a tenacious resistance to interracial mixing, whereby contact with the various Afro-Trinidadian communities is considered to be a sign of racial contamination. Patricia Mohammed explains that the very idea of racial interaction or creolization is regarded with suspicion by Indo-Trinidadian communities because "creolization was viewed as synonymous with the absorption of black culture at the expense of one's own".[18] Indians were thus able to maintain and reinforce the cultural duality between the two major ethnic groups in Trinidad through the idea of Brahmanic racial and cultural superiority, that justified to them their cultural insularity. Typically, the female body became the necessary ground on which the Indian resistance to assimilation and creolization was situated, as has been suggested by Paula Morgan.[19] Indian women, through their communal responsibilities, became the collective advocators of cultural closed-mindedness; their culinary parochialism reflected a larger racial parochialism. If the preparation of *prasadam* guaranteed the community's spiritual integrity, the "othering" and marginalization of blacks would ensure its racial purity. In this way, Indian women became proud defenders of their space by limiting and controlling the rights of access to this space.

The female characters in Persaud's *Sastra* illustrate the idea of territorial possessiveness in their disparaging attitudes towards a black woman, Milly. Milly's profession as a cook requires her to handle the preparation of different kinds of meat. For Hindus, contact with meat is an act of contamination and communication with demonic forces. Milly is discriminated against immediately for her culinary preferences as well as for her religious sensibilities as a meat-eating, meat-preparing Christian woman. The women's antagonism towards Milly grows when they learn that she also cooks beef. They consider the defiling of the sacred Hindu cow to be the ultimate act of sacrilege and a sign of flagrant disrespect for the Hindu religion: "Wealthy Indians employed Negroes, but not as cooks. . . . To kill, cook and eat the sacred cow, as well as an animal that wallowed in mud and made grunting sounds was sacrilegious and obscene, especially when freshly picked green, leafy spinach, bygan choka, dhal and paratha were so delicious and nutritious. So, to have the hand that put those meats in its mouth touching one's pillow, one's cup, was deeply repugnant to these brahmin ladies" (56). By affirming the superiority and sanctity of their own cooking habits, the women reduce Milly to a state of untouchability, reminiscent of the caste disparities along occupational lines upheld by Hinduism. Milly is victimized by her professional and racial status, like the members of the *chamar* class of cobblers and tanners in India, who face severe discrimination because their profession involves the preparation of leather and the fabrication of leather products.

The women interpret Milly's employment by an Indian man who has converted to Christianity to protest Hindu hierarchical privilege as a sign of cultural treason and debasement. They consider the presence of a black woman in a (former) Hindu kitchen to be a direct violation of the sanctity of the kitchen and its rules for individual and group well-being. The trespassing of sacred space, together with disregard for the codes that govern its safekeeping, can have only negative consequences, according to them: "Milly's employment as cook was seen, therefore, as a sign that Surinder Pande had been on his own too long, and that this was what happened to a man cut off from his roots, his culture – like a cow grazing on the open savanna, alone, exposed, he was certain to be brought low, seduced" (56).

It is interesting to note how attitudes towards food promote a certain sociology of gender relations, deeply rooted as they are in traditional perceptions of culture, as a basis for identity formation. Linda Brown and Kay Mussell explain: "Foodways bind individuals together, define the limits of the group's outreach and identity, distinguish in-group from out-group, serve as a medium of inter-group communication, celebrate cultural cohesion, and provide a context for performance of group rituals."[20] Food, as a symbol of communal identification, serves as an indicator of the sexual division of labour that maintains the dynamics of the food politic within a society. In other words, foodways promote a hierarchical organization of gender relations within the home by creating a binary division between men, as income earners and providers of food, and women, as preparers and servers of food.[21] This gender dissymmetry is a function of class, whereby upper-class membership for women is not necessarily accompanied by gender-role flexibility. In this way, it is easy to observe how upper-class Hindu women would use kitchen space as leverage to correct the gender imbalances within their homes by discriminating against "other" women, who do not conform to the Hindu model, thereby instituting a racialized imbalance that is (self-)vindicating.

Aisha Khan explores the idea of *juthaa*, or food contamination, in the Indo-Trinidadian cultural context as a way of analysing the differing categories of hierarchical discrimination and patterns of inclusion/exclusion that are institutionalized through food discourse: "The very nature of juthaa requires a focus on pollution as it applies to food exchange, since food is both a principal conduit of pollution in India and a key medium of social relations in Trinidad. In all societies, obtaining and sharing food contain symbolic messages about the way people construct and express their social relationships."[22] *Juthaa*, as a signifier of food that has been symbolically or physically polluted through contact with another person who has been identified as the "defiling other", expresses a certain ideology of Hindu caste and class relations that maintains its impervious influence in the Indo-Trinidadian cultural repertoire.[23] In other words, food discourse offers microcosmic insights into a particular Hindu world view that is maintained as a means of preserving ethnic wholeness in a diasporic location. As Khan confirms, "The concept of juthaa has significance for ethnicity because it speaks directly to the creation or maintenance of boundaries based on a common cultural heritage and/or definitions of affinity."[24] Hindu foodways justify the demarcation of insider/outsider groups and establish the parameters of exchange/non-exchange between these different groups.

However, the spices curiously assume an autonomous presence in Persaud's novels when they communicate an important lesson in cultural and racial harmony by showing how the blending of spices from different culinary traditions can produce an even more appetizing curry, *colombo* or callaloo. Just as cultural intermingling leads to the removal of the blinders of ignorance and racial prejudice, so also the sharing of spices between different communities of women will initiate the necessary cultural thawing of relationships. The Hindu cook

Draupadi in *Sastra* experiences this sentiment when she is asked to share her culinary experiences with Milly. Milly initiates the first step towards racial understanding by expressing her interest in learning how to cook Indian food, but Draupadi initially refuses to respond to her. However, she experiences a dramatic change of heart when the spices urge her, during a dream-like trance, to develop her cultural sensibilities. The spices "speak" with a certain authority as culinary history reveals the well-known fact that spices themselves have known a long tradition of cultural transmigration and culinary mixing. Draupadi exclaims,

> I had a choice of becoming a spice that was fragrant, rich, exciting, a warm spice that had not lost its aroma for this young black student, or of becoming dust, charcoal of no use to her. While I was still breathing, while *Bhagwan* was performing the miracle of life through me, I was opting to be of no use, fit only for weevils and mould. And the more I thought about it, the scales of ignorance, of meanness, of my narrowness, fell from my eyes; for the very spices that I had all my life treated with great care, these minuscule grains and buds, were now showing me such a large, magnificent way. I would never have thought . . . that I, Draupadi, would one day be so obligated to my spices. (168)

Draupadi learns that the miserly hoarding of spices over a long period of time will destroy their potency while encouraging the growth of mould and infestation by weevils. In a similar fashion, a society that continues to remain ossified in its traditions will hasten its own destruction by suffocating in its self-created glass bubble. Spices advocate the urgency of a creative "masalafication" or creolization of cultures as a prerequisite for achieving dynamic cultural plurality in the Caribbean. This dynamism can be accomplished by an effective dialogue of spices across cultures, as spices provide the necessary common ground for different varieties of Caribbean cuisine.

Similarly, Ramabai Espinet stresses the efficacy of "cultural enlargement",[25] in her eight-page short story "Indian Cuisine", as a stepping stone to the creation of a multi-ethnic heterogeneity of experiences through the parameters of hunger, creolization and creative cooking. This story demonstrates the reconfiguration of Indo-Caribbean female identity through the language of food to represent an initial engagement with creolization by an Indo-Caribbean Christian woman writer. It situates Indian creolizations in an in-between space of intermediary negotiations of blackness and whiteness in an Indo-Trinidadian context. In other words, food discourse provides the essential technique – or, as Edward Brathwaite would call it, the "seasoning"[26] – to posit Indian attempts at creolization from a woman's point of view.

The term *Creole* initially represented a certain anathema for Indo-Caribbean communities. Simon Gikandi attributes the ambivalence of the Indo-Caribbean participation in creolization in Trinidad and elsewhere in the Caribbean to the particular problematics of Indo-Caribbean history.[27] He associates the tentativeness of the Indian efforts with a particular anxiety that is directly linked to the contradictions inherent in Indian history. Gikandi highlights certain historical paradoxes in his analysis to explain the uneasiness demonstrated by the early immigrants to experiment with new initiatives. He states that while indentureship was supposed to be voluntary and temporary, it soon became an institutionalized form of labour discrimination that was patterned after the insidious workings of the African slave trade. Confounded by the arbitrariness of the newly imposed rules and regulations, Indians closed ranks internally by seeking comfort in the familiarity of their culture. Cultural introspection was one way of making sense of the trauma of transatlantic vulnerability, by reflecting on the instability of the Indian position, aptly described by the Trinidadian writer Sam Selvon: "As for the Caribbean man of East Indian descent, he was something else. He wasn't accepted by those from India, and he wasn't wanted by the others because he wasn't a black man so he couldn't understand what was going on."[28] Selvon's reflections evoke a sense of cultural alienation and existential displacement experienced by the Indo-Caribbean man, who suffers from a state of symbolic orphanhood, rejected by the motherland (India) and remaining unidentified by the politics of the new fatherland, represented by colonial authority and the Afro-Trinidadian majority. While Indo-Caribbean men remained in a relative state of unease in the pre-independence years, both Patricia Mohammed's and Rhoda Reddock's studies demonstrate how "lower-class" Indo-Caribbean women, in contrast, were able to negotiate the complexities of creolization with a greater sense of comfort.[29] Women in particular had everything to gain by "coming out" because this exposure placed them at a midway point between the cultural dynamism of the outside and the traditional fixity of home.

The desire to transgress the closely delineated parameters of domestic space through self-initiated intercultural explorations highlighted the greater adaptability of Indian women to their new environment and their greater facility in dealing with issues of race and ethnicity in a multi-ethnic society. These "infractions" by Indian women, who were accused of selling their culture short, accounted for the pejorative connotations of the term *Creole* when applied to them in a Trinidadian context. As Mohammed indicates, *Creole* was an offensive word when it referred to Indo-Trinidadian women because it was popularly used to designate women who "consorted with people of African descent, especially men, Indian women who changed their eating and dress habits and who adopted non-Indian social customs".[30] Creolization, as an agent of transformative change for Indian women, was looked upon with suspicion and trepidation by men and by more traditional upper-class Hindu women because it implied that creolized women were "out of control", overstepping their prescribed boundaries. Several historical documents on the indentured Indians have indicated that despite the scarcity of women during the early phases of immigration, Indian men were unlikely to be sexually involved with African or non-Indian women, whose sexual otherness was less than desirable to them. Hence, the supposed sexual audacity displayed by Indian women, who were more inclined to engage in intercultural liaisons, led to a serious wounding of the Indian male ego.

However, in post-independence Trinidad, creolization has become an everyday reality and a new means of survival in an ethnically diverse society where cultural purity is fast becoming a myth of antiquated reductionism, according to Mohammed. In fact, creolization has become a way of negotiating local representation in national culture by paving the way for the inclusion of "minority" ethnic, gendered and political discourses to create a more inclusive model of Trinidadian citizenship through creative adjustments and reciprocity.

This sketchy historical overview has been important to contextualize Espinet's story within the parameters of Indian creolization. The author uses fiction to reveal the ambiguities and tensions involved in the process of Indian creolization by using the model of culinary experimentation as a metaphor for a larger cultural and historical rearticulation. Additionally, it is important to note that individual and collective responses and reactions to creolization have varied greatly according to ethnic, gendered, regional and class specifications. Comparing and contrasting the process of creolization in anglophone and francophone Caribbean locations, Yannick Lahens stresses a fundamental difference between the two regions' preoccupations with creolization; while francophone Creoleness focuses predominantly on questions of language and identity construction, as a result of the normative influence of French, anglophone creolizations refer more specifically to cultural and behavioural practices.[31] However, Lahens's statement is not entirely accurate: it minimizes the efforts of Indo- and Afro-

Caribbean anglophone writers who have actively participated in linguistic creolization as a means of positing a particular "local" consciousness in order to deconstruct colonial paradigms of linguistic and literary authority. Linguistic creolization has been particularly important for contemporary Indo-Caribbean writers, to help them recover an initial loss, symbolized by the marginalization of Indian languages within the national language scheme, and to deal with the simultaneous alienness imposed by the colonial language in its capacity to falsify meaning through its inability to translate indigenized experiences.

Espinet's "Indian Cuisine" uses linguistic duplicity within a culinary framework of feminist consciousness to engage in cross-cultural celebrations and imaginations that, according to Wilson Harris, institute genuine change by converting totalizing reductionisms into new and liberating aesthetics.[32] By using an energized aesthetics of Creole food preparation, Espinet's story embraces a double articulation by remedying the historically created inequities of the past while proposing creative cultural models of recuperation for the future.

The story begins with an ironic exchange between an Indo-Caribbean woman and her presumably white lover:

> ". . . And since that night the taste of fruit cocktail has always been magical to me. . . . It was far from everything around . . . I open a cheap can of the overcooked, overprocessed, overripe fruit and the whiff of gramarye is overwhelming."
>
> He sighed and turned away. . . . "A childhood of privilege," was all he said. And I could see it through his eyes too but it was wrong, all wrong. And how to begin to excavate the difference from where his head had already settled in?[33]

The lover ironically associates fruit cocktail with a sense of privilege and, in doing so, reinforces the erroneous perception of Indians as privileged immigrants. In other words, the distortion of the woman's social status (her family's ability to afford the can of fruit cocktail) is magnified into a larger historical distortion that creates a disjunction between impressions of privilege and daily reality. On the other hand, the narrator associates this processed fruit product with painful childhood memories of desolation, emptiness and lack, especially on Christmas day: "Privilege? I don't know . . . the creeping inexorable smell of desolation" (564).

The can of fruit cocktail becomes a repository of processed memories of colonial domination and exploitation by serving as a desolate reminder of glaring disparities between the economic realities of colonizer and colonized. The indiscriminate exportation of tropical fruit from the Caribbean at a cheap price was followed by a subsequent rerouting of these fruits, in synthetic form, back to the islands, to be sold at a much higher price. Bananas, pineapples and mangos left the islands in their natural state only to return as artificial products that were a pale and lifeless imitation of the original. Fruit cocktail processed in England became a composite colonial ideal to be ingested by the local population, as a sign of colonial privilege, even though the prefabricated product had lost its vital juices, nutritious value and flavouring.

The overpowering odour of the sugary syrup that preserves the essential composition of the fruit mixture reminds the narrator of the driving forces behind slavery and indentureship. Through a process of free (and immediate) association, the can concretizes the history of the African and Indian labour that sustained the sugar plantation economy. The control of the fruit processing industry, like the processing and distribution of sugar, was thus a colonial prerogative that led to the ultimate destruction of indigenous economies through overcultivation and trade imbalances.

The lover suggests that for the "natives", the consumption of fruit cocktail symbolizes an act of identification with and acceptance of the colonial ideal, with all its benefits. Like the economic power imbalance instigated by colonial capitalism, the lover initiates a gender power imbalance in the relationship, by his false assumptions and his ability to speak for his native woman in his capacity as a white man. He ironically fails to recognize his own position of privilege, which he presumably takes for granted, leading to miscommunication and a lack of understanding of the fundamental differences that separate him from his partner. These sociocultural, gender and racial differences will remain compressed within the aluminium confines of the can of fruit cocktail until the narrator can tell her story in a language that is acceptable to and easily digestible by him.

The use of the term *privilege* receives a further twist when it is used to symbolize poor man's food in Barbados – food that is, however, fit to titillate the palate of a king. The narrator recalls "privilege which, now that I think of it, is a fabulous Bajan dish made of rice and ochroes, saltmeat and saltfish, all cooked down together. . . . Belize had serre, Trinidad had pelau and Barbados had privilege. When Barbados set down the steaming bowl they announced it as a dish fit for a king. That table was a queen's banquet alright. And it was all poor-people Caribbean food" (565). This passage expresses the transformative potential of food to "spice" the ordinary plate of life by injecting it with simple yet flavourful ingredients that produce a satisfying result. Food becomes the vessel to fill a void in life, created by social and economic disenfranchisement, in the same way that the narrator experiences a vicious craving for the right words to rectify a historical oversight.

The narrator's existential hunger for the appropriate language in which to write a counter-historical script, through her access to books and knowledge, parallels a more immediate physical hunger that is a symptom of prolonged economic deprivation: "And in between the books there was the hunger that came and went with the low, low whine of a mangy dog. The hunger came and stayed although there was never really a day with nothing at all on the table. Something always materialized somehow. It's like that with some levels of poverty. Want, hunger always there" (566). The narrator tries to feed her hunger by taking control of the family library and kitchen. Her early exposure to reading ("it's possible that my only real privilege was that our house was packed with old books" [565]) is complemented by her assumption of kitchen responsibilities at age twelve, when her mother is obliged to get a job out of economic necessity. The correlated existence of books as food for thought and cooking as food for the body culminates in the creative swallowing of a cookbook, whereby "the food on my plate turned into cookbook magic" (569). The *Boston Cooking School Book* supplies the necessary language/text to establish a sense of historicity, using food items as essential characters and food preparation as the necessary events to provide the structural basis for the story. Historical/textual discourse is posited through an orally ingested food discourse whereby oral accounts that are either lost or forgotten receive concrete articulation in specific recipes. In other words, food provides the testimony for lived-out cultural experiences that have been ignored by the more conventional, Eurocentric narratives of colonial history that have obscured oral, undocumented or unpalatable accounts of immigrant realities.

In other words, just as the recipes for the preparation of creole food reflect an inherent hybridization of different culinary experiences and styles, so the language used in the articulation of these recipes follows a similar pattern of linguistic mutation. Mikhail Bakhtin has explored the subversive aspects of linguistic hybridity by associating it with a particular decolonization of language. Describing hybridity as a process of "unmasking the authority of another's speech through a language that is double accented and double styled",[34] Bakhtin suggests that linguistic hybridity represents an effective voice-over that ruptures the fixity of authentic or true meaning. Hybridity creates a *trompe l'œil* or illusory effect of sameness for the uninitiated while simultaneously inscribing new meanings. Linguistic mutations displace the authority of the colonial dictionary through the inventiveness of indigenized vocabularies. In this way, the word *privilege* undergoes several levels of linguistic splicing to alter the fixity of epistemic signification. The white lover imposes a fixed definition of privilege – the rights and benefits of a particular group (colonial privilege) – as a homogenous characterization of what he perceives to be the special favours enjoyed by certain colonized subjects. When he projects his own interpretation of and experience with privilege onto disenfranchised people, his misuse of language exposes a certain displacement of signification through its irrelevance of meaning. His static use of language reveals his linguistic impairment when he gets caught in a particular linguistic freeze of colonial misconceptions and archaisms. On the other hand, the appropriation of colonial vocabulary to infuse it with new agency – that is, the ironic transformation of colonial privilege or entitlement into the local privilege of enjoying a decent square meal – symbolizes an act of active contestation by the colonized to expose and satirize the illogic of the financially privileged other, as indicated by Bakhtin. These ironic reversals subvert the validity of colonially determined systems of "original signification" in a Caribbean context through the adroit reconfiguration of linguistic codes of domination to create the necessary double-layered interrogative consciousness of decolonized subjectivities. This heteroglossic speaking in multiple tongues gives agency to repressed histories by creatively interweaving the multiple symbolisms of narrative inversions into dominant narratives. As Bakhtin states, "It frequently happens that even one and the same word will belong simultaneously to two languages, two belief systems that intersect in a hybrid construction – and consequently, the word has two contradictory meanings, two accents."[35] By undermining the false essentialisms that underlie colonial discourses regarding immigrant and other histories, hybridity inserts the voices of the underrepresented, creating multiple world views that negate the legitimacy of hegemonic appropriations of meaning.

In a similar fashion, the language of the *Boston Cooking School Book* is deprogrammed from its original agenda when the blandness, homogeneity and authority of colonial cuisine is first displaced and then radically transformed into tongue-teasing creolized possibilities. In other words, the learning of different cooking techniques parallels a course in historical methodology that includes careful documentation, fact-finding and research techniques. Consequently, the swallowed cookbook becomes a palimpsest that contains a coded history in the same way that a plate of "semi-stew of eggs, saltfish and tomatoes with bake" can be metamorphosed into "shirred eggs, braised tomatoes and saltfish soufflé" (569) through a process of imaginative decoding undertaken by the narrator.

Hybridity is the discourse of creative decoding, this "third space of counter-authority" posited by Homi Bhabha, that reverses patterns of dominance into active moments of intervention.[36] By creating the necessary space for the insertion of displaced histories, hybridity permits the chronicling of indigenized forms of resistance to colonial rule and sociocultural discontinuities that are a result of immigration and demographic deracination. In this way, Espinet uses ochroes (okra) as symbols of contestation to personify the history of the first Indian immigrants. The functional value of ochroes is compared to the strength and adaptability displayed by the immigrants, establishing a rapport between food and immigrant history: "Ochroes were our salvation. . . . They grew straight and tall – taller than usual maybe because they were half-starved of lights" (566). Despite the immigrants' cultural and socio-economic deprivation, they, like the light-deprived ochroes, demonstrate their resilience in a hostile environment. Moreover, the story suggests how the versatility of the ochroes, which can be "fried, stirred into cornmeal batter with a whisper of saltfish and made into fritters, dusted in cornmeal and deep fried" (566), can be compared with the fluid dynamism of alternative historical narratives in which passive victimhood is converted into creative subjectivity. Like the ochroes, the immigrants hold their ground by refusing to "bend with every stray wind that filtered through the grove" (566), thereby establishing a legacy based on hard labour, fortitude and a sense of dignity. In other words, "Indian Cuisine" narrates the history of its people, who are trying to come to terms with their past while negotiating their present citizenship as a minority culture. As Veronica Gregg says, "What 'Indian Cuisine' reveals is . . . the problems of history and culture, language and silences. A life shaped by indentureship, sexual and social interaction among African and Indian Trinidadians, denied and unspoken, duplicitous familial relationships, gender hierarchy, fissured 'realities', a focus on social mobility."[37] Food initiates a particular cartography of societal relations by permitting a mapping out of historical location. For example, when the narrator's family moves from a rural setting in Biche to the suburbs of La Plata, her experience of displacement is neutralized by a sense of culinary belongingness when her mother continues to prepare ochroes in their new home. Ochroes provide the necessary "salvation" (566) by creating a feeling of security in an unfamiliar and socially pretentious milieu: "Once while I waited outside Auntie

Semoy's kitchen and neat living room for the ice, she asked in her friendly way, 'How your mother always picking ochro so, eh? All Yuh like ochro, eh!' She followed this up by asking Muddie who confirmed that we were almost passionate in our taste for ochroes" (569).

At a later stage, the narrator's mother continues the tradition of creativity and resourcefulness demonstrated by the first immigrants when her family's inability to afford a decent meal whets her appetite to search for nutritious substitutes. Hunger, like passion, stimulates the mother's creative potential, enabling her to perform transformational magic in the kitchen, thereby setting an early example for her daughter. She converts meagre provisions into a healthy meal with her talent for using whatever she finds in her yard, especially in times of financial distress. The narrator marvels at this ability to make the most of existing material: "She would snip the youngest ochroes from their bushes and serve them lightly steamed with a dot of butter. In front of the house a stand of dasheen had sprung out of the drain. She cut the young leaves of these, mixed them with ochroes and made a bhaji. A little bit of flour for roti and we ate a whole meal" (567).

The mother becomes an effective role model for the daughter's own culinary experimentation when the latter's self-managed apprenticeship in the kitchen begins at an early age. The kitchen becomes the workshop of everyday life, where the hunger for knowledge becomes a means to transcend gendered marginality and social confinement. Culinary mastery supplies the essential tools needed for self-mastery: "I devoured material on how to bake, boil, shir, braise, roast, how to make puff pastry and how to identify a variety of fruits and vegetables like turnips, kale and kumquats although I never saw these until many years later" (569). In other words, food supplies the necessary ingredients to chart a genealogy of origin by tracing the narrator's trajectory from her early experimentation with cooking as a young girl of twelve to her formalized establishment as a recognized professional caterer in her adult years. However, this success story is inscribed within the politics of hunger and prolonged deprivation to show how the process of creolization has essentially been class- and gender-based. As Reddock states, "The increased acceptance of creole culture as a national culture has to be seen as the result of years of class struggle as it was the poorest and working class who were the most creative and tenuous in their re-creation and indigenization of cultural forms."[38] Hunger, as a symbol of political consciousness, provides the necessary motivating force to transcend the limitations imposed by class-based and gendered infirmities.

The narrator's desire to expand the parameters of her cooking expertise parallels her desire for upward mobility by breaking away from traditional gender-role expectations to reach a stage of economic self-sufficiency. Her growing autonomy from household-related duties and obligations to personal independence follows the same channels of experimentation as her ultimate mastery of Creole cooking: "I got tired of cooking the same things over and over", she states (570). Impelled by the desire to innovate, she "made coo-coo with ochroes and cornmeal", finding the recipes in a "thin blue hard-covered West Indian cookbook hidden in one of the cardboard boxes" (570). The choice of coo-coo as a primary experimental dish is not coincidental: the preparation of coo-coo involves the mixing of boiled ochroes with cornmeal and the blending of these ingredients into a fine paste-like mixture, as stated in several Caribbean cookbooks. The initiation into Creole cooking serves as a rite of passage for the narrator to move beyond cultural constrictions by embracing a pluralistic world view. A sense of one's own culture, together with the required open-mindedness to exploring new horizons, leads to a certain control over one's circumstances. Mastering the cookbook while adding one's own innovative recipes equals the act of acquiring transcendental knowledge about the self and history. This newly found level of expertise becomes the prescribed antidote to hunger that leads to the narrator's current state of privilege. This privilege is acquired through her culinary entrepreneurship that permits her financial and personal autonomy: "Privilege is the life I lead now. I can do just about anything I like in this city because I earn enough and am my own woman" (572). Moreover, she *earns* her privilege when she transforms a childhood occupational necessity into the profitable trade of a "designer of cuisine" (572).

As a designer, the narrator's cooking skills have been raised to the level of artistic creation; she is able to produce individualized, custom-tailored meals that are reflective of the multifaceted, overlapping and complicated parts of an individual's identity: "I design cuisine to integrate every aspect of a person's special event so that the table looks like your life quilt laid out as a feast for eyes and palate. Home, childhood, history, nationality, personality, seasonal produce – no stops allowed" (572). Her recipes for life are based on the vital ingredients of inclusion, personal affirmation and a simultaneous celebration of transcultural experiences. The menus she prepares for her clientele are personalized case histories of Patricia Mohammed's definition of *creolization* as "a commitment – political and social – to the new society, as well as . . . engagement with the society so that the existent cultures are mixed and enriched in the process".[39] Through creative cooking, the narrator is able to negotiate existing sociocultural and racial boundaries to finally reach a space of "privilege . . . fruit cocktail and all" (573). In other words, Indian creolization reveals a dynamic Caribbean cosmopolitanism by offering a contemporary model of cultural cooperation to promote and sustain multi-ethnic interactions.

The narrator's personal story also reflects the dramatic changes that are taking place in the traditional position of and roles ascribed to Indo-Caribbean women as a result of sociocultural transmutations. Creolization has been instrumental in elaborating these changes. As Patricia Mohammed states, "The stereotype of Indian woman as primarily keeper of the culture, sacrificial and passive, can no longer apply to all. Indian women have become more integrated into the society, a process accelerated in the post-independence era by the increased opportunities available to them in education and employment out of the home."[40] In other words, creolization has provided women with the necessary education to negotiate gender-role flexibility and to promote a shift in attitude from traditional stereotype to actualized prototype. In Espinet's narrative, the kitchen supplies the essential site for creative learning by enabling the protagonist to master traditional Indian recipes as a stepping stone to the production of culinary re-creations.

However, Indian creolization has been fraught with internal tensions within the home, thereby revealing divergent intergenerational attitudes towards this process. While the younger generation has associated creolization with greater access to national culture and personal mobility, parents have regarded it as a serious threat to the integrity of Indian culture through unwarranted cross-cultural fertilizations. These conflictual reactions can be attributed to growing insecurities on both sides, whereby, as Kelvin Singh asserts, the gradual erosion of traditional Indian culture has led to "the increasing meaninglessness of that culture among the younger Indians, a generation gap between parents and children in the rural areas and intra familial conflicts over such emotionally vital problems as romance, selection of mates and lifestyles".[41] In other words, parents' inability to communicate with their children has been predicated on the loss of a traditional linguistic and cultural base. In contrast, the children's attempt to circumvent the alienation enforced by the supposed meaninglessness of ancient traditions in a contemporary context has prompted the creation of a common plurivocal creolized language that is more reflective of day-to-day experiences and realities.

In a similar fashion, in Espinet's story, the narrator's efforts to introduce an element of creolization into her Indian household through the creolized language of food are met with stiff opposition, especially by her mother. The mother's violent rejection of coo-coo seems ironic, especially since she had already prepared a dish with similar ingredients for the family on a previous occasion but under a different appellation and using a different technique. The mother's "ochroes stirred in cornmeal batter with a whisper of saltfish" (566) resemble the narrator's "coo-coo with ochroes and cornmeal" (570). However, the latter "receives a terrible boof and nobody would touch it" (570). The family's resistance to something different is uncompromising, so that "late as it was, Muddie had to quickly make up some sada roti and butter for them" (570).

In this way, mother and daughter are placed on opposing ends of the cultural spectrum, reflecting the stereotypical dichotomy represented by tradition and modernity, whereby "Muddie never even tried the West Indian cookbook because by this time she had given up on the kitchen" (571). Ironically, it is the father who supports his daughter's cooking initiatives, because of his suspected extramarital affair with a Creole woman. Coo-coo provides him with the vicarious sensual pleasure of "eating creole" at home. In other words, his appetite for Creole sex fortifies his enjoyment of Creole food, leading to his wife's accusing questions: "Yuh know bout coo-coo? Where yuh know bout coo-coo?" (570). While the mother's fidelity to Indian food is associated with her desire to preserve the sanctity of family traditions, the father is more inclined to engage in a duplicitous code of sexual morality, whereby he hypocritically conforms to the ethos of the inner sanctum of the Indian home while reserving his sexual escapades with a Creole woman for the outside. Father and daughter are united by their common bonds of complicity wherein the daughter's culinary transgressions fuel the father's sexual transgressions, thereby creating a common discourse of creolized communication through extra-domestic/extramarital sexual and culinary experimentations.

Espinet's story also highlights the critical relationship between artistic contribution and national pluralism within the newly emerging nation state. The protagonist's culinary agency initiates an effective chronicling of history, providing the basis for a national revisioning that includes the contribution of women. "Indian Cuisine" opens up the space for the integration of the woman artist's input in the construction of the national imaginary by establishing a parallel between food discourse and the articulation of a dynamic national discourse, rooted in what C. L. R. James calls a "future in the present".[42] This future-inspired present receives its support from a sense of participatory ownership that fosters healthy ties between the individual and his or her community through the principle of inclusiveness. As James proclaims, "The good life . . . is that community between the individual and the state; the sense that he belongs to the state and the state belongs to him. . . . [T]he citizen's alive when he feels that he himself in his own national community is overcoming difficulty."[43] The woman artist, as a cultural visionary, creates new models of national agency that facilitate this system of reciprocity through her effective feeding of the nation. In other words, national wholeness is predicated by a culinary wholeness, whereby a healthy nation is sustained by a balanced diet of cultural reimaginings that advocate and maintain pluralisms. The contributions of women provide the vital missing ingredients to spice the national smorgasbord of Caribbean realities by offering palate-titillating alternatives that negate cultural binarisms and archaisms.

Indian women's negotiations of identity through food discourse have involved them in complicated and contradictory journeys of self-affirmation that have been characterized by successful fruition or by failure. Whatever the outcome of these explorations, however, it is important to emphasize that women have always negotiated change by elaborating indigenous forms of activism that have depended upon local culture and social standing. Persaud's characters fight against cultural syncretism by concentrating on cultural revisions within patriarchal Hindu society, wherein the affirmation of female subjectivity either remains precarious or is achieved at a tremendous cost. Espinet's characters look outwards for intercultural, multiracial dialogues that explore the "permeability of boundaries and identities within a shifting multi-racial society".[44] While both models of identity formation carry levels of ambivalence, they should not be seen as constituting mutually exclusive paradigms of representation that perpetuate a state of antagonism or resistance. The finding of an in-between space that encourages the formation of distinct yet inter-culturally composed identities could inspire the synthesized third space whose creation would provide a possible resolution of the problem. As Veronica Gregg concludes, "it is the name of a problem whose solution is our promise".[45]

4

Orality, Indo-Caribbean Feminism and Aji Culture

> Per-Ajie, in my dreams
> I visualise
> Thy dark eyes
> Peering to penetrate
> The misty haze
> Veiling the coast
> Of Guyana
>
> – Rajkumari Singh, "Per-Ajie: A Tribute to the
> First Immigrant Woman"

The preceding chapter established the importance of the kitchen in the negotiation of Indo-Caribbean female identity; this chapter extends the argument about the relationship between women and space in the Indo-Caribbean household by demonstrating how women try to redefine the gendered segregation of space in Hindu culture by politicizing and sexualizing inner, and thus feminine space, in a diasporic context. The need to reconceptualize spatial configurations and their pertinence to female subjectivity can be traced to women's problematic and highly paradoxical access to space in Hindu culture. Space in India has traditionally been defined and polarized by essentialized, gendered dichotomies between the domestic (*ghar*) and the public (*bahir*), the spiritual and the material, the "invisible" feminine interior and the "visible" male exterior.[1] The segregated distinctiveness of space has thus known a long cultural tradition in which the invisibility of women has been sanctioned by patriarchal discourses that have legitimized women's relegation to inner courtyards, kitchens and women's quarters.

However, confinement ironically provided Indian women with a oppositional space in which to assert themselves. The foundation of home was constructed on a tenuous contradiction whereby home was simultaneously the site of gendered repression and of self-affirmation. Home space was thus a contradictory space for women in India and a site of dilemma for Indo-Caribbean women. This dilemma reflected women's powers of renegotiating space (within limitations) during the process of migration. Indo-Caribbean women's negotiation of space was thus located within a particular spatial disjunction that created multilayered interstitial cracks, exposing the vulnerability of patriarchal binary structures. The parallel between female subjectivity and the idea of spatial splintering established the necessary preparatory ground for cultural revisionings that would initiate a more favourable mapping of home for women. As Meena Alexander notes in her memoirs, *Fault Lines,* reimaginings of home are possible "only through a resolute *fracturing of sense,* a splintering of old ways of holding that might have made the mind think itself".[2] Fault lines assure the necessary cracking of the essentialized paradigm of home as an always already constituted construction to pave the way for alternative meanings.

In Lakshmi Persaud's *Sastra* and *Butterfly in the Wind,* Jan Shinebourne's *The Last English Plantation,* and Narmala Shewcharan's *Tomorrow Is Another Day,* the female characters follow a pattern of contestation and assimilation to create a three-dimensional level of spatial reintegrations. Women's renegotiations of space in the Indo-Caribbean household are an attempt to claim cultural authority through the creation of active (fictionalized) subjects who resist cultural erasure by elaborating alternative scripts that guarantee female representation. While women were undoubtedly confined by Hindu patriarchal strictures, they have also resisted confinement at home. How have women, who have not had access to a foreign education and the option of life abroad, made a difference in their own lifestyles at home? How has the notion of home been reconstructed by women and transformed home into a more amenable location for them? These are some of the questions that structure the following analysis, which demonstrates how Indo-Caribbean women use the "inner" space of the houseyard in a rural Trinidadian and Guyanese setting as the necessary site to draft a certain politics of relocation. This blueprint enables them to circumvent cultural and gendered displacement through collective and creative agency.

The idea of home for women has thus been based on what I call a "paradox of positionality". Whereas the Hindu patriarch associates home with a series of nostalgic evocations captured in clichéd expressions such as "home is where the hearth/woman is", for Indo-Caribbean women home symbolizes a source of disruption since women's occupation of home space has not been accompanied by the necessary deeds of entitlement. Homi Bhabha reformulates the Freudian concept of the *Unheimlich,* or the unhomely presence, in relation to the diasporic home. Referring to the idea of home as a ruptured belonging or a strangely (un)familiar place, Bhabha states, "The unhomely . . . captures something of the estranging sense of relocation of the home and the world in an unhallowed place."[3] Describing the diasporic home as something at the same time external (foreign/strange) and internal (familiar), Bhabha relocates home within the parameters of a synthesized third space that welcomes and celebrates the manifestation of the repressed, the invisible or all that is "lost" in the process of migration. In the newly formulated space, "private and public, past and present, the psyche and the social develop an interstitial intimacy. It is an intimacy that questions binary divisions through which such spheres of social experience are often spatially opposed. . . . This . . . represents . . . a difference 'within', a subject that inhabits the rim of an 'in-between reality' ."[4] The dynamic complexities of space in transformation upsets the structural dissymmetry maintained by hetero-patriarchy through the process of fusion in which un-differentiation favours the mutuality of experiences. Un-differentiation eliminates the principle of otherness that is located within binary polarities by celebrating the notion of multiple internal heterogeneity or expansion. Like the process of osmosis, undifferentiation permeates the very fabric of society to liquidate self-imposed and culturally imposed boundaries. This neutralization of space marks a certain liberation for women who can contest male strictures that are in a state of suspension during this process of structural transformation.

This study establishes how the houseyard, in addition to the kitchen, becomes the major locus of historical and cultural production through a spatial undifferentiation that positions the female characters in the novels as feminist agents of history. The yard represents the very site of Indo-Caribbean feminism through its enabling location of belonging. Patricia Mohammed indicates that Caribbean theories of feminism revolve around issues of identity politics: "Identities are affirmed and constructed on the basis of real struggles which people and groups are engaged in and which they communicate to each other in coded messages within a culture. . . . Political struggles for identity which have taken place in the Caribbean must themselves be historicized and culturally investigated if they are to have meaning."[5] Therefore, postcolonial feminist identity politics translate a particular desire of affiliation to transcend nationalist exclusions and the imposition of a male-inspired national and cultural imaginary wherein women have suffered from a certain territorial dispossession. Indo-Caribbean women politicize the yard by symbolically transforming it into a microcosm of the nation whereby women's control of the yard parallels an effective "sexing" or reclaiming of the nation by women.

The construction of yardspace within the Indo-Caribbean home goes beyond mere architectural design to function as an important meeting point for women. The centrality of the houseyard is maintained by its duality of purpose: it serves as the site for interpersonal exchange between the women of the household, transcending class and ethnic distinctions, as well as as a point of economic exchange in which women from the nearby marketplace come to sell their products. The gender-specific use of yardspace situates it as a particularly female space that occupies an intersectional position between the household interior and the more commercial exterior. The in-between positionality of the yard, which favours the historical agency of women, negates traditional associations of history-making with male-dominated public spheres of influence. The creation of intersectional space leads to the rupturing of the inside/outside distinction by locating the yardspace itself within the interstices of the public/private dialectical implosion.

In Indian culture, the houseyard has served as a centre for female activity, whereby women have assumed the responsibility for designing, maintaining and decorating yardspace. Embellished with fragrant *tulsi*, or basil leaves, and with intricate flower designs made with *rangoli*, or rice flour, yards have come to symbolize loci for female well-being and autonomy, as all yard-related services have been supervised and maintained by women. R. T. Smith describes yardspace in the Caribbean by stating, "Women organize and oversee the various activities that support the social and economic reproduction of the yard, providing continuity from one generation to the next."[6] Serving as community space, the yard also provides the necessary location for a centre for political and social advising for women, resembling a village *panchayat*, or council.

While women have traditionally been excluded from local self-governance in village *sabhas*, or committees, their exclusion has often been countered by the creation of *mahilasabhas*, or women's groups, within the home. Women's control of the yard has facilitated the communal hosting of a variety of activities that include counselling sessions, story telling, entertainment, planning and policy making. In other words, women's ownership of the yard has counterbalanced their patriarchal tutelage within the confines of the home by permitting a certain transgressional crossing of boundaries to negotiate both spaces simultaneously.

Female power is thus located in the dual capacity to negotiate one's way both through the inner machinations of the home and through life's forces, represented by the yard and its capacity to function as a microcosm of a more global, external exchange. This exchange is made possible by the yard's internal dynamism, functioning as it does as the repository of an interconnected cultural, political and economic contestation by women. In other words, the yard becomes the necessary preparatory ground for the enhancement of female empowerment through a strategy of collective influence that is sustained by the process of female re-membering within its parameters.

The reconstruction of the past into a more favourable location for women takes place through the creation of alternative female histories that offer women the potential for creative agency. In *Sastra* and *Butterfly in the Wind*, the female characters spend time telling stories and exchanging information in their yards. While "woman talk" has often been dismissed as idle gossip and playful bantering, the political significance of these stories cannot be dismissed. The yard provides the necessary supportive space within which women's stories are narrated. The traditional exclusion of women's histories from the male text corrects itself when women create a counterscript that gives voice to their forgotten and forbidden histories.

The repressed mother tongue finds a new articulation in female space, in a language that Bhabha describes as a "speak(ing) in tongues, from a space 'in-between each other' which is a communal space".[7] This "in-between" language represents the emergence of a linguistic repossession after centuries of ancestral silencing, whereby women recount their day-to-day experiences as a means of self-expression and validation. The voicing out of personal narratives and the communal hearing of stories builds up a storehouse of collective knowledge that provides valuable archival documentation of women's histories, thereby ensuring the preservation of those histories.

In Indian and other cultures, women's creative agency through story telling has known a long tradition. As Trinh Minh-ha says, "The world's earliest archives or libraries were the memories of women."[8] Locating women's stories at the level of primal memories, Minh-ha's statement suggests that the divine logos was, in fact, the word of woman, the Mother, as the original creator and maker of stories. Consequently, women's role as the oral transmitter of historical agency served as a motivation for the initiation of a female legacy, even though patriarchal culture was to later institute a programme of cultural silencing to minimize women's participation in the elaboration of plurivocal histories.

Lakshmi Holmström establishes Indian women's oral heritage by claiming that "women in India have traditionally been tellers of tales. They have used not only the mythic materials of the epics in their local versions, the lives of the gods and the animal fables of the *Panchatantra,* but also the more realistic material of family histories and memories".[9]

This heritage has been complemented by a rich tradition of woman-narrated Indo-Caribbean folk tales, proverbs, jokes and maxims for everyday life. Kenneth Parmasad indicates that 80 per cent of the Indo-Caribbean folk tales that he researched for his collection *Salt and Roti* came from the mouths of women.[10] The very title of his collection reveals women's dexterity in "seasoning" (salt) the quotidian (roti) through their inventive resourcefulness while grounding the tales in local rural culture. The popular Sakchulee, or trickster-figure, stories demonstrate the title character's creative machinations to alter reality to his own specifications. Disenfranchised villagers could immediately identify with Sakchulee because these stories mirrored their own attempts to survive, using their wit and wisdom. Through story telling, women have tried to affirm their subjectivity, using these stories as sounding boards to question issues of gender inequality, sexual oppression, female marginalization and invisibility, thereby creating a revisionist version of the primarily male-centred epic tales. Chandra and Satya Mohanty pinpoint these revisions in their introduction to a collection of contemporary short stories by Indian women writers: "Women's stories raise questions of gender identity, of location, agency and the reimagining of the social. . . . Each story engages questions of sexual politics (the regulation, control and use of sexuality) as it expresses the conditions and moments of resistance to dominant patriarchal paradigms."[11] It is this very moment of resistance to patriarchal domination that provides the *fil conducteur,* or binding force, of cultural continuity between women from India and their Indo-Caribbean counterparts. The retrieval and sustaining of ancestral memories is guaranteed by a process of "matrifocal generational continuity"[12] that finds its basis in the common displacement of Indian women under patriarchal control. This locus of commonality helps to refigure ancestral space as a geography of diaspora. The idea of dispersal helps to dislodge the primacy of the experience of the Indian nationals, posited as the original or authentic experience that often invalidates the specificities of diasporic realities. National chauvinism is neutralized when the initial sharing of the umbilical cord is later ruptured to create geographically and culturally specific modalities in the Caribbean.

The wise mothers Kunti and Chandi in *Tomorrow Is Another Day,* Kamla's grandmother in *Butterfly in the Wind,* and Nani ("grandmother" in Hindi) Dharmadai in *The Last English Plantation* control the politics of the houseyard. Represented as the wise elders, or *ajis,* who have reached a stage of distinction through their mastery of ancestral knowledge, these women can be compared to the original *griottes* of Indo-Caribbean female history. Their presence as the ancestral mothers goes beyond mere archetype to indicate their importance as sociocultural and historical interpreters who initiate transformative re-evaluations of women's history and cultural resistance.

As the preceding chapters have shown, Indo-Caribbean women occupied a marginalized position in history until the recent scholarship of Caribbean feminists. Even though women automatically wrote themselves into history through their economic productivity on the plantation estates, their commercialized, wage-producing activities were neutralized into mythically constructed patterns of dominance at home, inscribing women within an apoliticized cultural imaginary of passivity and subservience authenticated by the sanctity of founding Hindu texts such as the *Ramayana,* as analysed in chapter 1. However, in a conference paper entitled "Singing *Ramayana*: The Text of Sita's Fidelity", Ramabai Espinet indicates that even though both men and women recited verses from the sacred text in the early days of indentureship, women at that time creatively problematized the text on women's fidelity and self-abnegation. The women reimagined the epic as a text of contestation by inscribing resistance to cultural dictates over domestic virtue. Espinet pays homage to these women, whom she positions as the first revolutionary Indo-Caribbean story tellers who, through creative reimaginings, de-emphasized the importance of mandatory behavioural prescriptions for women in order to elaborate their own stories.[13]

These stories were generally narrated at twilight in the open-air theatre of the *angan,* or yard, when the mellow and diffused after-sunset light would create a warm ambiance of fellowship after the travails of a long day. Several Caribbean writers, such as Edouard Glissant and Wilson Harris, have ascribed a particular importance to what they call a "twilight consciousness", located in a midway space between dusk and dawn. Symbolizing hope and renewed possibilities for the future that were offered by the new day through a process of forward thinking, twilight consciousness was synonymous with re-creations of intent. As Harris states, "The twilight situation enables the language of consciousness to rediscover and reinform itself in the face of accretions of accent and privilege, the burden of 'sacred' usage of one-sidedness."[14] Through oral re-creations, the twilight consciousness resurrects the stories of the repressed or the marginal that are buried under the loftiness of "sacred", unitary impositions of signification. By revealing an inherent multiplicity or plurivocality of experiences and points of views, the twilight consciousness affords an immediate resource for women to organize their private revolutions as a means of diffusing the fixity of Hindu and colonial cultural mandates. In other words, twilight consciousness stresses the primacy of orality and pre-discursive modes of communication as a dynamic counterculture of alternative expression. Describing the contrapuntal value of such alterations, Ernest Pépin and Raphaël Confiant emphasize their importance and relevance to indigenized cultural, linguistic and historical realities of the Caribbean: "It leans on the true memory as a matter of urgency for an itinerary more suitable to our time space — through the revising of systems of dating, positioning in space, legibility of the obscure — and all this by differing from colonial chronicles."[15] By advocating a politicized revisiting of colonial timelines and points of reference, contrapuntal affirmations reveal the infirmities of mnemonic disfigurement through an active decolonization of memory.

The colonization of Hindu memory in the Indo-Caribbean context has resulted from a three-tiered structure of cultural and historical alienation. This structure has been imposed by indentureship and its disenfranchising consequences, a misidentification with falsely constructed notions of Hinduness that were imported from the homeland, which was, itself, reeling under the impact of sustained intellectual and physical colonization, and further misinterpretations of Hindu culture by patriarchal readings that were aimed at redressing colonized male subjectivities through the gendered domination of women. Distortions in memory created falsified historical referents of discredited knowledge in colonial texts that enforced normative models of compliancy on colonized populations, as a means of control. These structures were later replicated by Indian men within the confines of the home, to salve their frayed egos, which had been demoralized by systematic assaults on their masculinity and by other forms of humiliation suffered at the hands of the white masters.

As the primary "beneficiaries" of gendered and cultural victimization, women were driven to devise protective modes of alternative knowledge in order to make some sense of the anomie that surrounded them. Orality gave them the essential strategies to effectively decipher social dis-ease through the documentation of previously unrecorded histories that, according to Evelyn O'Callaghan, established a "woman version" of diverse and empowering Caribbean experiences wherein patterns of confrontation were replaced by models of collective mutuality.[16] Carolyn Cooper associates orality with a form of folk wisdom, "that body of subterranean knowledge that is often associated with the silenced language of women and the 'primitiveness' of orally transmitted knowledge".[17] Orality, as a model of underground female expression, refers to all forms of communication that have been repressed by canonical structures of ordered rationality and discursive transparency. Orality stresses the importance of primeval bonds among women, the creation of politicized female spaces that override the uniformity of colonial and patriarchal readings.

—·—

The novels discussed in this chapter are examples of culturally grounded texts in which Indo-Caribbean women reclaim a sense of self through *aji* culture. The Indo-Caribbean *ajis* are communal healers who are responsible, through their personal example, for providing inspirational models of affirmation for Indo-Caribbean societies that have been victimized by colonial and racist ideologies. The late Indo-Guyanese poet Rajkumari Singh pays tribute to these grandmothers as the original makers of Indo-Caribbean history, women whose fortitude, cultural authority and sense of pride in themselves provided stabilizing forces to combat sociocultural and political displacement. Singh erects a commemorative (poetic) statue that immortalizes the presence of the *ajis*:

> *Per-Ajie*
>
> I can see
> How in stature
> Thou didst grow
> Shoulders up
> Head held high
> The challenge
> In thine eye.[18]

The resolute political and social tenacity demonstrated by these women was strengthened by their growing mastery of challenging circumstances through a particular "third eye" consciousness that was developed by the harnessing of women's creative potential to face adversity. Within these parameters, *ajis* complement Alice Walker's definition of a womanist, who is "committed to the survival and wholeness of entire peoples" as a result of her sense of self and her love for her culture.[19]

The communal mother is thus a mobilizing force in her community, providing a model of female authority. In this way, she offers a counter-model of female representation to idealized abstractions of a mythical, timeless mother figure. *Aji* mothering illustrates a dynamic role in formation that addresses the needs of a community in transition between pre- and post-independence stages of transformation. It can be better characterized as a process (of being) that postulates a certain philosophy of social conduct developed under the tutelage of the *aji*, who provides basic paradigms for day-to-day life.

Moreover, *aji* mothering broadens the limited connotations of the term *mother* by extending itself to include a community activist of feminine orientation. Traditional cultural values that have upheld male-centred prescriptions for women have tended to equate "ideal" womanhood with a woman's reproductive capacities. Positing the biological mother as the paradigm of all femininity, motherhood has been fixed as the norm by which women are evaluated for ultimate social approbation. The valorization of the mother has reached mythical proportions of representation in the works of conservative Indo-Caribbean men and women writers, who have converted motherhood into a mystical abstraction that has obfuscated the harsh realities of motherhood in several rural-based Caribbean societies (malnutrition, lack of resources, unhealthy environment, physical strain on women). The image of the idealized mother (represented physically or symbolically as Mother India or Mother Earth and her powers of regeneration) has led to the immobilization of women in traditionally convened roles in which mothers have been presented as symbols of an essentialized femininity. The reduction of womanhood to a purely biological function has favoured a one-dimensional, stereotypical and exclusionary paradigm of female representation, seeking to confine women to a subcaste based on a rigid sexual caste system that has dispossessed those who have remained childless out of choice or necessity.

In this way, *aji* mothering broadens the scope of womanhood by removing it from its narrow biological confines. It provides a creative alternative, to be "other mothers"[20] through a communal birthing of values and group effort. By acting as rehabilitative centres, yards provide the preparatory ground to sustain such birthings. Mediated by the recuperative powers of the *aji*, who finds her support among other women, yards represent a certain space of solidarity whose parameters are controlled by women through a strategy of collective influence. Female power lies in its collectivity, that is, in the construction and preservation of communal knowledge that provides the necessary countermemory of decolonized subjectivity. In other words, *ajis* become symbolic "granny midwives"[21] who facilitate the birth of an indigenized oral literacy through the exorcism of interpretational misinformation or misreadings provided by colonial and patriarchal documents.

As a result of these corrective revisionings, yards become highly politicized space for women; all major decisions concerning individual and group welfare are made there. In other words, women not only control their own space and administer their affairs within the parameters of yardspace, but they also protect their own rights and interests as women by developing a certain socially motivated consciousness (of self), wherein subjectivity lies in a self-articulated politics of healing. A developed sense of *aji* consciousness provides a counterscript that gives Hindu women a sense of their history through an effective deconstruction of Hinduness. *Ajis,* as the original chroniclers of oral history, supply the necessary language to fill the gaping lapses in Indian memory that are created by the historical and cultural exclusions of women. By reaffirming a certain politics of the rural, the very site of the *aji*'s creative agency, these women transform marginalized areas of representation into vibrant loci of political contestation. In doing so, rural Indian women are afforded the opportunity to make sense of their physical and social dispossession on plantations and other areas of confinement through "curative transformations of reality"[22] that convert socioculturally imposed victimhood into active reconfigurations of Hindu culture.

Narmala Shewcharan's *Tomorrow Is Another Day* establishes a legacy of female assertion through the *aji* figure Kunti. Kunti serves as a point of origin to locate Indo-Caribbean women within an active history of labour production through their backbreaking work in the canefields. Ramabai Espinet has been particularly sensitive to the inclusion of the voices of these women in Caribbean history, in order to acknowledge their crucial input in the economic survival of Indo-Caribbean communities while maintaining the integrity of family life. Espinet bemoans the invisibility that these women have suffered in the annals of Caribbean history: "I want to begin by asserting that within the chorus of voices modulating the discourse on cane — its history, politics, sociology, culture and literature — one voice is notably absent. It is the voice of the female cane-cutter of Indian extraction in the Caribbean context. And because that voice has not been present, speaking out of the depths of her personal history, the experience of that woman has been denied."[23] Inscribing these women within a particular "female epistemology of cane", Espinet resurrects their voices from oblivion.

Likewise, Shewcharan pays tribute to their powers of endurance, sacrifice and economic entrepreneurship through the character of Kunti, whom she positions as the Mother of Indian female labour in the Caribbean. The novel establishes this tradition of female industry when the son remembers the hardships that his mother confronts as a cane-cutter: "She had worked hard all her life, bringing him up single-handedly after his father had died. He knew that her back still ached with the constant bending she had done in the canefields and her hands were scarred from handling the long stalks."[24]

The evidence of Kunti's labour is visibly inscribed on her body in the form of scars and an aching back. These signifiers of hard work provide the necessary text to create a discourse of rupture between stereotypical perceptions of Indian female passivity and women's day-to-day reality in the canefields. The working woman is thus an active co-worker in the fight for economic survival, struggling for equal participation in mainstream production and thereby disrupting any false notions about her dependence on her male partner. As a single, working-class mother, Kunti is her own agent of reliance, who has to look after herself and her son's welfare while braving the pernicious machinery of cane culture. In this way, her cane-cutting cutlass is a dual symbol of toil and resistance, symbolizing the affirmations and negations that are involved in survival struggles.

Kunti's cane labour represents her investment in her son's future: "He was a veteran politician. His mother had spent many years bending in the canefields to give him a reasonable education" (54). Kunti believes that Jagru's education and the subsequent possibilities of career mobility will compensate for her own professional immobility in the canefields. However, Jagru's errors of judgement, which lead to his ultimate downfall as a victim of political scapegoating, demonstrate his alienation from his environment. Protected from poverty, manual labour and the hardships involved in the cultivation of cane, Jagru's misplaced idealism reduces him to a state of helplessness in which, in the face of misfortune, he regresses to an infantile dependence on his mother.

The mother, on the other hand, is informed by the practicalities of cane culture, which advocate a sense of communal-mindedness, as reflected in her philosophy: "What a better place the world would be if people helped each other without looking for a return" (147). Her philosophy demonstrates the way in which Indo-Caribbean communities were able to survive the ordeal of the *kala pani* and the trauma of indentureship through the close *jahajibhai* and *jahajibahin* ties, of fraternity and sisterhood, that were established on the merchant ships that brought the Indian labourers to the Caribbean. Determined to continue the ethos of camaraderie maintained by the first Indian immigrants, Kunti becomes a communal mother who looks after the interests of others. Subsequently, the characters Chandi and Kunti develop intergenerational bonds of affinity based on the common absence of their spouses. Widowhood and desertion create common bonds of empathy and understanding based on the industry of the two women and their sense of responsibility towards their families and society: "She had grown to like Chandi, to admire the way she faced up to things and to realise that they were alike. . . . Kunti was pleased to help" (144). Chandi and Kunti are united by a common language of disenfranchisement that paves the way for sustained solidarities along the lines of race, class and age through the network of intergenerational continuity.

Similarly, Jan Shinebourne inscribes Nani Dharmadai within the *aji* culture as the keeper of a strong woman-centred Indo-Caribbean tradition. In Jan Shinebourne's *The Last English Plantation*, the protagonist, June, is raised by her biological mother, Lucille, as well as by Nani. While Lucille's motherly preoccupations for her daughter revolve around the creation of a colonial prototype through a misleading identification with Englishness, as was shown in chapter 1, Nani's maternal solicitude focuses on earth-bound traditions. Lucille's idealized fascination with colonial culture reveals her corresponding shame for all that Nani stands for, namely her "mati-coolie(ness)",[25] or primitive Hinduness. Misinterpreting the association between the earth (*mati*) and Indo-Caribbean identity as a form of regression or "primitivism", Lucille bases her knowledge of Hinduism on a colonized knowledge of this culture that has been re-created by nebulous distortions. Lucille's historical displacement reflects a more immediate territorial displacement when the airiness of colonial misreadings impede the groundedness of cultural identity.

Khal Torabully emphasizes the pre-eminence of the land in the construction of Indian diasporic identity: the first indentured immigrants were an agricultural labour force that toiled the land to make its first impression on non-native soil.[26] The Indian identification with the land was twofold, symbolizing a metaphysical umbilical affiliation with the rural lands of India as well as a politicized inscription of memory on the land. The politicization of the earth and earth-related traditions through the positioning of land as historical text avoided simplistic New Age romanticizations of the earth and earth mothers.

On the contrary, for the indentured labourers, the earth represented a historical palimpsest that inscribed the multilayered complexities of the immigrant's existence. In addition, the earthly traces of women's existence were crucial to maintaining the visibility of their experiences. In this way, Nani's earth religion located women's expressive agency and resistance in the soil as a means of safeguarding and sustaining the integrity of Indo-Caribbean female memory.

Describing memory as a variant of generational history and shared consciousness, Mary Chamberlain asserts that "the language of memory is the means by which tradition is transmitted, the means by which structure and values are internalized, passed on and inherited. Memories are imaginative recountings, representative of a set of meanings by which and through which lives are interpreted and transmitted, constructed and changed".[27] Memories, as sociocultural fictions, are endowed with fluid dynamisms that oppose the static fixities of colonial and patriarchal histories. Offering flexible and open-ended reflections of women's lives, these creatively adaptable expressions of oral culture are in consonance with the shifting patterns of Indo-Caribbean women's subjectivities. In other words, the language of memory projects the polyvalence of female realities to undermine representational closure and immobility. Earth-anchored memories promote a prismatic sensibility that reflects the earthy dynamism of the soil, which, while ensuring permanence and continuity on the one hand, simultaneously accommodates itself to the changing vagaries of nature's cycles as a method of self-preservation.

Nani's use of pure coconut oil illustrates the concept of an earthy prismatic consciousness through the use of natural products. The coconut palm is noted in rural coastal areas for its versatility and life-sustaining properties. Each component of the coconut palm has a functional purpose, including palm leaves for thatched roofs; coconut water for its nutritional and medicinal value; coconut bark for making lightweight rafts; coconut oil for cooking, massages and lighting of ceremonial *deyas*, or mud lamps; and religious offerings of the fruit to the various Hindu gods as a sign of devotion. Coconuts symbolize a particular village ethos by their ability to stand tall in rough sandy soil while offering bountiful harvests that ensure the survival of the entire community. The Guadeloupean writer Simone Schwarz-Bart compares her female characters to coconuts in a superbly crafted novel, *The Bridge of Beyond*, suggesting that even though women may bend in circumstances of severe adversity, their resilient spines prevent them from breaking under pressure in the same way that the coconut shell remains intact even after falling to the ground. The grandmother advises Télumée to develop a strong sense of self through her resoluteness, like the young coconut palm that learns its first lessons in natural survival at a tender age.[28]

In a similar fashion, Nani uses an effective coconut therapy to solder June's fragmented sense of self when the girl is confronted with the conflicting cultural values of her mixed Indian and Chinese heritage, which undergoes a third level of splitting through the imposition of Christian ideology in school and of informal indoctrination by her mother at home. June seeks comfort in Nani's home space after a particularly vicious fight with her mother, in the hope of putting her confused state of mind at ease with Nani's curative coconut culture. The following passages reveal Nani's powers of healing:

> Nani took her to the bedroom and laid her on the coconut sacking there. She covered her in a blanket and sheet. The room smelt of camphor and coconut oil. . . . She fetched a large drink of fresh coconut water from the kitchen which she made her drink, and a bottle of coconut oil. She helped June take off the uniform then bathed her hair in the oil. She laid her on her stomach and massaged her, then on her back and massaged her again, praying in Hindi all the while. . . . "Let my tongue speak, ears hear, nose inhale, eyes see, arms and thighs be strong, let all the limbs be strong." . . . When she finished the massage, she dressed her in a clean vest . . . telling her to go to sleep. (131)

Within the healing space of her inner sanctum, Nani's fingers establish a primordial contact with June's body to ease out feelings of pain and negativity that diminish the body's vitality. Massages relieve tensions from various pressure points in the body. This sense of relief is provided as a result of an intimate knowledge of the body's physical composition and internal chemistry, establishing Nani as a folk physician whose understanding of pre-institutionalized medicine, such as herbal cures, acupressure and natural remedies, provides an alternative to the white man's cure. Just as head massages with coconut oil restore the lustre and beauty of a woman's hair, so also body massages, while cleansing and softening the skin, provide emotional comfort by infusing the body with a new spirituality. In June's case, the new spirituality promotes a philosophy of reconciliation that neutralizes the destructiveness of binary alienations represented by cultural and religious confrontations between Hindu and Christian ethics. By providing an effective technique of conflict resolution, massages help June to drift off into a peaceful slumber in which "[t]he burning wood, ghee and camphor were meant to have healing powers, to purify the atmosphere, like the incense at the Anglican church – it was no different. The scents filled the room and the memory of her quarrels with Lucille vanished. Nani's prayers lulled her to sleep" (131–32).

Nani uses Hindu rituals as a means of purging the discomfort caused by existential indigestion. She masters the precise healing techniques that effectuate a holistic balance of the mind and body as a precursor to finding the appropriate words to heal and restore women's history to its rightful agency. The chanting of mantras, or incantations, represents the power to invoke the gods through repeated oral affirmations of their presence. Nani pays her respects to the gods of speech as the protectors of oral traditions that associate orality with the positioning of a divine female logos, as mentioned earlier. She recites the following mantra after making the customary offerings of ghee and water to purify her *bedi*, or domestic shrine: "Let the gods of speech purify our words . . . let the sun grace this sacrifice, its worshippers, let the gods grace us, let the gods of speech sanctify our tongue" (131). Her prayers call for a purification of bad intent symbolized by the unlawful truths of racism and sexism that jeopardize human integrity through violence, historical and cultural distortions and psychological subservience to authoritative systems of control. Invoking the gods parallels the act of exorcising communal dis-ease through the verbal power of conjure that receives divine sanctification.

Houston Baker indicates that in African and African American communities, the term *conjurer* generally referred to a "two-headed doctor" who possessed a dual consciousness or double wisdom to transform reality.[29] Similarly, the dual consciousness of Hindu fakirs, sadhus and shamans resides in their mastery of ancestral and local folk knowledge that positions them as venerable spiritual doctors, advisers and educators. I argue that because of gender disparities, women are obliged to add a third level of political (self-)consciousness that reflects their triple-headedness, or trinitarian vision. This vision projects the multiplicity of female subject positionalities whereby conjure, as a medium of spatial dissolution, has the power to "cause definitions of 'form' as a fixed and comprehensible 'thing' to dissolve".[30] Conjure situates orality as local memory by extricating it from the totalizing confines of patriarchal and colonial absolutisms. In this way, Nani's story-telling sessions demonstrate the timeliness of unearthing lost beginnings, especially for the children of her village before they are socialized into adopting institutionalized patterns of thinking and behaviour: "As she recited the story, it seemed to lift her to another plane and she rolled the legend off her tongue like a visionary, conjuring the mythical scenes so that the children felt they were hearing them for the first time" (180–81). Positive models of identification represent a more inclusive ownership of Hindu culture through an effective North/South collaboration, symbolized by the complementary affirmation of the Indian empires of Koshala and Sri Lanka (181). The security of cultural wholeness assured by mythical oral creations "absorbed the humiliations of their plantation existence" (181) by providing the children with a positive sense of anticipation for the future, through the celebration of Diwali lights. Each light, as an illuminated story of hope, reflects the agency offered by rejuvenated histories, whereby "June found herself on Nani's landing which looked out across the whole village. She took in the lights on the roof tops, landings . . . on the ground everywhere. On this one night of the year, the darkness was completely banished from New Dam and the power of the lights gave a feeling of hope and happiness which she felt the more for the feelings of loss and the dramas of the year" (182). Lights offer much-welcomed compensations for daily plantation humiliations by providing a temporary transcending of sentiments of despair and failure.

Nani's role as a cultural visionary provides another illuminated path of psychological and moral uplifting, judging by the vantage point that her landing/yard occupies in the village. Offering a panoramic overview of the entire village landscape, the landing's strategic positioning enables Nani to secure a broad perspective of her community. This global perspective accounts for the intergenerational support and learning within the yard, where the communal mother passes on her education to future generations to ensure the preservation of female cultural knowledge through a transformational model of learning that stresses the linguistic importance of Creole.

Creole, as a linguistic medium of oral cultural transmission, offers an alternative form of expression to colonial linguistic dominance in school and "public" life. As the populist language, Creole establishes a sense of indigenized identity that resists colonial conformity. Endowed with an inherent hybridity, Creole eludes any form of categorizing or systematizing to offer a certain freedom of speech. The personalized use of Creole initiates a broad-based gendered interrogation of "national" consciousness in the novel. Hence, the female characters' subversive use of Creole enables them to insert their voices and perspectives in hegemonically doctored historiographies. In other words, Creole represents the articulation of the suppressed collective imaginary by giving voice to the people through linguistic agency. Linguistic reclaiming is particularly important to rural Hindu girls and women, who find themselves at the very bottom of the totem pole of racialized class and gender discrimination.

Derek Walcott posits Creole as a language of deliverance from servitude, "a language that went beyond mimicry, a dialectic which had the force of revelation as it invented names for things, one which finally settled on its own mode of inflection and which began to create an oral culture".[31] Associating Creole with a certain autonomy of expression, Walcott valorizes the language for its capacities of inventiveness, which initiate a new cultural legacy distinct from the one imposed by the colonizer. Individual experiences and subjectivities are articulated by the people, in the language of the populace, thereby minimizing the imposed alienation created by the "foreign" tongue.

In Shinebourne's *The Last English Plantation*, Creole represents the mother tongue of the *aji* culture. Helen Pyne-Timothy indicates that Shinebourne makes use of an English-based Creole, a combination of European, Amerindian and African languages, together with a mixture of "informal" or working-class Hindi.[32] The creation of an Indianized Creole (as a *kala pani* language) can be attributed to the initial communications between Indian indentured labourers and the newly liberated African plantation slaves. Linguistic syncretism posits Creole as a language of dual articulation, represented by the ancestral language Hindi and its hybridized version of "creolese": "Nani spoke in creolese but she used Hindi for her prayers, and when the creolese could not keep up with her feelings" (133). This passage suggests, however, that superimposed linguistic polyvalence does not lead to the obliteration of the ancestral language. Hindi, as the language of interiority, emerges during moments of quiet reflection to create an autonomous, self-defined space of expression. In other words, Nani's access to Hindi as an interiorized private language and to creolese as an exterior or communal language endows her with a certain linguistic mobility that makes her an effective translator of different cultural experiences. The informed translations of local culture invalidate colonial orientalizations of these cultures.

As stated before, Nani initiates a three-generational model of learning between herself as the wise mother, a cane-cutter named Mariam Mootoo as a communal daughter, and June, the communal granddaughter. Nani, Mariam and June provide an indigenized trinitarian female force that threatens the immanence of the male-configured trinities of Hinduism and the Catholic Church. Nani's sense of authority mirrors Miriam's independence and economic self-sufficiency. As the "bread winner of the family" (53), she remains her own person by refusing to subscribe to conventional gender-role expectations for Hindu women. A free agent like Nani, "Mariam had never married and had children like most Indian women" (54). Her social unconventionality enhances her individuality, indicated by her aura of self-confidence: "Lucille did praise Mariam once for what she called her 'carriage' and told June that she should learn to push back her shoulders, hold in her stomach and walk erect like Mariam, but Lucille also said that it was sheer hard labour, the long walk to the backdam, the bailing of punts and swinging of the cutlass, not breeding, which gave Mariam such a good figure and carriage" (55). Like the coconut palm, Mariam's erect carriage symbolizes her inner control and her pride in her profession. Her hard labour as a cane-cutter contributes to the maintenance of the plantation economy in a significant way. Her tireless industry reverses traditional norms of respectability that automatically associate decorum with upper-class urbanized sociability. On the other hand, Mariam earns her respect when her unmistakable (working) womanly gait signifies a strong sense of rootedness and personal historicity.

Mariam's identity as a rural Hindu woman is further consolidated by her use of Creole and Hindi. Her refusal to learn "prappa English" (54) indicates her refusal to succumb to external authority. Her subversive deconstruction of the English language, through creolized syntactical reconfigurations, is a localized act of resistance to colonial authority and its suppression of linguistic plurality. Her informal learning in the everyday workshop of the canefields alerts her to the importance of preserving indigenized linguistic agency as an antidote to colonial displacement. Pyne-Timothy suggests that Mariam anticipates the ultimate demise of Indian languages under the aegis of colonial linguistic domination.[33] This annihilation would further marginalize the Indo-Guyanese populations by reducing them to a state of linguistic muting through the slicing of the mother tongue.

Mariam shares her visionary politics of ethnic and gender assertion with June, as the third recipient of informal communal knowledge. Stressing the importance of maintaining proficiency in Hindi, Mariam cautions June about the alienating consequences of linguistic displacement and its subsequent impact on national displacement: "You use fo' talk Hindi. You *bap* too, but you ma don' 'low y'u now. Now y'u going town, now y'u gon talk prappa English!" (54). The uniformity of "prappa English" will ironically perpetuate varying hierarchies of discrimination ranging from the linguistic mimicry of the assimilated elite to the supposed illiteracy of those "who can't speak English" (127).

Mariam also encourages June to politicize the education that she receives in school by appropriating formalized instruments of knowledge, such as text books (*kitab*), and writing implements, such as pens (*kalam*), to assume the (self-proclaimed) position of a new historian (*vidvan*): "Eh, eh *bachcha* yuh ta'n *vidvan* goin to *madarsa!* a wan prappa nice *kitab* dis, man. *Aray bapray Bahin,* now yuh mus teach me for write *chitthi* an' use *kalam*" (53).[34] Mariam's request to acquire the basic writing skills that will permit her to write a letter is reflective of a larger need to consolidate female oral knowledge into its scriptural form as a living and well-documented testimony of women's lives in the Caribbean. Women, as new historians, write their own histories to rectify their traditional invisibility from male-engineered partial transcriptions of oral history into its written form. However, the new historicity encourages the complementarity of oral and written modes of transmission to formulate "talking" texts that create an energized genre of literary expression that is more inclusive of different forms of literariness. The oral power of conjure, represented by the village women, sustains the transformative power of written conjure to deconstruct the ambivalence of hegemonically constructed texts in school by encouraging new patterns of agency for disenfranchised groups. In this way, the *chitthi*, or script, offers concrete historical documentation of women's otherwise invisible presence and their right to equitable participation in Caribbean citizenship. Pyne-Timothy confirms the need for such documentation that creates "spaces for the diversity of Caribbean cultures since only through the record of these dialogic encounters can the history and identities of these various communities be filtered to take their place alongside the whole".[35] In other words, the writing of the "woman version" in Indo-Caribbean history assures its insertion in the dynamic historical plurality of the Caribbean as a whole. Partial knowledge of or ignorance about Indo-Caribbean women's histories can lead only to a sense of moral and social impoverishment through antagonism, racism, sexism and historical obfuscation.

However, these comments are not meant to naively suggest that women's spaces are utopic, idealistic constructions. The very term "woman space" is, in itself, based on a paradigm of exclusion that indicates the way in which women discriminate against each other on the basis of age, class, race, religion and sexual orientation. At the same time, it is also important to acknowledge the necessity of woman-centred control of space within systems of power that advocate female spatial dislocation as a prerequisite for the construction of national transparency. The fact that these spaces can be transgressed and violated periodically testifies to their fragility and vulnerability.

Women's eviction from national space has often been facilitated by their economic disenfranchisement, as a primary element of discrimination. However, the female characters in these novels are also involved in an economic reclaiming to assert their rights of equal citizenship. As mentioned before, the yard provides the ground for economic initiative through the daily buying and selling of goods. The yard, which constitutes the very backbone of societal relationships among women, creates within its parameters matrifocal communities of economic self-reliance. Economic autonomy guarantees a certain upward mobility by which women are able to control localized space by asserting their authority. Economic control plays the dual role of ensuring female empowerment and, at the same time, guaranteeing women's inscription in history through economic entrepreneurship, which facilitates women's access to domestic and public spheres of influence. In other words, women's control of the household economy is complemented by their extra-domestic market activities that lead to their multifaceted, transgendered occupational input.

In Persaud's *Butterfly in the Wind*, the cook Daya's economic skills of thrift and careful budgetary organization enable her to acquire a sense of ownership of her house when her partner's growing alcoholism and squandering of money motivate a reversal of roles. The partner's increasing economic dependence on his spouse minimizes his influence at home, thereby permitting her to take control by transforming the inner dynamics of the house. In a conversation with Kamla, Daya admits,

> "It was I, Kam I, who saved and scraped and saved and scraped and if you see the house now, you wouldn't believe it is the same house. You haven't seen the house?"
>
> I shook my head knowing that she meant, not the outside of the house which I knew, but inside her home.[36]

Similarly, the fruit vendor Tara displays a superior knowledge of the economics of production and distribution activities that constitute a vital part of her worldliness, despite her lack of formal education. Trained in the school of yard politics, Tara's control of self amid severe hardships makes her the chief bread earner, thereby eliminating any misconceptions about her secondary influence within the family: "Thin, tall, hard-working, Tara was never sent to school, but she was equipped with that rare, valuable understanding called commonsense. All day she worked in the Tunapuna market, selling fruit, vegetables and ground provisions. Though she had a serious business-like side to her, which she needed to help her gentle, quiet husband support their two sons and two daughters, she smiled a great deal" (105–6). Tara's commonsensical understanding of day-to-day economics, as a means of survival, places her in the position of an effective small-scale businesswoman. Her personal example provides the necessary syllabus for the school of hard-knocks learning:

> When the Tunapuna market closed at half past four, Tara came home and did whatever housework, yardwork and shopwork there was to do. . . . But what came through in all her transactions, whether in the market place or outside of it, was her trust in God. . . . If things worked out well for her, she praised Him. If they did not, she simply tried harder.
>
> ". . . [W]hen you have that, no man can stop you." (106)

The passage implies that self-reliance and hard work parallel a certain godliness that is a source of power, even though this power is conversely achieved at a price: unreasonable working hours, exhaustion and a fatalistic acceptance of one's socio-economic situation.

While these women work without any support from their male partners, their financial initiatives receive the encouragement of the women of the community. As Kamla reports, "Tara provided my mother with good quality vegetables at a price that satisfied both ladies, and my mother, in return, allowed Tara to carry over her debts to the following month when things were tight with her. But more important, there was a magnanimity of spirit between them both" (107). Kamla's mother and Tara meet on common ground: they are united by the mother's economic dependence on her husband at home as an upper-class Hindu woman and by Tara's social disenfranchisement as a Brahmin of a "lower" class. However, as in the case of Daya and Tara, their relatively lower-class status provides them with a greater freedom of movement to negotiate boundary lines. Their capacities of spatial negotiation expose the marginalized position of their upper-class counterparts, who remain confined to gender-role limitations and codes of behaviour.

Tara and Daya exemplify the transitional in-between roles that women assume during cultural revisions by situating themselves at the very fulcrum of these modifications. All cultural readjustments are instigated at an enormous price for women, whereby their control of space is based on a mediation of power or a converse affirmation in negation. However, this instigation/investigation propels the pioneering winds of change that displace the stranglehold of tradition by locating female affirmation within the very interstices of this displacement.

Commenting on her niece's accomplishments as a teacher, Kamla's aunt asserts, "Who would have thought of a day like this when our grandmothers and great grandmothers left India not knowing where they were going? All they were told was that there would be work. They came in good faith. . . . And look at this now, look at this success story" (200–201). This charting of new ground by the next generation can be seen as reparation for the enforced journey across the *kala pani* undertaken by the ancestral mothers as well as a consequence of the *ajis'* long history of activism and sacrifice that paves the way for a younger generation's "success story".

Indo-Caribbean women have reconfigured their lives through their active recreations of private and public space that have led to corresponding re-evaluations of institutionalized norms and expectations for them. Women have always been making history through their personal revolutions at home. These revolutions have gained a more public articulation through socio-economic reorganizations offered by *aji*-mothering, linguistic non-conformity and orality. These three authors seem to favour a rural-based historical contestation by Indo-Caribbean women, to suggest that integral change takes place at a microcosmic "earthy" level and not within the institutional walls of academic departments. By advocating a "the political is rural/the rural is political" ethos, these writers pay tribute to the rural ethics of the founding *ajis*, who supplied the very structure for the elaboration of Indo-Caribbean history — a history that has been fraught with its internal and external tensions, ambiguities and exclusions, while simultaneously providing a complex model for rejuvenated feminist beginnings.

5

From Dispossession to Recuperation

Spatial negotiations by women have transformative value in terms of gender ideologies while simultaneously creating dissonance in terms of women's alienation and exilic dispositions within patriarchal and colonial systems of power. The trope of exile constitutes a major theme in twentieth-century Caribbean writing by providing a valuable basis for the comprehension of the complexities of the postcolonial Caribbean exilic predicament, which has been shaped by the disenfranchising forces of colonialism and mass migration, racism, sexism and class stratifications. In Indo-Caribbean fiction, V. S. Naipaul's exilic explorations have received widespread academic attention and have served as a vital starting point for examining the specificities of Indian preoccupations with exile and displacement in a Caribbean context. Linking exile with the notion of a colonized subjectivity, Naipaul has defined exile as "one's lack of representation in the world; one's lack of status".[1] Presenting exile as symptomatic of colonialism's politics of disempowerment, which have configured/disfigured the postcolonial state and immigrant realities, Naipaul has simultaneously associated exile with the "historical darkness" that has shrouded Trinidadian history in general, and the Indian community in Trinidad in particular.[2]

The traversing of the *kala pani* by the first immigrants has come to symbolize the primordial journey into exile for Indo-Caribbean communities, whose origins have reflected the tenuousness of uprooted affiliations. While it is true that Indians were allowed to retain primary elements of their culture and traditions, unlike the systematic sociocultural genocide experienced by enslaved Africans, it is also expedient to indicate that indentureship and mass transplantation created a historical vacuum, a particular black hole where the Indian past was plummeted into the "chasm between the Antilles and India".[3] The obfuscation of the historical past as a structuring agent condemned Indians to a state of physical and symbolic exile represented by the strangeness of the new lands and by the precariousness of the Indian dilemma of preserving ethnic identity in the face of creolization. The enigma of arrival, to use Naipaul's phrase, promoted the development of a certain exilic consciousness as an antidote to historical orphanhood. Huma Ibrahim defines the exilic consciousness as the desire to belong both to one's country of origin and one's country of adoption.[4] The exilic consciousness translates the anxiety of (non-)belonging by evoking the ambivalence of losing one's birthplace while simultaneously attempting to adjust to the land of exile. Within the parameters of Ibrahim's definition, exile situates itself in an imaginary in-between space of negotiation that provides the necessary magnetism to repel and attract by creating a primary psychic splitting between the *now* and the *then*. The absence of historical anchorage to firmly moor floating insecurities of exiled origins leads to the formation of nomadic identities that are in transit between the disruptions of forced and voluntary arrivals and departures.

Similarly, the Palestinian critic Edward Saïd emphasizes the historical and cultural orphanhood that has accompanied the modern age: "We have been accustomed to thinking of the modern period itself as spiritually orphaned and alienated, the age of anxiety and estrangement."[5] Inferring that modernity has been achieved at the price of an irrevocable loss, Said locates the thematics of exile within the dual problematics of metaphysical angst and political self-consciousness. In other words, for Saïd, the annihilating effects of exile are counterbalanced by a particular logic of political positioning that has motivated the necessary historical subjectivity as "an assertion of belonging".[6] Highlighting the inherent paradoxes and tensions that animate the exilic sensibility, both Saïd and Naipaul inscribe exile within the parameters of an active contestation or decolonization of self and community by positing "the executive value of exile that can be converted from a challenge into a positive mission, whose success would be a cultural act of great importance".[7] Saïd and Naipaul, like other Caribbean and Third World writers and critics, have situated exile within a binary power dialectic that has oscillated between disinheritance and self-recovery. ·

Preoccupied with the insecurities of the colonial male, these writers have curiously accorded negligible (if any) attention to gendered perceptions of exile, perceptions that have further complicated the insecurities and vagaries of sociocultural and historical displacements and alienations. As stated before, reflections on exile have characterized a predominantly male-defined literary tradition, in which the experiences of women have been relegated to a mere appendix or footnote. Myriam Chancy's ground-breaking study on Afro-Caribbean women writers in exile has been an important point of departure to rupture the centrality of dominant male discourses by relocating the "secondary" female voices from the periphery to redress the traditional narrative imbalance of experiences.[8]

While Chancy's text provides valuable insights into Afro-Caribbean women writers' preoccupations with exile and identity, this study asserts that the corresponding muting of the Indo-Caribbean female voices has established the authority of the exilic experiences of Indian male writers as representative of a universal Indo-Caribbean experience. The absence of a gendered interrogation has compromised the scope for a more inclusive, transgendered engagement with the problematics of exile. The inaudibility of Indian women's voices has thus exposed a serious literary omission in the area of Caribbean postcoloniality by creating a wide gap in the thematics of exilic positionality.

—•—

The poetry of Mahadai Das (*Bones*), Lelawattee Manoo-Rahming (*Curry Flavour*) and Rajandaye Ramkissoon-Chen (*Ancestry*), together with Ramabai Espinet's short story "Barred: Trinidad 1987", address the question of the suppressed exilic consciousness of Indo-Caribbean women through an effective claiming of exilic space to assert their right of authorship. Their writings explore the complexities of exile from the vantage point of disenfranchised Indian women who have had to negotiate the physical, sociocultural and psychologically (self-) imposed levels of exile, both at home and abroad. Their work represents a palimpsest that codifies the different ways in which the female body serves as an external signifier of exile in an attempt to articulate its multiple alienations. Through a series of interrogations of the past and through its moulding of the Indo-Caribbean female imaginary, these writers have sought to examine how the female body acts out its exile in order to determine whether it eventually finds its point of transcendence by relocating itself into a three-dimensional space that favours reintegration or a coming to terms with self. Positing a particular aesthetics of corporeality in their works, these women broaden the parameters of our understanding of exile by extending it beyond the confines of metaphysical abstractions into a dynamic process that is based on a three-stage trajectory of physical and spiritual recuperation, leading to the rediscovery of the female self. The emergence of the revised self is brought about by a cyclical process of physical mortification and spiritual disconnection that is, ironically, a prerequisite for the last stage of holistic integration and final resurrection. The physical and mental abjection of the body motivates its rearticulation, or "backward resurrection" as noted by Wilson Harris,[9] by providing the necessary framework in which negation, fragmentation and physical degeneration become the necessary elements to transcend the exiled self. Harris questions the assumption that progress, whether social, material or personal, is contingent upon a movement forward. He compares the backward resurrection to a revisioning or a transformative strategy that Rhonda Cobham defines in the following manner: "Rather than claiming the non-space of ultimate victim or constructing an Other in relation to which her claims to humanity may be judged . . . , the Caribbean writer has had to look for ways of accommodating her subjectivity as well as that of her oppressors . . . to confront the whole notion of otherness and the allocation along racial or gender lines of specific properties and values."[10] At the same time, the exploration of exile that exemplifies the very politics of othering provides the framework for an alternative positioning of female subjectivity, whereby the de-figuration of the female self becomes a precursor to its reconstruction in an attempt to break the mould of gender and racially based typecasting. Indo-Caribbean female authorship and, by implication, readership of the female exilic script bears testimony to women's efforts to speak (out) their own texts through a concerted contestation of otherness. In *Parole des femmes*, Maryse Condé indicates that the stifled feminine voice, whose muffled utterings are barely audible, is "loaded with anguish, frustration and revolt"[11] in its initial attempts to confront alterity. The anguished female voice that Edouard Glissant compares to the "frenzied scream" becomes a voice of self-assertion to counter the forces of alienation, ambivalence and exclusion.[12]

The narrative/poetic screams of Manoo-Rahming, Chen, Das and Espinet create a certain fracturing or disruption of traditionally defined Caribbean exilic space, to demonstrate the violence with which these voices are unleashed from the periphery. This violence is a symptom of the political, literary and sociocultural dispossession that has characterized the lives of Indo-Caribbean women, whose strategies of resistance and self-affirmation have been conversely located in pregnant silences, disruptions and creative spatial intrusions. However, these re-memberings of exile have not constituted erratic or errant meanderings through an elusive historical past. They have, in fact, been anchored by a four-tiered organizational model in which the problematics of exile have been involved in an interactive exchange with the insecurities of dispossession, the exploration of ancestral memory, the effective writing out of the female text through the articulation of the female body and the positing of alternative feminist mythologies through the spiritual reclaiming of the land and self. In other words, the naming of exile by Indo-Caribbean women has reflected their desire to transcend the trauma of exile by creating safe spaces of empowerment and belonging through certain strategies of narrative reclamation.

The physicality of exile, as reflected in Indo-Caribbean women's writing, can be compared to a graphic inscription on the female body that reveals a particular cartography of dislocation. The body, in turn, introjects and reacts to this dislocation in the form of actual symptoms of physical illness in which it is dismembered by a virus, resembling a cancer, that seems to chew into the very bones of its structure. The dislocated body becomes the privileged signifier of Indo-Caribbean women's amputated histories, in which women have been denied active participation. Françoise Lionnet positions the female body in Caribbean literature as an emblematic space that is marked by a disenfranchising history represented by the slave trade and its aftermath of indentureship and *métissage*, as well as by the social, sexual and political constraints that have been imposed on women.[13]

The female body in exile exhibits a mutilated presence that resembles the progressive stages of corporeal amputation prescribed to eliminate organic disease. In fact, images of amputation and death-related themes and metaphors punctuate Mahadai Das's collection of poetry, in which the poet links exile with the idea of premature death. The very title of the collection, *Bones*, reveals the inner structural discourse of the female voice that exposes (in skeletal form) a profoundly visceral engagement with the trauma of exile. Although Das's poetry does not describe a culturally specific Indo-Caribbean female experience, her personal example of estrangement serves as a microcosmic representation of a more globalized preoccupation with Caribbean women's sense of exile that results from their sociocultural and historical displacement. In the poem "Unborn Children", the poet laments, "I mourn unflowered words / unborn children, inside me".[14] The body suffers a certain violation through its inability to (pro)create, symbolized by the linguistic prefix *un-* as a signifier of negation and non-existence. Impressions of atrophy and immobilization restrict the full expression of the female self by locating it within a certain dysphoric space of representation, whereby exile serves both as a metaphor and as a reality for women. The intersection of physical and symbolic exile results from several levels of societal dispersal that make women prisoners of their physical selves (confinement of the body) as well as of their social selves (relegation to second-class citizenship). The barrenness of "unflowered words" and "unborn children" reflects a larger territorial sterility whereby women are exiled in a land of no return in which they are confronted by alien laws that render them powerless, thereby making them social exiles in their own country. Outlawed by a system of arbitrary control within patriarchal systems of justice, the female body succumbs to a strict regime of regulation or censorship.

Elaine Scarry inscribes the censored female body within an invisible geography of pain, whereby pain becomes an expressive outlet to resist the stifling of self: "Pain makes overt precisely what is at stake in 'inexpressibility' and thus begins to expose by inversion the essential character of 'expressibility', whether verbal or material."[15] In other words, pain speaks the language of the female body by articulating the inexpressible or the repressed. Associating exile with women's repressed memories, Das describes her despair in terms of a deep moral pain that is more intense and inconsolable than any physical pain that can be treated or cured eventually. The poet tries to characterize this feeling of pain in her poem "Pain":

> It is not tears, rain
> upon a willow tree. Ophelias
> hanging desolate upon backyard boughs
> but ugly dark clouds rumbling without
> consideration. It marks a sorrow. (36).

Through a system of inversion, Das describes what pain *is not*. This disavowal or negation, while symbolizing women's negated experiences, simultaneously exposes the body's inability to effectively voice out its pain in a conventional and easily identifiable way. On the other hand, Ophelia's watery grave becomes a visible signifier of her disenfranchised status by locating women's resistance within a well-established literary tradition that equates female suicide with the desire to transcend the confinement of sexualized otherness. The visibility of victimization results from direct action to reverse a subaltern status through a manifestly physical expression of pain, unlike the mental dislocation that torments the female body in *Bones*. In Das's poetry, the body absorbs the physicality of pain in terms of an integral moral malaise that Lionnet attributes to a process of "deculturation"; instead of exteriorizing its pain, the body internalizes it as a longing for (self-)castigation and mortification to compensate for its sense of worthlessness or nothingness.[16] The ambivalence projected by the female body results from its inscription within patriarchal systems that are based on the politics of restriction and subjugation. The patriarchal economy posits the female body as lack and absence by denying the autonomy and subjectivity of that body. At the same time, it positions the male as a self-reflecting subject who masterminds and controls his own destiny through his access to law, authority and language.

Situated outside representation, the female body becomes a defective organ, an "infected kidney" as evoked in Das's poem "Secrets" (43), resulting from its sexualized and racialized alterity. Strategies of alterity trap the body in a schizophrenic impasse between external expectations of conformity and acquiescence and an inner creative reality that remains repressed. Schizophrenic demands made on the female body heighten its alienation by giving rise to feelings of despondency and low self-esteem. Consequently, the body introjects externally imposed levels of societal ambivalence to participate in its own negation.

Ernest Pépin remarks that a woman's perception of her body is motivated by her sense of (self-)consciousness: "We cannot pass over the body; it is the inexorable of existence. . . . Inhibited bodies, alienated bodies, transcended bodies, no matter what the case, the image confronts the reality in a relentless one-on-one, where psychological equilibrium is at stake. In the end, the body, despite being the natural property of the subject, does not escape from society."[17] Pépin's analysis implies that the commodification of the body by societal prescriptions results in its subjectlessness or state of suspension. The body's secondary status can be transcended only by its castigation as compensation for its devalued instance. Reading the language of pain and its inscription on the female body serves as a preface to the reading of female exile, which, in turn, bears witness to women's sociocultural invisibility in male scripts. Pain transcribes a particular female language aimed at self-definition and creative assertion.

Pain, as the return of the repressed, speaks a fragmented language that mirrors the amputation or the dismembering experienced by the female body. The body's dispersal into a series of fragmented body parts that are out of touch with themselves epitomizes the sociocultural colonization of the body.

In Das's poem "Beast", the body's colonization is likened to a violent act of rape that leads to its mutilation:

> In Gibraltar Straits,
> pirates in search of El Dorado
> masked and machete-bearing
> kidnapped me.
> Holding me to ransom,
> they took my jewels and my secrets
> and dismembered me. (48)

The physical conquering of the female body through rape is an example of a dual corporeal dislocation: the forcible kidnapping from the homeland as a result of colonial piracy and the subsequent violation of one's person through the imposition of masculine sexual aggression. The premature separation from home parallels the premature breaking of the hymen, leading to a double loss of identity. Hortense Spillers describes this double dispossession as "the seared, divided ripped-apartness of the flesh", whose dispersal undermines the integrity of a certain totality of representation.[18] In this instance, the male does to the female what the process of indentureship and slavery has done to home and community. Territorial patterns of colonial aggression on the homeland are replicated on the female body, revealing the body's dual disembodiment by colonial and indigenized patriarchal control.

Das's poetry links the politics of female estrangement to the imposition of a conceptual framework of female disenfranchisement that typifies a particular process of psychological orientalism. I define this process as a pervasive – or, more aptly, an invasive – strategy of confronting and controlling otherness through a manipulation of imposed images and sensations in an attempt to re-present the feminized other. In his seminal work on political orientalism, Edward Saïd defines *orientalism* as an imposition, leading to the creation and occupation of space. Orientalism, as Saïd asserts, is based on a power dynamic to maintain the Orient in its position of alterity, thereby affirming the superiority of the orientalist, the master fabricator and manipulator of false images.[19]

The application of psychological orientalism to the reality of women is another attempt by the male psyche to fathom and control the "mysteries" of the feminine. Psychological orientalism bolsters man's reconstructive/ reconstitutive capacities, in which women's realities can be altered by him. Das describes this transformation in "Beast":

Limbs and parts eventually grew:
a new nose, arms skilful and stronger:
Sight after the gutted pits could bear a leaf.
It took centuries.

In the cave where they kept me,
a strange beast grew. (48)

The idea of physical strangeness exposes the way in which the master surgeon orchestrates and manipulates the reconstruction of the dismembered female body to create a new being that is alien to woman herself. In other words, the male subject/author participates in a creation myth of his own making, in which Pygmalion creates his female object. Reduced to a non-presence, women become fetishes for the male magician, who is more interested in his powers to conjure the image-ideal irrespective of the ontological reality of the women in question.

The imposition of a unitary masculine refashioning reinforces misogynist representations of the feminine that soon become part of the socially acceptable cultural heritage. These unitary refashionings include stereotypical depictions of essentialized femininity that strip the body of its individuality. Consequently, the power of the image of idealized womanhood fascinates and seduces the male, relegating women to an inferior position in which they serve as easily replaceable substitutes for the preferred, idealized image. As a result, the image has a more enduring impact than does the woman herself. John Berger evokes the specificity of the image in *Ways of Seeing*: "Images were first made to conjure up the appearance of something that was absent. Gradually it became evident that an image could outlast what it represented."[20] As reproductions of an original master image, women are confined to a level of psycho-social alienation that results from this displacement. Feelings of alienation have led to a psychic splitting, in which women are partitioned and deprived of multiple parts of themselves. This sense of depersonalization reduces the body to a non-presence in which the body exists solely as a phantom of a presence, as Das's poem "For Maria de Borges" illustrates:

I am a pair of hands.
A pair of feet.
Eyes without candle.
Bird stricken. (22)

Stripped of its individuality, the body is compartmentalized into a series of visible signifiers that, because of their dislocation from the rest of the body, assume an autonomous presence. The body is accorded a secondary status when it becomes a mere appendage of the signifier, much like the serial number in prison, which receives a greater value than the person it designates.

Finding their specificity in division, women's corporeal deprivation manifests itself in feelings of loneliness, depression, lack of self-esteem, sexual exploitation and other forms of societal violence. Das's "Unborn Children" is a violent indictment of socially motivated crimes against women that go unnoticed or unreported because of an insidious system of arbitrary justice that engineers and encourages society's indifference to this repeated violation:

> Who attends the funeral of the desert rose;
> wears dark rags and solemn faces
> for the doing-away of the unborn?
>
> O widows of old Greece with your black shawls!
> Raise your voices with their seasoned
> sorrows
> to my invisible funerals. (12)

While expressing its grief in private mourning, the body seeks, at the same time, public articulation of its private violation to provide living testimony of its disfavoured status. The poem is shrouded by a certain funerary darkness of imagery that links the obscurity of death with the language of repeated or seasoned sorrow and negativity.

The language of pain ironically finds its most graphic expression in love, which Das describes as a unilateral relationship based on a power dynamic that works to the detriment of women. The poem "Bird" highlights this ambivalence:

> Out flew this bird.
>
> . . . . .
>
> You clipped
> its wing, kept
> it a pigeon anklestrung
> homefed
> homespun. (42)

Love does not usher in a certain expansiveness of self or a joyous celebration that should lead to personal rejuvenation. Instead, love is a sign of possession and conquest that results in a particular branding of the female body to show male ownership of it. "Diamond" exposes the commodification of love in which the poet admonishes her ex-lover:

> Alright, medieval
> knight. Exhibit your trophy
> from your Holy Crusades. (33)

Das associates a romantic relationship with the feudal system of serfdom that guarantees the success of the master–slave dialectic. Within this oppressive structure, love becomes a trophy of conquest that translates the anomie and distrust that exists between the sexes. Love is a mere smokescreen of violence to destroy women through its mechanisms of domination. "For Anna Karenina" highlights the sadomasochistic aspects of love that lead to the untimely suicide of women:

> A woman's broken body remains
> robbed of its sweet, wild breath.
> In being robbed, passion could
> but flee, for its badge must
> be worn but well. (18)

The tragedy of love speaks the language of the mutilated female body by exposing its infirmities. The disempowered body speaks a fragmented, invisible text in which, according to Lionnet, it has "a presence which is both striking and disturbing. Victim of the entropy generating its slow disintegration, this body is a revealing text, one which draws attention to and denounces the necrotic ideology of our culture".[21] As prescribed by hegemonic readings, a woman's relationship with her body is synonymous with her relationship to death, a self-cancelling and requited censorship of the body and spirit that inscribes itself within a suicidal tradition represented by Ophelia and Anna Karenina.

The mutilated body typifies women's confinement within an exiled identity that is a consequence of its social and political ostracism. The poet recounts her own reclusion in the male Academy, where women's knowledge is devalued and spurned because of its explosive, transformative potential. Knowledge is power. By placing women outside the discourse of power, by monitoring and thwarting their access to "public" knowledge, men try to confine women to a state of ignorance. In her poem "Secrets", Das exposes the male conspiracy to keep women outside the system of academic production by denying them the right to equal participation:

That public address holds my purposes sealed.
Quiet, small bombs ticking without a clock,
they never explode in the Academy,
only in my mind. (43)

The continued implosion of creative knowledge initiates a state of madness, leading to a certain disintegration of mind and spirit that parallels the physical atrophy experienced as a response to confinement. Madness becomes a metaphor for female cultural and intellectual exile, a sign of protest and rejection of conventionally defined female roles and expectations, reflecting the desire to transgress the limitations imposed by such forms of exile on women. Phyllis Chesler indicates that madness is a "mirror image of the female experience and a penalty for being *female*, as well as for desiring or daring *not* to be".[22] Mirroring the search for female uniqueness, madness symbolizes the muted forms of female self-expression behind a veil of silence. However, these symbols of suppressed discontent often manifest themselves more overtly in sublimated forms of expression such as heightened intellectual activity, creativity, female initiative and other forms of "unwomanly" behaviour that need to be regulated in patriarchal institutions such as the prison, asylum or academy. Intellectual exile confines women to a certain impasse, where, according to Chesler, "they cannot survive as just 'women', and they are not allowed to survive as human or as creative beings".[23] Her statement implies that women's creative talent remains invisible because it cannot be measured in economic and tangible terms within male-centred capitalist systems.

—·—

Lelawattee Manoo-Rahming's poem "Caged Soul" graphically locates this impasse within the confining limits of the infernal:

Caging her
In that hell
Where
Leaves drop upwards
Rivers flow to the mountaintop
Babies explode
From the womb
Old and senile
Laughter and love
do not exist.[24]

Confinement in hell predicates a certain illogic of natural inversion that reverses the chain of being, causing leaves to drop upwards and rivers to flow backwards. Like the system of reverse logic that governs the functioning of the asylum, in which individuality is suppressed by the laws of institutional conformity, the tragic impasse reveals women's "doomed search for potency"[25] by thwarting the very means of expression by which women can achieve a certain wholeness of representation. The following verses reveal the annihilating vacuum of silence that surrounds women when they are placed in solitary confinement, where their cries of desolation reverberate in hollow echoes that reflect the emptiness of their environment:

> Laughter tinkles
> outside her world.
>
> Her only link
> to that teenaged laughter
> A little window
> with one-way glass
> through which
> She cries out
> But is not heard. (19)

Communication with the outside world becomes a futile one-way act demonstrating society's unresponsiveness to this seclusion. Like the frantic screams of the disfavoured Indian labourers that were ignored by the crews of the *Fatel Rozack*, the *Whitby*, the *Hesperus* and other ships that transported them to the Caribbean,[26] women's cries for recognition echo back their invisibility and voicelessness. The unmaking of the female body complements the unmaking of Indo-Caribbean history, establishing a correlation between immigrant displacement and female displacement that nevertheless situates the female immigrant at the lowest level on the pyramid of discrimination.

Primal cries of pain express themselves at a pre-verbal, archaic level of language acquisition to posit a particular consciousness of dispossession. The Indo-Caribbean woman writer's anxiety (like that of other Caribbean authors) to find the appropriate utterance to voice out her pain as a means of claiming her space in society "expresses the anguish of a writer overwhelmed by a history of slavery, death and deportation so devastating that it leads to silence, or at best to the fragmented utterances of the dispossessed. Her story bares the word's power to unleash the frustrations of the disinherited into revolt."[27] Like the primal screams associated with the process of childbearing and labour, words are unleashed by painful intra-uterine spasms that reflect the hesitant and powerful, albeit ambivalent, aspects of creation.

—•—

Ramabai Espinet's short story "Barred: Trinidad 1987" reveals the writer's ambivalence towards language when she describes the linguistic inadequacy that she experiences in her attempts to articulate the specificities of the Indo-Caribbean experience in Trinidad. Associating the newness of the Indian arrival with feelings of strangeness in a new land, the narrator agonizes over the most effective medium of expression in which to describe the alienation experienced by the Indian communities. Like June in *The Last English Plantation*, Espinet ponders the effectiveness of English, as the official language of colonization and patriarchal domination, to accurately and passionately convey the trauma of displacement. In other words, the narrator asks herself whether English, as the very source of linguistic exile, can creatively sensitize itself to communicate the vulnerability of immigrant dislocation: "Which one is right, what the books now say or what we uttered in the peasant newness of this settlement? We are lost here, have not found the words to utter our newness, our strangeness, our unfound being. Our clothes are strange, our food is strange, our names are strange. And it is not possible for anyone to coax or help us. Our utterance can only come roaring out of our mouths when it is ready, set, and can go."[28] Espinet's text implies that the immigrant status of racial and sexual otherness predicates an objectification of this experience. Colonial subjects have historically been made passive receptacles of the colonizer's languages. When one is denied access to language, always being spoken for, the deprivation of linguistic agency implies the denial of one's identity. The narrator experiences an acute identity crisis at the very beginning of the story when she loses her keys and wallet: "I lost my keys a few days ago. That and my wallet. All my life I have flirted with the fantasy of losing these two things – a fantasy of being locked out and thrown absolutely upon my own primary resources" (80). Keys, as symbols of access or entry, and wallets, as markers of personal identification and economic security, signify primary possessions. The loss of a wallet containing photo identification, a driver's licence and other tangible proof of one's existence implies an immediate anonymity. The inability to express feelings of depersonalization and exclusion engenders a state of existential castration in which the immigrant finds herself in an alien reality where she is estranged, both from herself and from other members of the community, precisely because of the "inability" to articulate this disempowering experience. Espinet's narrative illustrates the aphasia, or temporary loss of the power to speak, that results from the restrictions imposed by the colonial tongue in its inability to translate otherness.

The gendered othering of women places women at an added disadvantage through a further complication in the problem of self-representation. If woman is situated as the sexualized and racialized other, can she then speak? Does the subaltern have a voice, as Gayatri Spivak would ask?[29] If so, whose voice, whose language would she use, given the fact that she is silenced within and by the patriarchal economy? The French feminist Luce Irigaray asks the all-important question, "What if I thought only after the other has been inserted and introjected into me? Either as thought or as mirror in which I reflect and am reflected?"[30] In other words, wonders Soheila Ghaussy in response to Irigaray, in a system that is shaped by masculinist practices and in which women themselves have either consciously or unconsciously internalized the very same practices that favour their marginalization, can they recognize these patterns of victimization themselves?[31] The denial of subjective agency to women leads to the imposition of alien realities that women often mistakenly identify as an "authentic" point of reference. On the other hand, does the elaboration of a specific "womanspeak" provide the necessary space in which women can affirm their subjectivity as sexual, social and political beings? Or is womanspeak, which is an exclusive language aimed at a selective female audience, in itself based on a pattern of exclusion that undermines the creation of a common, plurivocal language, accessible to both men and women, in which a multiplicity of voices and experiences can be affirmed?

The narrator of Espinet's story seeks to determine at what point language can be indigenized to demonstrate a certain homeliness, to dispel the isolation, fears and insecurities associated with the ambivalence of one's origin. She confesses, "This is the land that spawned me, far from the continent of my origin. Can an island be someone's real home, I wonder? My ancestral roots are far from here and I don't even know really what they are" (81). Anxious to figure out whether language can fill the void created by homelessness, the narrator stresses the importance of articulating a particular discourse of Caribbeanness as a strategy for claiming the island as home. Situated in limbo between ancestral land and adopted home, the narrator's rootlessness exemplifies the rootlessness of Caribbean history. This history has been located within a certain disjunction created by the absence of localized, internal cultural referents, which were supplanted by colonial value systems, and the alienation motivated by the nebulosity of undetermined ancestral affiliations. Referring to Naipaul's characterization in *The Overcrowded Barracoon* of West Indian societies as "manufactured societies", Renu Juneja asserts that "personal and cultural identities have had to be negotiated in an area that offers either the taint of replication and mimicry of the colonial culture or a seeming cultural vacuum".[32] The denial of historical (self-)creation through colonial disenfranchisement and alienating alliances imposes a definite sense of deterritorialization, in which the land, as a primary text, loses its inherent potential to regenerate its natural resources, revealing instead its fallowness and unproductivity. J. Michael Dash, in his introduction to Glissant's *Caribbean Discourse*, links the notion of territorial disinheritance with "the inability to locate *la trace* or the primordial track. With the disappearance of *la trace*, not only a sense of the ancestral past is lost but the land is so transformed that it no longer allows for the exploration of past associations".[33] The land, as a signifier of mirrored alienation, as a no-man's-land, displays an exilic landscape that remains elusive and unfathomable.

Espinet's short story reveals a particular insecurity of being. This is a symptom of the precariousness of the Indian situation in Trinidad where displaced Indians are confounded by an impassive landscape. The narrator ruminates, "And then I rise and throw open the doors to my balcony high above the ground. I look up at the peaks of the Northern Range. . . . Unto the hills around do I lift my longing eyes. Only I have no idea what I'm longing for, or if I do, it's still only an apprehension of something" (81). Ironically, the land does not provide the security of a stable footing or grounding but projects instead a sense of foreboding. The towering hills of the Northern Range do not promote a lifting of the spirit through a feeling of boundlessness. On the contrary, the spirit cowers before a sense of impending doom when the landscape assumes an authoritative and menacing presence that threatens the fate of the immigrant.

Michelle Cliff uses the Jamaican neologism *ruination* to explain the ambivalence displayed by the land:

> *Ruinate*, the adjective, and *ruination*, the noun, are Jamaican inventions. Each word signifies the reclamation of land, the disruption of cultivation, civilization, by the uncontrolled, uncontrollable forest. When a landscape becomes ruinate, carefully designed aisles of cane are envined, strangled, the order of the empire is replaced by the chaotic forest. The word *ruination* (especially) signifies this immediately: It contains both the word *ruin* and *nation*. A landscape in ruination

means one in which the imposed nation is overcome by the naturalness of ruin. As individuals in this landscape, we, the colonised, are also subject to ruination, to the self reverting to the wildness of the forest.[34]

Exhibiting the lawlessness or arbitrary rule of colonial regimes with respect to colonized populations, the landscape in ruination becomes a predator that preys on vulnerable sensibilities. Through a process of organic inversion, the land loses its life-sustaining properties to reveal its emptiness. Manoo-Rahming's poem "Emptiness" emphasizes the land's depletion when the land is reduced to a parasite that feeds on immigrant trauma and anxiety to compensate for its "milkless breasts" and the "lifeless red drippings" that are shed from its womb (12). The earth's belly lies bare, negating its powers of regeneration to confirm Glissant's claim: "Our lands do not contain treasures that can be transformed."[35] While Glissant's statement expresses the tragic impossibility of creating an energized Caribbean landscape with impoverished roots, land in ruination impedes the effective excavation of buried histories/roots that remain confined to the earth's underbelly.

Obscured historical origins have led to the creation of falsified Caribbean histories by external sources, relegating Caribbean subjectivity to an irreversible victimhood. Espinet's story illustrates how Indian immigrants are forced to recognize themselves in alienating stereotypes that are formulated by racist and misogynist misconceptions. These distortions allocate a pre-natal exilic disposition to communities that are born into exile. The following passage associates the creation of Indo-Caribbean identity with an imaginary, preconceived fabulation, wherein "Indians ain't have no backbone, no stamina. You ain't see how at the slightest sign of stress they does run and drink Indian tonic? (Boy meets and love girl but the arranged marriage gets in the way. Boy and girl drink GRAMAZONE and perish together – desire literally burning a hole through their bowels.) Indians ain't fraid to die. They does kill easy too. It is because they believe in reincarnation, don't doubt it" (83). The reduction of Indo-Caribbean history to a tragic and violent love story demonstrates the dual precariousness experienced by Indians as colonial subjects and as disfavoured ethnic and cultural minorities in Trinidad. Stylized re-presentations expose biased readings that confine Indians to a permanent backwardness and savagery of expression. While all stereotypes do contain subliminal half-truths, their creative manipulations into absolute truths often justify hegemonic impositions of control to keep these "truths" well contained. Ralph Premdas attributes this containment to a particular historiographical dislocation that has marginalized the Indian presence in the Caribbean through an overemphasis on Europe and Africa.[36] The characterization of the Indian as the bastard child of the Caribbean family has conferred a level of illegitimacy on Indians by establishing race and ethnicity as the prime suspects in the creation of exclusive citizenship and identity, as was discussed in chapter 2.

—•—

The exilic estrangement experienced "at home" became magnified into impressions of monstrosity in Das's poetry when the poet temporarily relocated to an urban US environment to pursue graduate studies. The idea of physical strangeness in a foreign land is transposed onto physical space or the location of exile to demonstrate the close association between monstrosity and exilic space. This correlation translates the feelings of displacement experienced by the newly transplanted Indo-Guyanese exile that are projected onto the alien territory.

The poem "Chicago Spring" describes the city as a gloomy subterranean space ("Chicago winters are grim" [10]), a living hell that resembles a descent into the abyss:

> Hooded shadows.
> Wrap themselves into night.
> Rainsticks, slender-snaked,
> hang from resolute limbs
> of staid office-racks.
>
> The air's complexion
> is as grey as a corpse. (10)

The poem evokes a certain petrification and immobilization in time and space that symbolizes all that is static, lifeless and impervious to change. Even the change of seasons, which is a natural process in the cycle of life, remains "reluctant", "unwanted" (10). The de-structuring of nature parallels the mental and physical atrophy of the "unthawed eyes" of the "wintered unbeliever" (11). Physical exile is an unnatural state for the poet, who remains indifferent even to the slow transition of the seasons that do not bring about a renewal of the spirit.

Das's "For Maria de Borges" develops the idea of monstrosity to an extreme in which the connection between exiled space and death is literal and uncompromising:

> Death, black moon, high mark
> on night's blue canvas.
> Stumped shadow beneath the lynching-tree.
>
> A star hangs over me.
> Dark sore.
> Is it death? (21)

Impressions of darkness dominate the poem, obscuring any glimmer of hope that the new city might offer. Images of the city as a site of imminent death are concretized in symbols of the black moon, lynching trees and a general panoramic scarification that resembles a dark, malignant sore.

The poet compares the city to a destructive machine that annihilates its citizens by trapping them behind its walls of steel. The confining walls of the city remind the poet of the forbidding walls of the penitentiary, whose claustrophobic atmosphere triggers an inescapable and recurring Kafkaesque nightmare:

> Between its iron teeth, mechanical, regular;
> in escalators, prisonlike elevators,
> I am lifted indifferently, dropped
>
> like a stone,
>
> borne, like a jumbie
> beneath stony earth.
> Shadowless, I descend, deeply
> into nightmares of childhood;
> down to steel-lined metros,
> to summerheat that beats, insistent,
> at my temples. Down, down to carriages,
> grimy steel-boxes caging men like packhorses
> being driven to a mill.
>
> Down to obsessions caged underground –
> down, down, down.
>
> Phantomlike,
> I move in long narrow streets. (21)

Compared with the forbidden cell of solitary confinement that is hidden beneath the labyrinthine recesses of the prison, the city obscures the possibility of contact with other human beings and with nature. In this way, exile creates an atmosphere of anonymity that characterizes the situation of the immigrant/

foreigner who is lost in the big city. At the same time, the dedication to Maria de Borges indicates that exile ironically establishes a sense of community among the dispossessed. Even though Das seems to suggest that exile typifies the human condition, she carefully distinguishes between the differing levels of exile that are based on racial, gender and class discrimination. While she empathizes with the migrant woman worker, she does not compare her personal sense of estrangement with the tragic specificities of daily life for the female worker.

Maria de Borges's story personifies the story of the desperate migrant worker/immigrant who is lured into buying the American dream in the hope of securing a more favourable existence in the metropolis. Instead, the city organizes itself like a gigantic factory, in which the workers are denied their basic human rights, often at gunpoint, to become mere cogs that will ensure the smooth functioning of the wheels of production. The myth of the metropolis exposes a new set of alienations that are more disconcerting than patterns of disenfranchisement experienced at home:

> He grabs my tiara, my bangles
> of silver. He gives me tokens
> to send me to his factory,
> send me to his store,
> cage me in his offices,
> keep me in his kitchens.
>
> At gunpoint, he steals rubies in my cheeks,
> my full curve of hip. (23)

The city, which would like to present itself as a generous benefactor through its so-called welfare schemes, is instead a slave master that offers employment in exchange for complete subservience from the workers to support a capitalist economy. Within this structure, the economically disadvantaged are exploited and women are (sexually) abused even further:

> He bestows me coppers —
> so I may buy
> a jacket for my shoulders
> from his huge garment-store,
> hose from his hosiery, wine from his cellars. (23)

In other words, the metropolis supports a contemporary model of sexual and economic slavery that complements the first European colonizations, thereby awarding a certain permanence to the colonial legacy in the Caribbean. Diasporic dislocations strengthen colonial authentications when exile, as the very condition of deterritorialization, becomes a "reading and rereading . . . [of] the colonial narrative of history and the canonical text", as stipulated by Simon Gikandi.[37] Exile concretizes the groundedness of colonialism by serving as a visible manifestation of this experience. However, while exile, as a creative palimpsest, provides official documentation of a master experience, it also subversively exposes other, unofficial versions that have been partially or completely erased or replaced by the primary text. These imperceptible traces resemble the "shards of memory" evoked by Salman Rushdie in *Imaginary Homelands*, sharp and jagged reminders of repressed recollections that remain imprisoned in isolated cultural and historical fragments.[38] These fragments represent the shattered collective unconscious that has been denied the opportunity to effectively piece together or articulate the trauma of separation and the corresponding creation of an exilic sensibility that results from hegemonically imposed amnesia or mnemonic erasure.

——•—

Rajandaye Ramkissoon-Chen's poetry demonstrates an initial attempt to cure amnesia through an exploration of the ancestral past as a means of rewriting Indo-Caribbean history and unblocking petrified memories of separation, perilous crossings and the negative aftermath of immigration. Memories initiate a forced entry into history through a creative interrogation of the past as a necessary first step to establishing present citizenship and future reassurances. Positing a reciprocal association between history and memory, Betty Wilson states, "It is only through memory or 'going back' – what Toni Morrison calls 'self-recollection' – that one can re-live, understand and open a way to heal past trauma."[39] Similarly, Ramkissoon-Chen's poetic re-memberings underline the recuperative dimensions of such journeys that afford a sense of reconnection with and ownership of the past, as an effective means of transcending exile. At the same time, her poetry reveals the ambivalence associated with such ancestral confrontations.

The poet's nostalgia for the past is linked with her desire to familiarize herself with Indian history. She associates the omnipresence of memory with a particular anxiety of forgetting the past. In "My Old Book Prize", she states, "I burn the street of memory / like a sunset loath to retreat".[40] The tenuous links with a yet-to-be-defined past ("its fifty years might just dissemble" [10]) engages the poet in a parasitical relationship with her past as a means of holding onto a valuable starting point of reference. She admits, "I had clung on time like a mollusk / on roots above the water" (11). Just like the mollusk receives its sustenance from the resources of the sea, so also the past provides nourishment for the soul in its quest for a sense of belonging or identification. Stressing the importance of this commitment to remembering, especially in the case of colonized peoples with displaced histories, Myriam Chancy makes the following recommendation: "It is through this ancestral memory that resistance will continue to be enacted, and it is at the point at which that memory becomes cherished in our present communities that the empowerment necessary for the dispossessed to overcome their imposed oppressions will be gained."[41] In other words, Chancy associates memory with an active contestation of past negations by providing the necessary point of connection to solder together the severed ties between self, land and community.

The poet compares her search for the remnants of the past to an archaeological dig to uncover the lost symbols of yesteryear that have been replaced by contemporary signifiers of modern-day life that seem out of context. In "Village Revisited", she states,

> I search like a native returned
> for the old symbols
> for some pieces of the old jigsaw
> where neighbours fitted closely
> like aunts and uncles. (15)

Comparing the past to a snug-fitting security blanket or a well-composed jigsaw puzzle, the poet's idyllic consciousness is nevertheless forced to confront the realism of the "filling of the years" (15), where the past becomes a movable scenery that does not provide the security of rootedness. The poet expresses her disappointment when she says, "Even the copper, so large so heavy / had seemed immovable, fixed" (15). The illusion of permanence offered by the copper pot initially reassures the poet about the timelessness of the past. Copper, as a rich, earthy element, debunks the prior notion about the non-productivity and fickleness of the land, offering instead concrete proof of the soil's enduring potency. Associating the copper pot with a sign of territorial repossession through its immutable presence, the poem also highlights the negative consequences of separation from the land as a result of one's inability to make any territorial claims on it. As Chancy states, "In systems where people are denied access to the land for their basic survival and are instead exploited for their labor, a very crucial cultural connection is severed."[42]

The deprivation of a psychic connection with the land, as a primary source of identification, creates a state of meaninglessness instead in which disfavoured communities in particular are isolated by an imposed orphanhood that symbolizes loss and absence. The progressive shattering of the poet's delusions regarding the rehabilitating powers of the past reveals itself in the following lines: "Its domain is buried / in a sidewalk of concrete" (15). The land erects an impenetrable barrier to the past, which remains in suspension in the same way that the myth of displaced ideals remains unreachable in the sky. The following verse demonstrates the disjunction between reality and myth:

> Only the sky above seems the same
> the starry depiction of myths
> like punctate traces
> the unreachable things
> and in the silo of memory
> the untouched grain. (16)

The use of agricultural references is particularly pertinent in describing a culturally identifiable Indo-Caribbean experience that links the trauma of indentureship or plantation labour with blocked memories that remain repressed in the storehouse of the mind.

Ramkissoon-Chen's poem "The Beach on a Weekday" likens preserved memories to truncated fragments of the past, represented by stumps and hollows:

> There are the old preserved things:
> a bowl-like tree-stump
>
> . . . . .
>
> the hollow of a shell-horn. (27)

Once again, images of amputation dominate the poem to show how the colonized's association with the past can only be based on partial, truncated memories in the absence of historical wholeness. In "Surgery May 17, 1995", the poet compares colonized memory to a "pictoral hieroglyph" whose effective decoding could, indeed, reveal a counter-history.

However, any effective deciphering of memory to posit a decolonized Indo-Caribbean subjectivity involves the necessary critical thawing of frozen, dormant primary impressions. The poet relates this arrested level of development to a state of decomposition caused by a chemical imbalance in the process of preservation. As "The Old Station-Master's House" reveals, this imbalance leads to the creation of tarnished memories:

> Time lets its rust —
> a weathered red on the roof's
> sides. It clings to its crust
> like chemistry's reaction
> on memory's recall. (17)

Nevertheless, an outer veneer of rust often camouflages a hidden secret, like the old station-master's house that, despite its physical decay, still bears testimony to "the experiences of former royal rulings" (17). Despite its seeming displacement in a contemporary setting, the house is a glaring reminder of a negative history that cannot be ignored or forgotten: "It still stands above the rest / like an unbeaten age" (18). Reminders from the colonial past serve as activators to jog the memory from its imposed lethargy or inaction. Petrified memories are a manifestation of the exilic sensibility that is animated by the tension between the desire to reclaim the past and the inability to do so effectively.[43] Saïd attributes this tension to the "median state" created by exile, which leads to the formation of "half-involvements" and "half-detachments".[44] The in-betweenness of partial associations links the problem-atics of partial remembering to the particular situation of the physically and psychically exiled Caribbean writer who finds himself or herself on unsettled ground. In the introduction, I asserted that by adopting a median or intermediary position, the Indo-Caribbean presence created a primary fracturing in the very definition of Caribbeanness, which has traditionally been posited in terms of a black and white dialectic. However, the reality of in-betweenness has also confronted Indians with the dilemma of cultural isolation in the face of rapid creolization, as stated earlier. As Juneja states, "Thus within the larger context of the West Indian struggle to create and celebrate a local culture as distinct from that of the colonial masters lies the attendant struggle of the East Indians to validate their attitudes and expressions as integral to that larger culture."[45] Juneja's assertion implies that the perceived alienness of Indo-Caribbean traditions has located their expression outside the sphere of local culture as a readily identifiable marker of difference. Hence the urgency to recognize the dynamism of *kala pani* hybridity as an expression of contemporary Caribbean identity. The following comments by Glissant could aptly describe the ambivalence attached to the situation of Indians: "The truth is that exile is within us from the outset, and is even more corrosive because we have not managed to drive it into the open without precarious assurances nor have we succeeded all together in dislodging it. All Caribbean poetry is a witness to this."[46] The adjectives *precarious* and *dislodging* reveal a certain tentativeness of expression that questions the authenticity and accuracy of such trips down memory lane as a definitive strategy to establish cultural authority. Comparing partial recollections to gaps in memory, Ramkissoon-Chen refers to this void, in "Still My Teacher", as "nibbled out knowledge" (38). Associating exile with an interstitial subjectivity that is located in gaps and fractures, the poet suggests that fractured memories are faded prints or missing photographs in an album whose absence ironically indicates a partial trace of presence. These partial traces create a space of disruption in the chronologically organized sequence of family recollections, as the poem "To Mr Ramlogan's on the Tortuga Hills" demonstrates:

> The guests are an album
> of his memories
> the fading prints of long ago. (20)

Exilic memories are a source of rupture, bursting through the stranglehold of (colonial) historical preservation to assume an autonomous position. This autonomy is achieved through the development of a hybridized consciousness as a means of coming to terms with exile, as reflected in Ramkissoon-Chen's poetry. Through a process of transferral, the hybridized consciousness posits an ideal reality by serving as a point of transition between two worlds. Transferral represents a perfect synthesis of two conflicting realities into a harmonious whole, creating a newly found, recreated reality. Feelings of exile are confronted by a compromise with the self through the creative potential to fabricate a counterexistence. The poet describes the hybridized sensitivity adopted by her grandfather in his attempts to dispel the insecurity of alienness. In "Some Childhood Memories of My Father", she writes,

> He wore his white tunic of the Orient
> perfumed with the attar of roses
> . . . his moustache
> of the Rajput aristocrat,
> the East and the West
> the old and the new
> hybridized for elegance. (121)

The poet equates her grandfather's achievement with a certain creolization of customs that nevertheless leaves a bittersweet aftertaste, "this lemon-sweet smell of memory," evoked in "Aushee Dies" (58). Bittersweet memories of exile combine the agony of the forcible severing of ties with the ancestral land as a result of the Indian Middle passage – "Their sweat in runnels and knots / strangled their memory of the old homeland ("Ancestry", 23) – together with the sweetness of creating new memories in the adopted land, where "impressions remain like unwashable mouth-stains in a napkin" ("To Mr Ramgolan's on the Tortuga Hills", 21). The grandfather's exilic sensibility is thereby accommodated at the cost of a vital compromise between mythified idealizations of the past and cultural assimilations of the present.

—•—

Manoo-Rahming describes her ancestral rememberings in terms of a pungent curry flavour that symbolizes a sensory invocation of the past. The spicy tang of "onion, turmeric, crushed black mustard seeds" ("Curry Flavour", 52) are vital ingredients in the recipe for creative recollections, where these spices flavour the imagination in its reminiscences. However, as the title of the poem indicates, flavours, as spicy aftertastes, represent tasty but intangible remnants of the original repast. Flavours, like distant memories, lose their potency with time, thereby eliminating a certain concreteness of sensation.

The poet's desire to establish a certain tangibility of experience prompts her to associate memory with exilic recreations. "Incarnation on the Caroni" highlights the presence of living monuments from the ancestral past that are immortalized in local representations, whereby the holy waters of the river Ganges are magically reincarnated "on the banks of the Caroni River" (2). Re-creations from the past are maintained through the observance of ritualistic ceremonies that guarantee ancestral permanence through repetition. Even though the poet herself remains distanced from the actual experience of indenture, her regular participation in "the ritual at Cedras Bay on Indian Arrival Day" (2) connects her with the original experience through a particular mnemonic reclaiming. Memory serves as a vital link to the past by establishing a sense of personal historicity, whereby, as the poem "Footsteps in This Land" indicates,

> . . . they can
> bring to me
> a cry
> a footstep

> a voice
> from my ancestral spirits
> in that faraway land
> in the east. (10)

The poet experiences a sense of urgency to restore umbilical affiliations with the ancestral land in order to overcome the instability of historical dispossession in the new land wherein

> I am alone
> without a story
> in this land
>
> . . . . .
>
> where I have
> no umbilical cord. (9)

Searching for traces of the ancestral land in the new surroundings as a means of guaranteeing cultural continuity, the poet seeks refuge in the comfort of rituals, as mentioned earlier, rituals whose stabilizing and structuring effects re-establish her psychic equilibrium. Rituals offer the antidote of security to the confusion and disappointment that results from the nostalgic pursuit of inaccessible ideals, represented by

> . . . this land
> where my mothers
> my fathers
> have not lived (9)

However, the poet's newly acquired level of accommodation to the Caribbean land remains short-lived when her relocation to another island instigates a second bout of separation anxiety. The pangs of a second departure indicate a dual engagement with exile when the poet comes to the tragic realization that home can offer only temporary residence in an age of diasporic estrangements, which characterize the postcolonial condition. Imaginative and adaptive re-creations of "home" provide the only assurance to survive the transience of the contemporary age, as the following verse from "Trini Tabanca" indicates:

> Now flying in de plane
> above the mountain
> away from this land
> pain have meh crying

> in meh heart
> for where home is. (69)

Home ironically symbolizes vagrancy and errancy, like the ships of indenture that provided an unstable and portable home for the first immigrants during the long months across the *kala pani*. Manoo-Rahming's images of exilic homelessness betray the poet's desire to come to terms with her restlessness or existential limbo in order to claim a certain ownership of home through permanent residence or dreamlessness ("A Dreamless Man", 18). Dreamlessness offers the possibility of anchoring oneself in the present, in the here and now of reality. The poem reveals the feelings of resignation, expressed by the poet in response to this uncreative solution to survive displacement:

> So, now dreamless,
> I'll just sit on the beach
> And snatch the fish
> which swim past me. (18)

The poet grounds herself in the routine of sitting on the beach and snatching fish in an effort to eliminate her previous exilic wanderings.

In *Bones*, Das's exilic interrogations are formulated in terms of a search for the ancestral self through a remembering of ancestral history, as the point of Origin. When the poet tries to reconnect with her ancestral past, she confronts the hapless reality that the original homeland is itself located in a primordial fracturing of experiences. "The Growing Tip" offers a microcosmic view of colonial history in the Indian context, in which fragmented images of the homeland are a result of its original exploitation and disembodiment by the colonial authorities:

> They assumed a garden.
> . . . . .
> They assumed a gardener.
> . . . . .
> They assumed a house.
> . . . . .
> Perhaps they assumed a car or two. (51)

British residency, while displacing Indians, maintains itself for over three centuries through the abjection of the local people. Das juxtaposes the physical and spiritual chaos imposed by colonial rule with the neatly ordered world of the colonialists that sustains itself by the systematic dispersal of the colonized:

> Perhaps they assumed a car or two,
> a dog, a cat, a singing canary
> hanging by its wiry prison on the porch;
> a jolly postman, a friendly milkman, an ever-so-often handyman.
>
> What she sent reminded no one of a garden
> pieces of skin, a handful of hair, broken
> teeth, bits of glass. . . . (51)

The idyllic image of the British garden of Eden with its tea party–like joviality contrasts with images of the prisonhouse, where the light-hearted ambiance of jocularity is replaced by the ominousness of perdition.

Ancestral identification thus leads to a dual displacement that obfuscates two potential sources or origins when the original violation of homeland is duplicated by the later rape of the (forcibly) adopted land. The process of affiliation with the ancestral past locates itself in a double loss or separation evidenced by the tenuous links with India and by the equally ambivalent relationship with Guyana as a result of its unenthusiastic reception of the Indo-Caribbean political and cultural presence.

The motherland represents a primary signifier that provides the very basis of identity. Das's relationship with the motherland can be best qualified as an often-questionable stepmother relationship. "If I Came to India" describes the poet's hesitation and lack of conviction through a series of questions that do not, however, display any well-posited affirmations. She wonders, "If I come / will I find my self" (47), or

> Shall I be Methuselah
> in my tradition, a foreign vine
> Grafted to the Deccan Peninsula. (47)

The poet's major concerns are formulated in four basic questions:

1. Does a return to the ancestral land lead to a recovery of self in which the body overcomes the original trauma of separation?
2. Does the rupturing of ties with the homeland symbolize instead a point of no return?
3. Will a return to the homeland only accentuate the poet's foreignness?
4. Can a reconnection be effectuated amid apparent disconnection?

These four writers unequivocally highlight their own insecurities during their individual journeys of ancestral affiliation. At the same time, they unanimously suggest that the dislocation of the self, as a symptom of suppressed/repressed memory, can be relocated through the act of writing, which urges the female body to author itself. Writing gives body to voicelessness in the same way that the text assures the physical presence of its author. Gikandi asserts that "to write is to claim a text of one's own; textuality is an instrument of territorial possession; because the other confers on us an identity that alienates us from ourselves, narrative is crucial to the discovery of our selfhood".[47] The self re-creates itself in writing by defining and establishing its own parameters of expression through an active rewriting of the master narrative. Like the process of naming, writing is a ceremony of repossession through linguistic claiming. Writing (out) of exile and dispossession is a way to transcend exile by creating the necessary textual space in which loss is re-membered. In this instance, self-expression *is* self-empowerment, through strategies of transgressive confrontation and self-deliverance, confirming Trinh Minh-ha's claim: "More and more women see writing as *the* place of change, where the possibility of transforming social and cultural structures is offered. . . . Feeling the urgency of a decentralizing movement, they take up speech not to identify it with themselves or to possess it, but to deliver it from its enslavement to mastery."[48]

Minh-ha associates women's writing with a particular linguistic decolonization that effectuates a simultaneous liberation of the body. The body's pain resulting from its submission to mastery is converted into a site of creative self-fashioning,[49] in the same way that the colonizing aspects of the oppressor's language are neutralized into indigenized patterns of expression. Highlighting the body's capacity to transform the language of pain into the language of transcendence or self-knowledge, Lionnet remarks: "The body thereby becomes a text on which pain can be read as a necessary physical step on the road to a higher moral state, a destiny, a way of being. . . . This aspect of reformation and rebirth through suffering is, paradoxically, part of a philosophy of life which binds the mortification of the flesh to a certain vital principle, a spiritual vigor through which the individual may graduate to a higher plane of existence."[50] In other words, the inscription of pain on the female body becomes a prerequisite to its re-presentation based on a calculated strategy to circumvent its subaltern status. Pain alters the specificity of the body by motivating a spiritual quest to rediscover the self, whereby the body's very abjection leads to its (perverse) triumph in negation, as Das's poem "Resurrection" demonstrates:

> Triumphant, from dark days of starvation
> I rise from the grave,
> blood thin, body weak, will too
> exhausted to claim glory for my victories. (13)

Even though, after repeated acts of aggression against it, the body is too weak to celebrate its own victory, the poem underlines the body's capacity to transcend its infirmities. In this case, the severed mother tongue is reconnected to the body through the painful process of restorative suturing, thereby permitting the formerly silenced voice to ensure its immortality. The birth of voice coincides with the birth of text. Words come surging forth after centuries of silencing, like angry flood waters that make their mark by refusing to be contained.

The violence of expression in Manoo-Rahming's poetry exposes the explosive power of words that advocate a new militancy. In "Battlefield for Freedom", the poet compares her pen to a gun:

> my words
>
> on this battlefield
> I write
> with this gun
> I fight
> for my freedom
> with this pen. (28)

Describing her words as an eruptive, torpedo-like force, the poet associates writing with an act of linguistic exorcism that bursts through the impenetrable wall of societal prisons to claim the autonomy of those words. The physical body writes out its alienation through the liberating power of the written word, exemplifying the close rapport between writing and the body in the act of writing the text as a means of articulating the body. The female body insinuates its presence through the interactive rapport between body as text and text as body to assure its presence. "Battlefield" describes this interchange, which takes place in a combat zone:

> poems
>
> slither around
> the undersea world
> of my mind
> submarines jettison

torpedoes through my eyes
Shatter cataract stillness
and newborn vision screams
in that first breath.

short short stories. (28)

Words erupt like an explosion to delineate their own territory. Words as rupture
typify repressed narratives that seek to expose "bleached" historical falsifications
through the creation of new perspectives. This vision is achieved by the ripping
apart of

worldly trappings
of useless flesh
exposing
bleached hollow bones
conduits of truth. (28)

The poem "Eve of Creation" advocates the rewriting of myths and feminine
mythologies to correct culturally inscribed falsehoods about women. These
revisions deconstruct stereotypical and essentialist readings of women to provide
them with a certain totality of representation. The debunking of images of
self that are alien to female representations demonstrates the power of the
pen to expose and destroy beliefs and value systems that have been sustained
by age-old traditions:

Finding Eve was not tempted
so she never fell
there was no sin
so the veil never existed. (47)

Through the retelling of the story of Eve, who has been positioned as the
primordial sinner in the Bible, responsible for the treachery and downfall of
all womanhood, and mankind, the poem reveals that this story has been
fabricated by well-maintained illusions about women, through creative
manipulations.

The poet recommends the formation of communities of feminist consciousness that will collaboratively expose universalized untruths through the creation
of woman-centred databanks of information that she compares to a "primeval
soup" ("Making Soup", 54). The collaborative making of soup suggests the
inauguration of collective female effort, wherein

all rememberings
are blended and a poem
gurgles forth (54)

The nutritious, rehabilitative qualities of soup, which fortify the body, parallel the sustenance offered by "liquid memory" (54) to displace the fixity of structurally maintained origins that have symbolized alienating points of reference for women. Providing women with a certain fluidity of expression, the reclaiming of liquid memory asserts their right/write to re(produce) through a process that Minh-ha refers to as the appropriation of the womb.[51] She states that women "use womb to re-appropriate it and reunite (or re-differ) themselves, their bodies, their places of production. This may simply mean beating the master at his own game. But it may also mean asserting difference on differences."[52] The appropriation of womb permits an integral articulation of women's experiences that eliminates binary distinctions or separatism to signify a primary subversion of gendered differences. The either/or paradigm of exclusionary otherness is replaced by the mutual interplay of difference that highlights and celebrates pluralism. Pluralisms expropriate the alienating void of exilic space by realigning the fissured tensions created by gender, race and class alienations to bring about a holistic sense of self-perception and sociopolitical consciousness.

These writers suggest that the positioning of this consciousness can be achieved by the cultural reclaiming of the land through symbols of female spiritual transcendence, represented by rivers, the moon and ancestral connections with those gods and goddesses of the Hindu pantheon that have provided positive models of identification for women. Reconnection with the earth is an act of birth that infuses the self and land with new energy. Prior feelings of depersonalization experienced as a result of the land's alienated presence are re-expressed in terms of "the emergence of possible being"[53] through creative reincarnations that overcome death by a series of rebirths, as Manoo-Rahming's "Incarnation on the Caroni" indicates:

Your lifeforce curls upward, like wood-smoke;
then, like a rainy drizzle, falls upon me
caressing my full breasts, my round belly
and enters my womb
implanting new life
in the ripe richness of placenta

for your fourth incarnation
on the banks of the Caroni river. (3)

The regenerative powers of the earth are resuscitated by the impregnation of
Indian history in the earth's entrails, to establish its legitimacy while giving new
agency to this history. As Glissant states, "Our landscape is its own monument;
its meaning can only be traced on the underside. It is all history."[54]

In "Footsteps in This Land", Manoo-Rahming invokes Atabeyra, the Great
Mother of the Caribbean Sea, to fill the chasm of exilic uncertainty by bridging
the gap between the Caribbean and the Indian Ocean. The vital link between
these two bodies of water will establish a sense of diasporic continuity by
creating a revitalized consciousness of Indo-Caribbean history through its
transatlantic connections. The poet demonstrates the urgency of creating this
new awareness when she prays to Atabeyra:

> Goddess of childbirth
> hear my prayer
> hold my hand
> build with me
> the tunnel
> for my children to cross. (9)

She simultaneously invokes Hanuman, the monkey god of the *Ramayana*, as
the god of successful diasporic crossings. In the epic, Hanuman carries Sita to
safety after her abduction by the demon king Ravana, reuniting her with her
husband, Ram. In a similar fashion, the poet indicates that Hanuman secured
the preservation of Indian history during the perilous *kala pani* crossings and
assured the survival of the brave immigrants who undertook this journey. Under
Hanuman's guidance, the churning waters of the sea offered "safe" passage by
resurrecting the muffled voices and overpowered bodies of the ancestors to
honour them as the primary survivors of Indo-Caribbean history, as the poem
"Carifesta Five-Rebirth" indicates:

> I see men and women
> in each hand a lighted lamp
> standing straight and tall
> black and brown faces softened
> in the flickering flame. (73)

Identifying the *deya*, or lamp lights, with triumphant returns, such as Ram's
celebrated return from exile, the poet seeks to rescue a silenced history from

the thunderous reverberations of "reggae   soca   zouk" whose pulsating rhythms have obscured the "injustice of genocide / indentureship and slavery" under effective cover-ups of "carnival masks" and "white sands and waterfalls" (72).

In "Full Moon Healing", historical wounds are nursed by the recuperative powers of the moon, which provides effective healing to eradicate deep tissue scarifications. These scars are compared to "stains that would not wash, / for hands that would not stop bleeding" (36).

In her collection of poetry *Nuclear Seasons*, Ramabai Espinet continues to use the imagery of natural healing by evoking Mama Glo, a powerful female figure from Trinidadian folklore, the symbol of a revised woman-based Caribbean spirituality. Also called Mama De l'Eau or "mammy water", this figure promotes an environmentally safe consciousness by protecting rivers, streams and lakes. Associated with fertility, Mama Glo is a creation figure who epitomizes the birthing of an autonomous female experience:

> I am fertile now
> Rivers of creative memory
> Running
> Through my veins
> finding
> The streams of my own voice
> Dread and wise
> And unknown to me.[55]

Water enhances the body by energizing previously desensitized areas to create a new awareness of self and environment. The reconnection with the land assures a complementarity of expression between the flow of rivers and the birth of voice to indicate the inscribing potential of all creative action.[56] Minh-ha associates inscription or writing with the creative power of childbirth: "Hand/writing carries with it life — one life gives, remakes, maintains another. It is the mother: The one who experiences childbirth neither as a loss nor as an augmentation of self."[57] In other words, the mother's divine benevolence lies in its selflessness, that is, in its promotion of female self-assertion through a system of reciprocal maintenance. By creating a space of mutual intra-uterine affirmation within the circular dynamism of the womb, the mother passes on her legacy to future generations of daughters, who remain nourished by the womb's amniotic secretions. The poet admits,

And if I am fertile now
this birth
I bring . . .
A birthing of
My womanvoice, green
And glowing. (29)

The primary debuting of "womanvoice" provides a radical point of departure to establish a genealogy of female chorales that resonate in polyphonic harmony to create new symphonies of expression.

Mahadai Das seeks the empowering presence of the goddess Kali in her quest for transcendence. Identified as the most powerful goddess of the Hindu religion, Kali has been simultaneously deified for her benevolence and vilified for her perceived ambivalence. The very personification of *Shakti*, or primordial female energy, Kali symbolizes the spirit that refuses to be contained by societal pressures. Displaying qualities of self-reliance, inner creativity and autonomy from male tutelage, Kali's multifaceted representation has endowed her with a certain wholeness of being. Associated with the protection of women and children, Kali worship in the Caribbean has also been politicized to include the empowerment of the marginal and the dispossessed. Dennis Bassier attributes the revival of Kali culture among the Indo-Guyanese working class to their desire "to counter tendencies of alienation and anomie in a system in which they feel themselves unable to secure a fulfilling and satisfying life".[58] Apart from its overtly religious manifestations, Kali worship expresses a certain critical questioning of prevailing systems of power in the Caribbean, in which Indo-Caribbean women in particular, continue to remain an underrepresented subclass, as stated earlier.

The poet invokes Kali to destabilize the status quo through a purging of bad intent. The contact with Kali initiates a breaking of new ground through a final confrontation with and destruction of hegemonic structures as an act of redemption. Das describes this confrontation in "Sacrifice", where Kali demands reparation for male-orchestrated violations against women, children and other pariahs of society to create a new beginning of mutual understanding and cooperation:

Kathakali, blue queen,
black-nosed Mother of the Cosmos,
Jewess of Death, do not call us.
We are the sons of morning.

She beckons and beckons
offering, a necklace of skull,
a bloodied pair of lips, a sword on hip.
O insatiable Goddess,
mother of the damned,
death will claim us all if we listen.

Entranced,
he gallops to her breast,
eyes fixed to her face.
Behind her back, she hides
her quick sword. (50)

Kali-identified female empowerment is guaranteed by the destruction of ambivalence or opposition to it. Kali's omnipotence, symbolized by her terrifying presence, ensures this destruction in her capacity as the guardian of a female heritage.

Additionally, it is important to note that Kali has been linked with the pre-Aryan cultures of India. As David Kinsley states, "her roots seem to be among the peasant and tribal cultures of India that eventually leavened the male-dominated Vedic pantheon with several goddesses associated with power, blood and battle."[59] Kali's position of distinction within pre-Aryanic systems of worship exposes the Aryan ethos to contain women within imposed models of second-class citizenship in an attempt to undermine their spheres of influence. By representing the very power by which women adopt creative alternatives to oppression, Kali has come to signify the paradigm of Indo-Caribbean female resistance to exile and confinement.

Exile "speaks" a powerful, multilayered text in the writings of Indo-Caribbean women, for whom exile has been a source of creative strength and social repression. Their negotiation of exile and of its manifestations reveals the desire to establish historical and cultural agency by inscribing their voices in a permanent legacy of Caribbean postcoloniality. Their exilic explorations are reflections on the daily struggles and insecurities of Indo-Caribbean women who fight for exposure amid erasure and for validation in the face of systematized disempowerment. These journeys testify to the hesitations, contradictions and affirmations involved in such struggles, which nevertheless make a powerful statement about Indo-Caribbean women's capacity for autonomous action to overcome exilic alienations.

6

Sexuality, Violence and the Female Body Erotic

Sexuality has represented an important marker of exile and affirmation for Indo-Caribbean women. The issue of Indo-Caribbean female sexuality remains hotly contested among Indian communities in the Caribbean and other diasporic locations. Inscribed within a particular culture of violence and shame, this sexuality has been subjected to the machinations of elitist Brahmanic prescriptions for Hindu femininity elaborated in India as well as the colonizing effects of British colonialism and the impact of the Canadian Presbyterian Missions in Trinidad. Evelyn O'Callaghan makes the following observation about the representation of female sexuality in the works of Caribbean women writers: "Female sexuality in the work of West Indian women prose writers is either shrouded in *secrecy* and *shame*, or a matter of casual and unfeeling acquiescence to male pressure. In most cases, it has negative consequences for the woman's economic, social and psychological well being."[1] Associated with a series of taboos and restrictions imposed by male-ordered strategies of confinement and inhibition, female sexuality has constituted the ultimate fetish for male and female writers alike. In the Indian context, novels such as Rooplall Monar's *Jhanjhat* have linked female sexuality with the forces of chaos and disorder that have led to the disruption of social order. V. S. Naipaul has located female sexuality within the realm of the grotesque and "unrelieved fear"[2], while women writers have portrayed their female characters as victims of sexual abuse and subservience. At the same time, the interrogations of female sexuality in the writings of Shani Mootoo, Ramabai Espinet and Lelawattee Manoo-Rahming have provided the very basis for active contestations of preconceived state and religiously legislated sexual mandates for Indo-

Caribbean women, contestations that have mirrored the primary sexual negotiations undertaken by women under indentureship. These negotiations have located female sexuality within the dual problematics of sexual repression and control on the one hand and a dynamic and often contradictory site of self-recovery and repossession on the other. A brief description of the sexual negotiations undertaken by indentured Indo-Caribbean women will be instructive to this analysis.

Kavita Sharma indicates that pre-colonial India revelled in a healthy celebration of sexual life in which women were accorded sexual agency in the form of sexual autonomy and the privileging of individual rights over rigid definitions of upper-class Brahmanic morality.[3] Tales from the *Kama Sutra* and other erotic writings, together with the sexual prowess demonstrated by courtesans and temple dancers, testified to a certain sexual licence that was frowned upon by patriarchal morality. Sharma asserts that the rigidity of sexual mores was largely confined to the Brahmanic classes and was thus imposed only on select populations. However, these rigid sexual specifications were soon to become unilateral normative codes of behaviour as a result of the collusion between the Brahmanic elite and the British colonial rulers. The superimposition of Brahmanic and Victorian moralities instigated a serious erasure of sexual agency for Indian women, who were victimized by misogynist patriarchal and colonial sexual control.

The crossing of the *kala pani* by Indian women led to a corresponding re-evaluation of gender roles and definitions, as has been discussed in previous chapters. Spatial dissolutions motivated the blurring of caste, class and regional distinctions that provided Indian women with the scope for a certain sexual mobility. Serious sex-ratio imbalances gave women the opportunity for greater independence in the choice of partners as well as the necessary freedom of movement to move on to other relationships with Indian and non-Indian men if a particular relationship proved to be unsatisfactory. By openly flouting the very idea of Brahmanic monogamy, with its thesis of allegiance to one man and one family, these women were able to challenge traditional cultural norms and Hindu familial structures that had been deeply embedded in the Indian psyche for centuries. Patricia Mohammed states that this disregard for the "patriarchal contract", formulated in India and carried over to the new diasporic location, hampered the effective reinstatement of that contract in Trinidad in 1917.[4] Mohammed distinguishes between three competing patriarchies that were vying for control during that period: the dominant white patriarchy as the ruling minority, an emerging Creole patriarchy composed of the Afro-Trinidadian majority, and an Indian patriarchy that was situated at the lowest level of this hierarchy. Considered to be the most disenfranchised group because of its lack of political, educational and national agency, the Indians, according to Mohammed's analysis, did not constitute a significant educated elite that could compete fairly, because of their primarily agricultural status and preoccupations:

> Thus the patriarchal contract as it existed in Trinidad in 1917 was that of a competition between males of different racial groups, each jostling for power. . . . In the face of a hegemonic control by the white group and another kind of dominance by the "creole" population, the contestation was both a definition of masculinity between men of different races, and for Indian men to retrieve a ruptured patriarchy from the ravages of indentureship and thus be better placed to compete in this patriarchal race. This required a consolidation of the traditional patriarchal system brought from India.[5]

In other words, female sexual "promiscuity", together with the demoralizing impact of being disadvantaged competitors in the scramble for patriarchal supremacy, led to the development of a fractured sense of Hindu masculinity. This state of suspended masculinity translated feelings of male powerlessness that were symptomatic of the trauma and insecurities instigated by indentureship and the forced separation from homeland. While immigrant Indian women were in a stronger position to negotiate the newness of their situation in lands that offered the promise of enhanced gender possibilities for the future (in the form of a revised balance of power within family structures), immigrant men seemed to suffer greatly from the vulnerabilities of new beginnings, especially in terms of their control over women. As Bridget Brereton observes,

> On the plantations, the traditional sanctions of village India against infidelity had been eroded, and the abnormal living conditions in the barracks with frequent absences of husbands in jail or in hospital, contributed to marital tensions. Furthermore, in a situation where women were scarce, the possession of a wife was an important symbol of status and masculinity on the plantation, a crucial element in the husband's self-esteem, which he could ill afford to lose. Traditionally, the Indian husband was expected to keep his wife in subjection; this was almost impossible in the plantation situation where women earned their own living and were greatly in demand; the shame of failure was wiped out by "the cleansing violence of self-righteousness".[6]

The post-indenture consolidation of Hindu culture provided men with the necessary defence mechanism to reconfigure and reinstate patriarchal sexual and social control over women, thereby establishing the primacy of the Hindu patriarchal model as a classic signifier of ethnic difference in Trinidad. The rehabilitation of the Hindu male ego was assured by "a masculine assertion of power in Indian gender relations, and for a masculine definition of the Indian community to emerge in the contestations of patriarchy in the wider society in Trinidad", according to Mohammed.[7] Male control, in the name of preserving ethnic distinctiveness, justified the use of violence to curb women's sexual transgressions, thereby ensuring the sanctity of the ancestral cultural heritage. The high incidence of rape, domestic abuse and murder during this period testifies to the attempts made by men to restrict and subjugate women within the narrow confines of rigid familial ties. Violence against women became a rationalized purging of "female bad intent" and an effective elimination of the stigma of whoredom and social marginality that was attached to sexually independent women who tried to rewrite patriarchal scripts of Hindu womanhood through their individual and deliberate acts of self-affirmation.

Patriarchal domination received its validation through mythical inscriptions in daily life that guaranteed the permanence and "respectability" of varying levels of control. This model eliminated the notion of male accountability or responsibility while configuring itself "as contingent on women's acceptance and collusion with the control of female sexuality".[8] As demonstrated by Mohammed, Sita's trial by fire to prove her sexual faithfulness to Rama during her abduction by the demon king Ravana received widespread acclamation in the scriptures, while no such proof was required by the husband during his long separation from Sita. The scriptures ironically condoned the use of force in the preservation of female purity, as demonstrated by the story of Draupadi, the common wife of five Pandava brothers in the *Mahabharata*. Draupadi's story highlights the violation of her personhood through her "free for all brothers" status, a communal possession that could be circulated or exchanged for multiple consumption, like a commodified object of barter. Pawned to the rival Kaurava kings when the Pandavas lose a dice game against them, Draupadi is forced to prove her chastity during an attempted rape by Duhsasana, the most diabolical of all the Kaurava brothers. While Duhsasana's actions do not receive widespread condemnation, all attention focuses on Draupadi's ability to safeguard her virtue and modesty by her refusal to be unclothed in public. As Paula Duncker states, "Draupadi's body is private property, the property of men. Like all property she can be bought, sold, exchanged. In the *Mahabharata*, the woman is property to be exchanged between men, she is held captive by the male gaze; the nakedness would be her shame. Shame is man's threat against women: a woman without shame is a woman without worth."[9] Draupadi maintains her sense of shame as a result of the timely intervention of Krishna, another male character who is entrusted with the task of preserving her dignity. Her shame is concealed within the unending yards of sari material that protect her nudity/modesty so that she can be returned to her husbands untouched.

The pervasiveness of myth in the reconstitution of diasporic identity offered the security of cultural permanence and social cohesion in the face of cultural uprootedness and the perceived laxity of Indian social structures, especially in terms of family organization. Designated roles and functions inhibited the development of healthy ties of intimacy between partners, which could have suggested a relationship based on reciprocity and a mutuality of experiences. Instead, the institution of a power dynamic within the conjugal unit guaranteed the negation of female sexual pleasure, which was limited either to procreation (as a familial duty) or to the satisfaction of male sexual desire. The denial of intimacy between partners was thus inscribed within the dynamics of Indo-Caribbean indentured history, beginning with spatial confinement in tiny barracks that thwarted any measure of privacy, later replicated by confinement in mythical structures advocating sexual prudishness and propriety.

Indian women, consciously or unconsciously, collaborated in the perpetuation of myths that were detrimental to the realization of their own full potential. Kim Johnson exposes the irony of this situation, stating that even though the scarcity of women during the early days of indentureship gave them a certain power to question a family system that marginalized men and women alike, their second-class social status prevented them from finding any long-term solutions to the problem.[10] On the other hand, Mohammed describes this "collusion" as a calculated strategy of defence to deal with particular material and emotional circumstances in which people found themselves through the machinations of history.[11]

Additionally, the role of the Canadian Presbyterian Missions and of the British colonials cannot be understated. Outraged by the displays of sexual "lasciviousness" demonstrated by the early immigrant women, the colonial state was a willing collaborator in the maintenance and enforcement of gender inequity and female sexual subservience in the name of safeguarding national interest. Describing the socializing effect of the Presbyterian church on the lives of Indian women, Ramabai Espinet claims that

> at first the Presbyterian missionaries were scandalized by the ease with which Indian women moved households, and they certainly tried to reinscribe ideas of fidelity which many women had already abandoned. The general independence of Indian women, coupled with the need to reestablish a workable family unit, produced a structure in which Indian women were policed rigorously. . . . This phenomenon does not exist among African-Caribbeans, a mixed race people like Chinese or Syrians. . . . Men also feel the need to protect their women folk, but not in the same manner of accusation and rage without any apparent cause.[12]

It could be affirmed that the collusion of patriarchal and state control over female sexuality instated the beginnings of a state of sexual apartheid for women, whereby state-legislated and patriarchally sanctified norms of standardized morality became an effective method of regulatory control. As Rhoda Reddock explains, "It was the historical conflation of interests between migrant Indian men, struggling to improve their socio-economic and caste position within a new and hostile environment, colonial capitalism, and the state's desire for a stable . . . self-reproducing and cheap labor force that worked to generate ideologies rooted in particular notions of morality aimed at curtailing women's autonomy."[13] Normative standards of moral conduct were scripted onto a juridical frame of reference ensuring their legitimacy and easy verifiability.[14]

However, it would be misleading to affirm that mythical models of identification in the Indian context have remained impervious to change since the beginning of the twentieth century. The compelling impact of creolization, together with the changing specificities of everyday reality, has created open spaces of contestation to outdated paradigms, especially among the younger generation, as reflected in chapter 3. Changing gender ideologies have instigated a state of flux whereby unilateral mythical impositions are being challenged for their applicability to a modern-day setting. As Mohammed admits,

> the task of unravelling gender identities becomes more elusive when we try to match stereotypic norm with reality as there is so much variation in real life, and many changes taking place at each historical moment. What emerges in the examination of myth, and symbolic interpretations of these myths, and the range of male and female experiences during the period after 1917 and 1947, is that some aspect of the traditional roles were definitely retained by a majority of the population – on the part of many men the idea of commitment to wife,

responsibility to family and so on were still part and parcel of the Indian family system and gender relations established therein. . . . The majority of women retained the reciprocal commitment to endure whatever hardships this required, while remaining monogamous and faithful to husband, and an impeccable mother to one's children. But gender ideology had begun its imperceptible shift from mythological India to the western setting of Trinidad.[15]

This transition from mythical stereotype to concretized prototype has nevertheless been accompanied by a new set of tensions and insecurities. Women's increased participation in educational and professional occupations, a strong sense of feminist consciousness together with women's awareness of a multiplicity of choices available to them in the public and private sector have had the adverse impact of reinstating male fears of loss of control over women and their circumstances. The escalation of violence against spouses, daughters and girlfriends today is symptomatic of male psychic insecurity in the face of further renegotiations of social structures and options by women. As Espinet explains, "Perhaps some of the violence against Indo-Caribbean women occurring today is due to the fact that contemporary women are refusing to endure abuses as they used to. They are asserting different choices and the gender role structures in which they function do not allow them these choices, so they have to seize them against opposition."[16] In other words, if mythical incongruity seems to be losing its stranglehold of permanence, one structuring force that has maintained its hegemony in Indo-Caribbean communities has been the culture of violence that has, in fact, been motivated by the very violence of Indian history in the Caribbean.

Shani Mootoo's novel *Cereus Blooms at Night* is an interrogation and indictment of institutionalized violence against women within the "respectable" confines of the Hindu patriarchal family. Article 1 of the 1993 UN Declaration on the Elimination of Violence against Women defines violence against women as "any act of gender-based violence that results in, or is likely to result in, physical, sexual or psychological harm or suffering to women, including threats of such acts, coercion or arbitrary deprivation of liberty, whether occurring in public or in private life". Describing violence as an inherent violation of a woman's physical and psychic well-being, the UN definition collapses the inside/outside distinction that locates the inside with the personal and private domain of the patriarch, in which his authority remains unquestioned. However, theoretical formulations are sometimes a far cry from reality-based occurrences, wherein men have continued to engineer the privatized domestication of family life that has provided them with unrestrained and unaccountable sexual access to women. Consequently, the gender asymmetry maintained by the power imbalance within the Hindu patriarchal household has imploded the myth of ideal Indian family life that, according to Ramabai Espinet, is supposed to be based on the qualities of stability, nurturing and life-enhancement, leading to

> the formation of sound and healthy human beings. The assumption on the part of the societies they live in, Trinidad in particular, is that Indians have stable families. But, as in most societies, health can be measured in direct proportion to the morbidity of that society. In Guyana, in Trinidad and in Surinam, the rate of suicide among young Indian women is amazingly high. . . . The proportion of Indian prostitutes in these three countries is also alarmingly high. Put these factors together with the high incidence of batterings and wife-murder among the Indian population and that settled picture of domestic stability wears thin. . . . I'm talking about serious stuff here, which is not mentioned in the society from which I come, that of Trinidad, at least not in the official discourse. The subject is present in the tabloids but absent from the literature, present in the gossip of the society, while the formal dialogues still pays obeisance to the sanctity of Indian family life.[17]

Mootoo's novel exposes the well-maintained lie of Hindu familial respectability through the violent dynamics of rape and incest within the Ramchandin home. Through a series of inverted and perversely (mis)aligned triangles, the novel exposes an insidious family romance that has dire repercussions on the psychological development of the female protagonist, Mala Ramchandin.

It is interesting to note that the novel begins with a reference to the alleged criminality of the protagonist, thereby implying that women who defend themselves against sexual abuse are automatically regarded as deviant. As the novel indicates, "Even now a handful of people remained disgruntled about the dismissal and the ruling. They felt cheated of the rare opportunity to have a woman criminal in their midst. Some citizens believed that a crime was committed and that she was its perpetrator."[18] Like the irony indicated in the title, which reflects a certain floral blossoming of life at night, the protagonist's nightly deflowerings by her father conversely displace the locus of blame from the perpetrator to the victim. Incest, as the best-guarded family secret, is a glaring manifestation of patriarchal imbalances of power within familial structures that sanction unwarranted violence against defenceless children, especially girls. Shrouded by a veil of secrecy and silence, incest consolidates the power of the patriarch through intimidation, physical dispossession and a suppression of voice. The proverbial incest taboo is not so much an indictment of this heinous crime as a calculated strategy to stifle protest or the naming of the abuser by the victim. The perverse transferral of sentiments of culpability and shame onto the victim guarantees the endurance and enforcement of secrecy to create an outward facade of familial normalcy. The novel calls into question patriarchally accepted definitions of sexual normalcy in the following comments, made by the narrator: "I was preoccupied with trying to understand what was natural and what perverse, and who said so and why. Chandin Ramchandin played a part in confusing me about these roles" (48). Levels of acceptance of normal/perverse behaviour are closely related to patterns of gendered dependence within the family, where the father's sole custody of his adolescent daughters, after his wife elopes with her female lover, creates a morbid triangular configuration of desire and sexual control.

The novel highlights two instances of sexual repression experienced by the father, Chandin Ramchandin, when his English foster sister's parents quickly thwart his infatuation for her. Lavinia's father, Reverend Thoroughly, who has been responsible for Chandin's moral and spiritual education, admonishes him for the inappropriateness of his desire for his half-sister: "The Reverend walked to his desk and slammed the polished mahogany top with his fist. 'You cannot, you must not have desire for your sister Lavinia. That is surely against God's will. Do you understand? . . . Otherwise, otherwise . . .' " (37). The Reverend's chastisement of Chandin for his predilection to indulge in incestuous thoughts and feelings leads to the latter's humiliation and sense of frustration at being publicly exposed for improper behaviour. His internalization of feelings of despair and humiliation re-express themselves in certain bodily manifestations: "Chandin did not immediately return to the house. He stayed outside holding his stomach, which had turned into a hard knot. It cramped unbearably" (37).

His cramped-up frustrations are quickly displaced onto his childhood playmate and companion Sarah, whom he marries as a substitute for his cherished ideal. Despite his adopted status within the Thoroughly household, Chandin is reminded of his racial and social alterity as an ethnic minority from a disadvantaged economic background who lacks the essential credentials of gentility required to gain full entry into the family. His marriage to Sarah, apart from its substitutive, compensatory value, is also an attempt to erase ethnic otherness by marrying a woman of his own kind. Marriage provides a decorum of respectability to camouflage and contain previously free-floating libidinal anxieties. According to Monique Wittig, in her essay "The Straight Mind", the institution of marriage guarantees the installation of a patriarchal contract that reinforces obligatory social relationships between men and women.[19] In other words, the marital contract provides the necessary vocabulary that legitimizes the imposition of codes of morality, epitomized by virile masculinity at the expense of female marginalization. Jacqui Alexander equates marriage with the enforcement of a "hegemonic masculinity, procreative sex, subordinated femininity and vague but powerful notions of consent".[20] By regularizing social relations within the familial unit, marriage promotes a certain ordered rationality of control, appropriating female agency through obligatory sexual domination and other forms of private pressure exerted on female family members. The following lines from the novel are ominous in their implication: "Sarah gave birth to her first child ten months after the marriage, and a couple of years later she was pregnant again. Chandin thought often of Lavinia but his love for her had soured and mostly he felt betrayal. He was a dispassionate husband to Sarah though he enjoyed observing his two daughters, albeit from a distance. He was composed and diligent performing his duties" (48–49). The novel exposes the limitations imposed by rigidly defined sexual roles and commitments and their impact on human behaviour when the narrator states, "Over the years I pondered the gender and sex roles that seemed available to people, and the rules that went with them" (47). Implying that the Hindu social structure enforces a restraining framework of reference for men and women alike, the novel simultaneously highlights the intersectional positionality of race, class and gendered distinctions in the disenfranchisement of individuals.

However, the clearly hetero-masculinist delineation of Indo-Caribbean sexual morality sets up two barriers of exclusion for women when the primacy of the masculine norm inhibits the exploration of alternative sexualities by creating a situation in which "women who are 'wives' become the ground on which some very narrow definitions of womanhood are redrawn. . . . The very formulation of morality is underwritten in fundamentally gendered terms assigning women to a subordinated position while invoking some higher religious or natural principles in order to do so."[21] Sarah's role as wife and mother reduces her scope of influence to procreation as a "natural" and logical requirement of her marital status. Her supposed inability to produce the coveted male heir who represents the successful and expected outcome of a fruitful marriage in Hindu traditional culture further negates her sense of selfhood. The successive birth of two daughters mirrors her double disenfranchisement in the family, as a failed wife and failed mother. Ironically, her heightened sense of dispossession at each female birth is, in fact, a projection of her husband's own insecurities regarding his failed manhood or incapacity to father a male child. In other words, Sarah's abjection seems to mirror Chandin's perceived impotence, reducing them both to the same level of disinheritance. The father's suspended masculinity is the outcome of the mother's non-compliance with the rules governing the patriarchal contract, the enforcement and sustenance of which depends upon the presence of the male offspring as the legal and sole heir to the patriarchal heritage. Moreover, Sarah and Chandin's Christianized Hinduness, as a result of Reverend Thoroughly's tutelage, is a further negation and violation of the Name of the Father and the passing on of his authority to the Holy Son. This disruption of masculine space justifies the insinuation of a certain sexual lawlessness that invalidates the primacy of masculine or "natural" law.

The novel exposes patriarchally determined patterns of lawlessness in the growing intimacy that develops between Lavinia Thoroughly and Sarah Ramchandin. This relationship initiates a primary fracturing of masculinist space through an insertion of lesbian homoerotic desire that undermines the pertinence of socially legitimized categorizations of acceptable sexual partnership. Beginning with bonds of protection, companionship and comfort that unite the two ethnically and socially separated women — who, in their own way, are confined by patriarchal ideologies and expectations in their respective households represented by Reverend Thoroughly and Chandin Ramchandin — the friendship blossoms into a tender sexual relationship that nevertheless remains furtive in its expression. Pohpoh, the older Ramchandin daughter, perceptively observes the growing attachment/attraction between the two women: "The image stayed in Pohpoh's mind, fortified with a memory of Mama trying to send her and Asha out to play, and of Pohpoh feeling something was being concealed. . . . It frustrated her that Mama and Aunt Lavinia seldom spoke any more except in soft, abbreviated sentences. They seemed to communicate more with their eyes, and with long looks" (55–56). Like the thorny cereus plant whose beautiful flower remains concealed until the night, lesbian love constitutes a thorny issue in discussions of sexual morality, by either remaining invisible in official discourses or by being openly criminalized by oppressive sexual legislation, in the form, for example, of the 1986 Sexual Offences Bill of Trinidad and Tobago.

The lovers' plan to escape with the children "where we can be a family where we will never be separated" (59) is on the verge of being realized when, by a tragic turn of events, Chandin's unexpected appearance during their departure creates a situation in which the women are forced to leave without the children. Chandin's stunned reaction to the entire sequence of events exhibits a triple sense of inadequacy, demonstrated by his inability to control his wife's actions, his double rejection and humiliation by Sarah and Lavinia, and the displacement of the state-authenticated heterosexual contract by a supposed moral illicitness. His ensuing acts of violence and destruction are a defensive measure to restore his thwarted sense of manliness that results from his inability to consolidate his influence within the household. The novel demonstrates this violence: "The two children huddled on the verandah floor, unsure and terrified. He seemed oblivious to their presence. They watched as he swiped at the kitchen counter, sending pots and pans and cutlery crashing to the floor, clanging and spinning. . . . He rifled through photographs, pitching some on the floor. Those of his wife or Lavinia Thoroughly he crumpled into a ball, then spat on, all the while crying and making growling sounds. His children cried even more seeing him cry" (63–64). In this case, virility becomes a flimsily constructed imperative for Indo-Caribbean masculinity, judging by its fragility and susceptibility to contestation.

Entrusted with the task of ensuring male honour and prestige, the wife's supposed misdemeanours represent a serious loss of face for Chandin, whose only means of credibility and authority in society are located within a well-codified model of patriarchal masculinity. Moreover, his disfavoured ethnic status and the cloak of Christian respectability that he is obliged to wear as an official of the Christian church limit his possibilities to vent his frustrations outside the home. Referring to Indo-Caribbean men, Bridget Brereton makes the following observation: "The man whose wife had been unfaithful suffered a disastrous loss of self-esteem, and in the absence of other mechanisms for expressing anger and self assertion, violence directed against the other (murder or mutilation of the woman) or against self (suicide was almost as frequent in these situations) was the only way to recover his pride."[22] The condemnation of suicide as an act of violence against the Christian God leads Chandin to sexualize and externalize his aggression in the form of repeated acts of incest against his daughters, the older, Pohpoh, having to bear the brunt of his sexual impositions.

Pohpoh becomes a defenceless substitute for her father's sexual violations, whereby the permanence of masculine sexual desire is assured by the commodification of women and girls within a nefarious system of patriarchal consumption. The system of desire is perpetuated by male sexual control over women: each woman becomes a mere pawn that ensures the smooth functioning of the system. In other words, within patriarchal systems of power, women find their sexual specificity in their economic value as objects of exchange or commercialization. Within this mode of exchange, what matters above all is the efficient operation of the system in general, irrespective of the individuality of each woman in question. In fact, this dynamic imposes a level of sexual anonymity on women, who are reduced to a non-presence, deprived of sexual agency in the elaboration of male desire. The following passage is a powerful indicator of women's substitutive value within the economy of male desire, where the male gaze, with its myopic refractability, is unable to distinguish one woman from the other:

> For the first few weeks after the shattering of his world, he slept in his bed with a child on either side.
>
> One night he turned, his back to Asha, and in a fitful, nightmarish sleep, mistook Pohpoh for Sarah. He put his arm around her and slowly began to touch her. . . . Then he brought his body heavily on top of hers and slammed his hand over her mouth. She opened her eyes and stared back at him in terror. . . . Glaring and breathing heavily like a mad dog, he pinned her hands to the bed and forced her legs apart.
>
> That is how it started. The following night he sent the two children to sleep in their own room, but they both came to know that he would call for one or the other to pass at least part of the night in his bed. (65–66)

Pohpoh and Asha become the father's ultimate vindication for Sarah's betrayal and an "acceptable" outlet to satisfy his sexual cravings within the secrecy of the home, where his private morality remains concealed from public eyes.

This concealment is guaranteed by a particular culture of silence that surrounds domestic crimes, in which women are socialized into accepting their own victimization and into seeing themselves as sexual prey. Adrienne Rich attributes this disempowerment to the institution of compulsory heterosexuality, in which women become the sexual and emotional property of men.[23] According to Rich, compulsory heterosexuality is a political construction that has been inscribed in institutions that have traditionally dominated women. Rich suggests that, controlled by the politics of fear and domination, male sexual desire, in this case, can be motivated by feelings of female powerlessness and vulnerability. In the novel, Pohpoh's fear is inspired by her lack of control that leads to her father's repeated sexual aggressions against her: "Pohpoh, remembering her father's invasion, put her hand over her mouth and nose to stifle her panic and the nauseating smell of fear that rumbled from her insides. Pressed against the bush, she bit the inside of her lip and willed herself to think" (175). In many cases of incest, the victim's silence is mistaken for passive acquiescence instead of being seen as the manifestation of a certain corporeal amputation whereby the body's faculties are deadened in their capacity to express themselves effectively. The repeated physical colonization of the female body blocks its channels of articulation, leading to a robotic state in which it automatically, as it were, submits to its violation: "Her stone-blank eyes concentrated on the blackness of the night outside her window" (142). Kathleen Barry refers to a "sexual domination perspective" whereby the sexual abuse and terrorism experienced by women is rendered almost invisible because of its apparent natural inevitability. According to Barry, women, as victims of male consumerism, are subjected to a system of female sexual slavery whereby compulsory heterosexuality leads the daughter to "accept" incest/rape by her father.[24] Individual acceptance is extended in the novel to a societal level when the discovery of Chandin's violations do not lead to public outcry and ostracism. On the contrary, his crimes against his daughters are rationalized as the supposedly natural outcome of the humiliation suffered at the hands of his wife, thereby justifying the use of violence as a means of defending personal honour. Ironically, he is still awarded a certain respectability as a former teacher of the Gospel, implying that the patriarchal institution of religion can still be used as a mantle to camouflage sexual misdemeanours: "While many shunned him there were those who took pity, for he was once the much respected teacher of the Gospel, and such a man would take to the bottle and to his own child, they reasoned, only if he suffered some madness. And they further reasoned, what man would not suffer a rage akin to insanity if his own wife, with a devilish mind of her own, left her husband and children. Whether they disliked him or tolerated his existence, to everyone Chandin was Sir" (195). The convenient guise of insanity, as an effective cover-up for any form of accountability resulting from an "altered" state of being, is a further indication of a particular patriarchal conspiracy to disempower women and render them invisible by thwarting their appeals for justice before a male-dominated kangaroo court.

Pohpoh's sense of frustration at her powerlessness re-expresses itself in terms of an unarticulated rage that takes possession of her body. Repressed anger becomes the body's silent reaction to a losing situation, whereby "On relaxing she was overcome by the rage that seeped into her veins. At times like these she felt inflamed to the point of wanting to tear and scream into her father's room, of screeching so piercingly that she disabled him, of punching him in his stomach over and over until he cried like a baby, admitted how loathsome he had been and begged her and Asha's forgiveness" (143). The dynamics of anger give voice to voicelessness by transforming silence into the language of action, as demonstrated by Pohpoh's imagined acts of violence against her father. This violence is a symptom of her unwillingness to continue to accept her abject situation through her violent acts of self-affirmation. Qualified by its force and intensity, violence is associated with an active stance. Violence, in its pertinence to feminine representations, removes its subjects from a posture of passivity as it necessitates a reaction to a particular situation or condition. Exposing the tyranny of silence and compliance and stressing the need to reclaim a language that has worked against women, Audre Lorde makes the following observation: "We have been socialized to respect fear more than our own needs for language and definition, and while we wait in silence for that final luxury of fearlessness, the weight of that silence will choke us. . . . It is not difference which immobilizes, but fear."[25]

Pohpoh's first attempt at fearlessness is to find comfort in her love for Ambrose in her adult years. Her transformation from the child Pohpoh to the adult Mala is motivated by this love, which serves as an antidote to daily sexual trauma. The violence of sexual aggression converts itself into the sweetness of romantic love for a childhood friend, thereby demonstrating the body's inner resilience, its capacity to withstand violence by its ability to create an alternative and more favourable reality for itself: "That night Mala complied with Chandin Ramchandin's expectation that she lie down with him. She let him more easily than ordinarily lay his coarse hands on her belly, for she was in possession of a joy and hope that allowed her to block the whole thing out. She thought of Ambrose sitting with his mother in their house at the edge of the cane fields" (194). Ambrose's affections bring Mala to the realization that every sexual encounter need not necessarily be a painful one. A relationship based on reciprocity, in which each woman is afforded a sense of choice and the right to experience sexual satisfaction, can be a source of pleasure: "It was the first time, and her first time with someone of her own choice. . . . For the first time Mala felt no pain. It was the first time she felt what it was like to be touched and to have her nipples licked and tasted as though they were a delicacy" (218).

Mala reclaims her lost innocence through the physical reclaiming of her body, which experiences a virgin sensuality. This newly found sensuality heightens the body's excitability by re-sensitizing previously deadened emotional responses. The body comes to terms with itself after prolonged abuse to reclaim its autonomy and terms of desirability. However, this renewed sense of self is short-lived when Chandin discovers the lovers' liaison. Unwilling to be a player in the triangular configuration of desire that sets itself up between Mala, Chandin and Ambrose, Chandin's response to the situation is typical. His inability to relinquish his hold on his daughter confirms his proprietary attitude as well as his own slavish sexual dependence on her. The presence of a male rival leads to the ultimate branding of the female body by the father to show his ownership of it, through a brutal act of rape: "Chandin locked the bedroom door. He set the cleaver down by the bed. He raped her three more times that night. He made her stay in his bed" (223). Chandin's violence is aimed at showing Mala her "rightful" place of sexualized subalternness within the family and, by implication, within society, which considers female sexual agency to be a transgression of its rules of proper conduct. Women's continued internalization of socially imposed tenets of guilt and shame for supposedly improper behaviour sustains and legitimizes the unilateral culture of hetero-patriarchy through a lack of opposition to its disingenuous requirements. Mala's initial reaction to her father's actions is based on feelings of culpability: she berates herself for betraying her father. Buying into the ideology of the immutable status of sexual subservience, she displays her misguided sense of loyalty to her father in the following reflection: "After all, Mala berated herself, she should have known better than to cheat on her father. In the end she was to blame. She prayed that Ambrose had better things to do that morning" (224).

However, Chandin's renewed victimization of his daughter when he returns home from work later that night leads to a particular unleashing of Mala's pent-up energies and frustrations. By pushing his daughter to a point of no return, the father's violence instigates the unleashing of the fury of abjection, which culminates in his suspected murder. The ultimate voicing of subjection is realized by the elimination of the very source of this abjection as a final and desperate act of independence. The violence meted out by the perpetrator is turned against the abuser himself when he least expects the victim to fight back:

Mala's fury was so uncontrollable she didn't notice her hair being ripped out.
She forced her face toward the hand holding the cleaver and sunk her teeth deep
into Chandin's wrist. Chandin released his grip on her hair and curled his body
in sudden agony. Mala had drawn blood.

. . . Mala tore the cleaver out of his suddenly limp hand. With the back of
her other hand she wiped her father's blood from her face and spat at him.
(227)

Mala's fury, as an articulation of the repressed, is a symptom of women's
sense of helplessness when they are confronted by societal impasses that
physically imprison them in confining roles and modes of expression. According
to Shoshana Felman, women mourn this loss of self in terms of a certain
manifestation of madness, which she describes in the following manner:
"Madness is the impasse confronting those whom cultural conditioning has
deprived of the very means of protest or self-affirmation."[26] Mala's transformation into an apparent madwoman at the end of the novel is, in fact, a violent
indictment of social atrocities that are levelled against women. Her body
becomes a visible signifier of these monstrosities in the form of its altered
physical appearance and tenacity of expression. Ambrose is stunned when he
witnesses Mala's transformation: "Suddenly he heard a dreadful crashing. Mala
was calling out his name. He ran back up the stairs as though jolted by a
cord. In the kitchen he saw, instead of the woman he had made love to the
day before, an unrecognizable wild creature with a blood-stained face, frothing
at the mouth and hacking uncontrollably at the furniture in the drawing room.
He watched her smash a side table with a single powerful blow" (228). In other
words, Mala recovers herself in her apparent madness when she is finally able
to vent her innermost emotions and thoughts in an unconventional manner.
Unable to fathom – that is, control – Mala's newly metamorphosed self,
Ambrose commits a dastardly act of patriarchal self-defence by abandoning
her, despite her pleas to the contrary. Ambrose's inability to accept Mala's
attempts at self-definition exposes his complicity with the patriarchal conspiracy
against women; his cowardly disappearance becomes a tacit acknowledgement
and acceptance of the status quo. In fact, his action demonstrates the illusion
of fulfilment exhibited by hetero-patriarchal lovemaking in which his narrow
frame of experience with women limits itself to the sexual act and the emptying
of "his semen into a woman" (218). The novel exposes this final disillusionment:

"Ambrose, don't go. Don't leave me, Ambrose. Please don't go." Ambrose couldn't make out her words. Thinking she had gone crazy and fearing once more for his life, he turned and bolted from the house.

Mala gasped in disbelief. She rushed to the verandah, screaming his name. He had already disappeared. (228)

At a first reading, the reader gets the impression that Shani Mootoo's collection of short stories, *Out on Main Street and Other Stories*, makes the rather simplistic affirmation that heterosexuality is always associated with a certain violence of expression while lesbianism represents the ultimate utopia for all women. However, on a second reading, it becomes clear that the positing of this equation seems almost deliberate and politically motivated in its orientation, designed to shock readers into recognizing and acknowledging their own compliance with the patriarchal contract that seriously eliminates alternative forms of sexual expression for men and women. The violent exposure of disempowering patriarchal paradigms that regulate the heterosexual conjugal unit in the Hindu household provides the necessary rupturing of space to pave the way for other discourses on sexuality. As Monique Wittig argues in "The Straight Mind", "These discourses of heterosexuality oppress us in the sense that they prevent us from speaking unless we speak in their terms. Everything which put them into question is at once disregarded as elementary. . . . These discourses deny us every possibility of creating our own categories. But their most ferocious action is the unrelenting tyranny that they exert upon our physical and mental selves."[27] Mootoo's characters are driven by a certain sexual anxiety that reveals their lack of control to modify or significantly alter the rigid rules that govern patterns of marital conformity in their respective relationships. The stories focus on the way in which diasporic communities reconfigure themselves around issues of gender, whereby the community maintains its cultural identity through migrating notions of gender-role conformity. The diasporic women seem to be at a particular disadvantage because of their economic dependence on their husbands, their lack of contact with the outside world, their inscription within a Hindu maternal heritage of compliance and martyrdom, and the insecurities involved in being part of a diasporic community, in which women often become the scapegoats for men's economic and social vulnerabilities.

"A Garden of Her Own" describes marital space as a confined and confining space characterized by its lack of intimacy between partners:

A north-facing balcony meant that no sunlight would enter there. A deep-in-the-heart-of-the-forest green pine tree, over-fertilized opulence extending its midriff, filled the view from the balcony.

There was no window, only a glass sliding door which might have let fresh air in and released second- or third-hand air and the kinds of odours that build phantoms in stuffy apartments. But it remained shut. Not locked, but stuck shut.[28]

Marriage creates a depersonalization of experience whereby the couple is confined behind a wall of silence, "the rough wall. Cold from the wall" (16). The presence of the wall as an impenetrable barrier serves as a glaring reminder of the marital impasse experienced by the couple; the husband's long working hours reduce him to a phantom-like presence imprinted in "his indentation in the tired foam mattress" (16). The situation of the wife, confined to the role of the patiently waiting wife as part of the monotony of the marriage routine, exemplifies how immigrant dreams of a better life in the diasporic metropolis are compromised in the name of survival in the big city. The isolation experienced by the immigrants in the city parallels the isolation experienced by the wife in her marriage when she states, "Well, this is the first birthday I've ever spent alone" (20).

The husband's social marginalization as an Indian immigrant in the workplace displaces his authority in the public sphere. Patterns of victimization experienced on the outside are replicated with a vengeance against the wife within the home in an attempt to reclaim lost manhood. The husband's one-sided lovemaking re-establishes his parameters of control through his machinations of the sexual dynamic, machinations which leave his wife unsatisfied. The ejaculation of semen, as an effective release of pent-up frustrations, unilaterally transfers the locus of sexual and social repression onto the wife by depriving her of a similar outlet: "She feels his hands on her waist, leading her from behind to the edge of his bed. Her body is crushed under his as he slams himself against her, from behind, grunting. She holds her breath, taut against his weight and the pain, but she will not disturb his moment. She hopes that the next moment will be hers. She waits with the bed sheet pulled up to her chin. The toilet flushes and, shortly after, she hears newspaper pages being turned" (23). Codified sexual roles engineer a power imbalance in the relationship, in which the wife's participation is limited to the sexual servicing of her husband. A reciprocity of expression could destabilize this arrangement by awarding the wife some semblance of sexual agency. However, the story implies that the functional value of heterosexual sex creates a situation of double jeopardy for economically dependent immigrant women by enforcing their sexual and social negation.

Kavita Sharma highlights the ambiguous position occupied by Indian diasporic women who are afforded the illusion of greater mobility and control in the new location through the process of migration. Caught between past, present and future patriarchies, these women are simultaneously expected to "maintain homeland kinship networks and religious and cultural traditions in order to transmit them to their children. This tends to reinforce patriarchy and makes the domestic sphere both a refuge from the material and spiritual anxieties of exile and a trip in which the conflicting demands of family, work and old and new patriarchies have to be dealt with. The situation is painful."[29] As exemplified in Mootoo's short stories, diasporic crossings seem to strengthen the efficacy of the heterosexual contract in the name of cultural preservation. Women, as the protectors of cultural integrity, are awarded the dubious distinction of assuring group identity through a certain gender-role immobilization in time and space characterized by what I term the pathology of Hindu maternity and by its prescriptions for the transmission of a particularly disenfranchising maternal heritage to the daughter.

Mother and daughter do not seem to validate each other's presence in the story "Wake Up". While the son guarantees his mother the necessary passport to future security and validation, the daughter is perceived as a disappointment in her capacity as an inheritor of the mother's legacy. As the mother informs her eldest daughter, "You're the eldest, Angenie, if only you were a boy, but I have to call on you" (36). Daughters are inscribed within an easily identifiable pattern of victimization – "I know this pattern well" (33) – symbolized by the abjection of the maternal role.

The mother's sense of failure is projected onto the female child, who becomes living proof of the mother's negation precisely because she is female and hence an impediment to maternal actualization. The mother's situation of powerlessness reveals itself when she describes the restrictive nature of her wifely and motherly duties that are taken for granted by her family. She laments, "I can't go on like this any longer, I do everything for you all, I've devoted my life to you all, I have never neglected my responsibilities, I've been a damn good wife, and this is what I get in return. . . . [Y]our father does not know how lucky he is, I can't go on like this, what should I do? I only stay with your father because of you all, you know, not a damn thing has changed in these fifteen years since we got married" (36). Confined to her utilitarian function within the family, the mother's identity is based on a double displacement in which she is imprisoned by an imposed social reality that renders her defenceless and by her own inner psychological reality, which can never be articulated. However, in Mootoo's story, the mother expresses her powerlessness and repressed inner reality in the form of primal cries that echo her anguish: "She begins crying, a low wailing cry. More like a sound coming through her than from her. As if she were giving voice to all her female ancestors and they were all wailing at the same moment" (36). Ancestral voices of pain narrate the story of the mother's lamentations in moans and wails that reflect the limits imposed on her person. Her inability to articulate her suffering in a language that is comprehended by the public places her in an outer space of exclusion, outside of language and, consequently, outside of personal subjectivity.

The mother's valorization in Hindu culture is based precisely on her attitude of deference. The fetishized evocation of the mother resides in her back-handed exaltation, whereby she is validated for the very qualities that represent her abjection: silence, suffering, sexual passivity. She resembles the martyr who elicits the perverse respect of others by the extreme negation of her body and her sense of self. The negation of the mother is a prerequisite to her representation by the male order. The idealized, re-presented mother is glorified in her abstraction and reduced to a state of symbolic neutering whereby her mythical attributes lead to a loss of identity. In other words, the mother as autonomous presence does not exist in the patriarchal contract which contents itself with the perpetuation and propagation of its own mythology of the maternal. Love for the mother is consequently directed towards a satisfying ideal that is mummified in its deification. The discrepancy in representation between the glorified maternal image of Mother India and the mother's daily reality creates a certain disequilibrium between the mythical realm of fantasy and fixation and the social realm of the quotidian, wherein the social becomes an inverted mirror image of the mythic. The quotidian positions the mother as the negative, unsatisfactory opposite of the coveted ideal because she is limited in her capacities, unlike the all-expansive construction of the mythified mother.

The mother absorbs this sentiment of limitation and converts it into feelings of guilt, shame and inadequacy that she later passes on to her daughter as a symbol of maternal "love". The story exposes the feelings of inadequacy that are first experienced by the mother and then internalized by the daughter: "How inadequate I feel around her. Had I been, as the first offspring, a boy, I could have taken the situation more effectively in hand and offered her a strong, firm shoulder" (36). The daughter's comments highlight the way in which women are socialized into participating in their own alienation: each woman becomes the other's worst enemy. This distancing is demonstrated by the traditional mother–daughter antipathy, reflected in the story, where mother and daughter are separated by their lack of intimacy. As the daughter admits, "I want to reach over and touch her, but there is no invitation. To do so would be inappropriate, not the stuff that our relationship is made of" (36).

Mother and daughter are pitted as rivals for the father's attention. This rivalry conversely limits the women's influence in the father's life, whereby the displacement of female solidarity creates a situation in which "she has never, however, learned to redirect him, reprogramme him from the little niche she lives in inside his brain. Of what use, then, this infiltration?" (37). The mother's attempted infiltration of the male psyche, "where she can read his every twitch and thought" (37) in an effort to gain access to the authority of the patriarch, is thwarted by the imposition of a veil of shame that blinds her into inaction. As she states, "Utter chaos. Utter shame. A shame he has taught us to have" (38). The father's outward mobility and extramarital activities provide him with the coveted freedom of movement denied to the women of his household. As the daughter admits, "And as much as I cry inside at his rejection of her and so of us, his freedom looks more exciting, interesting. The freedom to go work, to go to meetings, to speak his mind. . . . The freedom, inherent in his maleness, to philander" (42–43). If masculinity is associated with mobility and freedom of expression, constructions of femininity are correspondingly associated with gender-role confinement and immobility: "Being female, my future looks grim, claustrophobic. I worry that I am expected, as a girl, to grow up to be just like her" (42), worries the daughter at the inevitability of inheriting the mother's familial identity. Consequently, as a compensatory and defensive mechanism, the daughter expresses her open identification with maleness and male-defined spheres of influence and her subsequent negation of femininity: "Still, the fantasy of modelling myself in his image . . . is more honourable than consenting to spending a lifetime trapped by the body of a female" (43). The daughter admits her collusion with patriarchal constructions of masculinity and femininity when she is manipulated into believing that female selfhood is contingent upon breaking off symbiotic ties with the mother from the very inception/conception through a violent severing of umbilical ties of affiliation.

As another example of the patriarchal stranglehold in diasporic communities,

Mootoo's short story "The Bright New Year's Eve Night" demonstrates the physical and emotional effects of the violence experienced by young women who find themselves in abusive relationships with displaced immigrant men. Tanya's victimization by her boyfriend, Bobby, begins when he is unable to read her innermost thoughts and feelings anymore: "You used to be so much fun when you were just an innocent kid. Now look at you. I can't read a damn thing on your stone-cold face" (69). Tanya's loss of innocence implies Bobby's corresponding loss of control over her inner being. His frequent acts of violence against her are a defence in order to control her physically through bruises and other visible male imprints on her body: "In his mind he can see the dark purple, green and navy bruises on Tanya's shoulder blade. A curious satisfaction, pride of possession comes over him when he watches them turn colour as the days go by. He often has an intensely sexual desire to lick and suck on the bruises" (71–72). The infliction of pain is accompanied by its eroticization as a source of sexual desire in the same way that a sadist experiences a perverse sense of erotic satisfaction when he brands his victim. The sadomasochistic dynamic at play in the Bobby–Tanya relationship reflects an inherent gender imbalance when Tanya is expected to be grateful to Bobby for his patronage of her: "I got it all for you, gave you everything money could buy. But nowadays you're too fucking full of yourself! I put a little class in your life, honey, and don't you forget that! I did it!" (69). Bobby's control is assured by his economic leverage over Tanya. He assumes that the financial ease with which he can give her everything money could buy will automatically ensure the buying of her affection. By instating the master–slave dynamic through socio-economic privilege and control, the relationship reduces Tanya to a position of serfdom in which her allegiance and unquestionable subservience become necessary prerequisites to guarantee the success of the relationship.

Female vulnerability in such a situation is part of a culturally inscribed tradition whereby women are expected to suffer in silence for their supposedly biologically constituted inferiority as the second sex. In positing the mother as the paradigm of womanhood in traditional cultures, Marianne Hirsch explains that because the mother is unable to articulate anger as a mother, she must step out of that culturally defined role of the mother as caring, nurturing and self-sacrificing.[30] In other words, the functional value of women is reinforced in relationships in which they are expected to show gratitude to their partners for having "saved" them. The cult of gratitude, like the culture of secrecy, constitutes another form of subjection that silences women's voices of protest to an unfavourable situation because the language of women's protest is not recognized as a socially viable discourse by patriarchal systems of power. The story highlights women's muted forms of expression in which the body nevertheless articulates an invisible text of inner violence: "When Bobby screamed at her not to spoil his evening, the bruises on her shoulder came alive, aching and cramping up her entire shoulder blade. She dared not flinch for fear of setting him off. The muscles at the back of her neck, under her skull, were taut enough to be plucked like the strings of a musical instrument. Her forehead was throbbing uncontrollably. Methodically, she bit off one fingernail after another, concentrating on the taste of bittersweet hand-soap trapped underneath her nails" (74). Tanya's attempts at self-mutilation, symbolized by the methodical biting of her nails, are evidence of the spiritual and emotional mutilation that she experiences with Bobby. Repeated abuse inspires moral and physical lassitude, whereby the victim loses the will to live when she is objectified into a punching bag, losing her human value. This lack of selfhood translates into feelings of low self-esteem when women's secondary position of sexualized subalternness receives cultural approbation. Violence thus has an enduring history, judging by the fact that the story presents the victimization of women as a well-inscribed family tradition: "My shoulder hurts so bad. This is how Mama's head must have felt every time Papa banged it into the wall" (76). The legacy of violence erects an impenetrable wall of resistance, which nevertheless displays certain indentations created by the banging of heads and other body parts against it.

The corresponding deadening of the senses leaves Tanya in a state of automation, in which her ultimate murder of Bobby, as in the case of Mala Ramchandin, becomes a vindication for the displacement women suffer in a society that offers them the limited option of serving as objects of socio-sexual exploitation. By refusing to perpetuate a violent tradition that forces women to conform to sociocultural typecasting, Tanya claims ownership of her body by eliminating the very agent of her victimization. Her indifference to the murder, as well as the sense of relief that accompanies her action, bears witness to this reclaiming of self:

> The red and blue lights whirled hypnotically across Tanya's face, mingling with several new bruises smudged along her cheeks and temples to create an eerie mask that made her look much older than nineteen.
>
> Already a crowd of men in different uniforms was taking over the kitchen. Without a fuss, she let herself be escorted outside.

    She left through the front door without a glance toward the kitchen floor.
(83–84)

Tanya's action provides the necessary chink that momentarily halts the self-perpetuating cycle of violence against women by dislocating a vital link represented by Bobby.

Bobby's death symbolizes a primary splintering of heterosexual space to accommodate the insertion of a certain sexual pluralism that subverts "naturally defined" sexual dichotomies of masculinity and femininity. Teresa de Lauretis attributes the reproduction of "just two neatly divided genders" to the heterosexual social contract that imposes monolithic ideologies of gender that negate the positioning of intersectional gender technologies, constructed along the lines of race, class and ethnicity.[31] Heterosexually constructed gender alliances obscure the presence of the grey, undetermined area of lesbian sexuality, "a gender dey forget to classify" (48), as indicated by the narrator of "Out on Main Street". The title of this short story is important for two reasons: first, it focuses our attention on the naming of a marginalized experience, the articulation of Indo-Caribbean lesbian sexuality; second, and more important, it indicates the urgency of recognizing this experience as a part of mainstream culture. The title highlights the importance of integrating ghettoized sexualities into the parameters of the acceptable, thereby invalidating the traditional binary dichotomies between "normal" and "perverse" sexuality. The story reveals the stereotypical typecasting of lesbian sexuality as a form of deviance: "I could see dey eyes watching Janet and me, dey face growing dark as dey imagining all kind a situation and position. And de woman dem embarrass fuh so to watch me in mih eye, like dey fraid I will jump up and try to kiss dem, or make pass at dem. You know, sometimes I wonder if I ain't mad enough to do it just for a little bacchanal, nah!" (48). Associated with a certain barbaric primitiveness because of its alleged emphasis on sexual bacchanal, lesbianism has been mistakenly identified with sexual licence and disruption in an attempt to posit the "normalcy" of heterosexual codes of conduct. The homophobic reduction of lesbianism to sex or cunt pleasure is a calculated strategy to eliminate difference through sexual othering by imposing a narrowly defined grid of sexualized citizenship whereby "not just (any) body can be a citizen any more", according to Jacqui Alexander. Alexander continues, "for *some* bodies have been marked by the state as non-procreative, in pursuit of sex only for pleasure, a sex that is non-productive of babies and of no economic gain.

Having refused the heterosexual imperative of citizenship, *these* bodies, according to the state, pose a profound threat to the very survival of the nation . . . as the state moves to reconfigure the nation it simultaneously resuscitates the nation as heterosexual."[32]

According to the heterosexual state, national interests are compromised by the spreading of sexual dis-ease through non-productive fornication, thereby necessitating the imposition of the "heterosexual cure" in order to contain the spread of "contamination". As the story demonstrates, "But if I ain't walking like a strong-man monkey I doh exactly feel right and I always revert back to mih true colours. De men dem does look at me like if dey is exactly what I need a taste of to cure me good and proper" (48). Intimidated by the narrator's self-assertive stance, whereby she can meet men on her own terms, the men in the story try to transform her self-assured strides into the demure womanly gait of "hip and thigh" (45). Convinced of their ability to cure the narrator's sexual malady through the injection of sperm, the men position themselves as self-appointed guardians of sexual morality.

Prescriptive and restrictive sexual norms have thus imposed a dual marginalization on Indo-Caribbean lesbians. While Shani Mootoo's diasporic relocation to Canada has enabled her to write about the experiences of Indo-Caribbean lesbians with a certain freedom denied to her in her homeland of Trinidad, this freedom has seemed rather heavy-handed ("Going for a outing with mih Janet on Main street ain't easy!" [48]) given the fact that Indo-Caribbeans in Canada have been relegated to a particular cultural bastardization by Indian and Canadian nationalism while lesbians have been reduced to a further level of sexual bastardization. The story reveals the two levels of "national" rejection experienced by Indo-Caribbean lesbians in the following outburst: "Cultural bastards, Janet, cultural bastards. Dat is what we is. Yuh know, one time a fella from India who living up here call me a bastardized Indian because I didn't know Hindi. And now look at dis, nah! De thing is: all a we in Trinidad is cultural bastards, Janet, all a we. *Toutes bagailles!* . . . I looking forward to de day I find out dat place inside me where I am nothing else but Trinidadian, whatever dat could turn out to be" (51–52). The collusion between the racist policies of the Canadian state with respect to its immigrant populations, the cultural high-mindedness displayed by South Asian nationals from India, and the hetero-patriarchal foundations of the home state (Trinidad) and the metropolitan state (Canada) creates an undeniable refugee status of nationlessness for Indo-Caribbean lesbians, by awarding irrevocable citizenship to heterosexual men. As Jacqui Alexander asks, "How do we construct home when home is not immediately understood nor instinctively accessible? Our challenge is to invent home in different spaces that cross geographically."[33] In other words, can Indo-Caribbean lesbian sexuality reconfigure the hetero-spatial configurations of home to create equitable rights of ownership for lesbian and heterosexual women alike?

The claiming of lesbian identity in an openly hostile environment demonstrates an attempt to de-nationalize the unilateral primacy of the economy of heterosexual desire through a certain decolonization of self. The correlation between the repression of queer sexuality and the colonial oppression of race and culture in the Caribbean and Canada exposes the patriarchal ideology of conflating questions of identity into a singularly masculine voice, according to the Indo-Guyanese poet and film maker Michelle Mohabeer.[34] The exploration of alternatives as a violation of the terms of nationhood displaces lesbianism into an outer space of non-representation, characterized by repressive regimentation and criminalization. However, the relocation of the margin to the centre is made possible through active contestations of hegemonically constructed paradigms of nationhood through the act of coming out. The personal desire to define the self connects with the social stance of re-evaluating existing societal norms through the politics of self-positioning.

Mootoo's characters are self-identified lesbians who live for themselves by refusing to succumb to societal prescriptions for womanly behaviour. By openly flouting their gayness, they position themselves as independent agents who vindicate their rights amid severe opposition by men and women: "Well, with Sandy and Lise is a dead giveaway dat dey not dressing fuh any man, it have no place in dey life fuh man-vibes, and dat in fact dey have a blatant penchant fuh women. Soon as day enter de room yuh could see de brothers and de couple men customers dat had come in minutes before stare dem down from head to Birkenstocks, dey eyes bulging with disgust. And de women in de room start shoo-shooing, and putting dey hand in front dey mouth to stop dey surprise, and false teeth, too, from falling out" (56). Reactions of disgust and disdain displayed by Indian men and women to the non-conformist appearance and behaviour of Sandy and Lise are an indication of the hetero-patriarchal socialization of Indian men and women and their resilient resistance to difference. The story highlights the cold response received by the characters in their open lesbian identification: "Well, all cover get blown. If it was even remotely possible dat I wasn't noticeable before, now Janet and I were over-exposed. We could a easily suffer from hypothermia, specially since it suddenly get cold cold in dere" (57).

The insertion of lesbian space within a predominantly masculinist social structure demonstrates its fragile positioning, whereby hegemonic insularity acts as an effective barrier to sexual identity. The narrator's discomfort at being exposed in public reveals her hypocritical stance of wanting to affirm her sexual difference without suffering the consequences of social disapproval. Her stance is also reflective of the limited opportunities for affirmation offered to women in Indian society, where individual desires and needs are often subsumed under the dictates of communal interest. The question of lesbian connections remains rather tentative in the case of the Indo-Caribbean diaspora reflected in Mootoo's work because of socialized alienations imposed on women that inhibit the formation of cross-sexual solidarities. Colluding with preconceived fabrications of "normal" masculinity and femininity, the heterosexual female characters' response to the lesbian women demonstrates the consequences of centuries of socially machinated cultural brainwashing that has transformed women into patriarchal stooges. These women have maintained the establishment of a female patriarchy and its enforcement of varying discriminations on other women. The story explodes the myth of sisterhood against patriarchy in its conclusion: "We say goodbye, not soon enough, and as we were leaving I turn to acknowledge Giraffebai, but instead of any recognition of our buddiness against de fresh brothers, I get a face dat look like it was in de presence of a very foul smell" (57). While the heterosexual women in the story are capable of limited solidarities with lesbians, in the form of their collective resistance to sexual advances from men whom they identify as the primary oppressors in the victimization of women, they fail to recognize their own role as oppressors when they victimize "other" women who affirm their individuality through their sexual and political difference.

It would be misleading to assert that Indo-Caribbean women writers inscribe their female characters solely within the narrow parameters of a passive victimhood as an irreversible social condition. These writers are making concerted attempts to reclaim female sexual agency through a particular erotics of the body as a site of corporeal reclaiming and affirmation. In her conference paper "The Absent Voice: Unearthing the Female Epistemology of Cane", Ramabai Espinet locates the Indo-Caribbean female erotic within the female-centred tradition of matikor, practised by the foremothers despite their sexual and social privation. Espinet describes this ceremony:

The Maaticoore is the vehicle through which the sexual knowledge of the women in the bride's circle impart this knowledge to her. The Maaticoore occurs on the Friday night before a Hindu wedding, which is traditionally held on Sundays. The only males allowed at a distance are the drummers. Many of the drummers are also women. There is uninhibited dancing depicting varieties of sexual positions, and sometimes women are dressed like men and simulate the sex act through dance. At other times they twist their skirts or saris into phallic forms, run races with eggplants between their legs and so on. They also sing — bawdy songs for the ears of women only — a general celebration and explication of sexual practices. This is one instance of cultural resistance which is strong and vibrant still, and deserves to be celebrated and preserved.[35]

During the matikor ceremony, as described in chapter 2, the female body is released from the restrictions imposed by the male gaze and can therefore fully participate in the expression of its pleasure or *jouissance*. The body is liberated from socially fabricated chains through uninhibited dancing and sexual suggestiveness, demonstrated by the parodying of sex roles and sexual transvestism. In this way, the women can openly mock the "sanctity" of patriarchal power by reducing it to limp eggplants between their legs or twisted skirts and saris. The bawdy songs, as signifiers of sexual foreplay often denied to women, are an even more important text of sexual knowledge imparted to the new bride to dispel her "virgin" knowledge of female sexuality. The matikor is thus an intergenerational ceremony of sexual repossession by Indo-Caribbean women who establish a legacy of feminist cultural resistance to sexual subordination. However, it must be pointed out that, for the most part, these sexual reclaimings are situated within a heterosexual model of affirmation, as a confirmation of the cultural constraints and of the fear of social ostracism that still threaten Indo-Caribbean women writers, who are forced to confront Hindu sexual prudishness and sexual censorship in their writings on a regular basis.

Ramabai Espinet's "Erotic Fragments" are an attempt by the author to break out of the stranglehold of sexual censorship by positing a certain erotics of language that is uncompromising and unapologetic in its articulation.[36] Espinet's unabashed positing of the female erotic displaces the primacy of cultural modesty and other social inhibitions that have limited the expression of the body's erotic power in the form of sexual victimization and passivity elaborated in male discourses on female eroticism. These one-sided sexual fabulations as projections of male mythologies of the feminine have created a situation whereby, as Marjorie Agosin explains, "eroticism, love and sensuality have been masculine reserves where intellectuals, historians and sexologists write – and still write – about women's sexuality and eroticism, telling them how to think and feel and giving them recipes for making love".[37] These "recipes" have consisted of unimaginative prescriptions for lovemaking that have equated "normal" female sexuality with vaginal stimulation – that is, with masculine penetration leading to reproduction – and "sexual pathology" or "lesbianism" with clitoral excitation, according to Freud and other male theorists. Confining definitions of sexuality have trapped women within an either/or exclusivity, thereby limiting the body's potential for simultaneous and multiple *jouissance*. Espinet's fragment "Carambola" fractures the very ground of binarism by redefining female sexuality in terms of an endless, uncontained/uncontainable fusion that transcends the limits of sexual confinement: "Ba-a-a-ad, unrepressed sexuality. Or pleasure maybe. Not confined to closed, stale rooms, small space, hot air, stifled moans, week-old sheets. Another kind altogether: high windowless rooms, a breeze from the sea, a man's brown iron arm, a sea-breath, a laugh, a song. Not sometimes. Always. A fearless merging with another – without distance – without drawing fucking breath" (47). The fragment exposes the inadequacy of limiting definitions of sexuality that lead to a containment of expression. On the contrary, by advocating a certain boundlessness or expansiveness, the fragment suggests that eroticism is a holistic experience, a source of power and self-revelation denied to women by patriarchal culture. Associating the erotic with the unleashing of inner creative energy, Audre Lorde in her essay, "Uses of the Erotic: The Erotic as Power", links the erotic with "a resource within each of us that lies in a deeply female and spiritual plane, firmly rooted in the power of our unexpressed or unrecognized feeling".[38] The erotic, as the rearticulation of repressed knowledge, can be compared with women's primal memories, which are located within the parameters of a female ancestral world. Women have been excommunicated from this world by a rupturing of primeval bonds with other women through the hegemonic practice of female dispersal, in which the mother tongue has been silenced and women's attempts at physical and emotional recuperation have been thwarted. The repossession of ancestral knowledge mirrors the search for female uniqueness wherein the erotic, as the very language of cultural and sexual reclaiming, provides an intimate basis for self-exploration. Leading to a heightened awareness of the self, these explorations transcend patterns of "ordinariness" that anchor the body in deep-seated anxieties and insecurities.[39]

The narrator of "Safe Sex?" seeks to re-evaluate sexual predeterminations through the agency of personal choice. When she asks, "So what does fucking consist of really? Different things with different people" (46), she posits the necessity to establish a pluralistic model of sexual affirmation based on individual need and circumstance. She proposes counterdialogues that will challenge normative sexual discourses in which duplicitous bourgeois moralities have reserved sexual gratification for men. By embracing a certain *"mala palabra"* (language of dirty words), the narrator calls for an alternative linguistic refashioning that will create the space for the voicing of female desire. Luisa Valenzuela stresses the urgency to "unleash the menacing differences which upset the core of the phallogocentric, paternalistic discourse . . . [through a] transformation of that language consisting of 'dirty' words that are forbidden to us for centuries, and of the daily language that we should handle very carefully, with respect and fascination because in some way it doesn't belong to us".[40]

Espinet's "dirty words" are formulated in terms of women's expressed sexual desires and feelings and their self-assuredness as sexual beings. The narrator's sexual longings are not masked by the florid clichés of romantic love but are articulated openly in the form of raw desire for her loved one. In this fragment. "In and Out of the City Where I Live", the dynamics of sexual pleasure focus on the narrator's multiple and uncontrollable orgasms that move her to heights of ecstasy instead of highlighting the proverbial moans of male satisfaction. Moreover, her sexual energies are limitless and all-consuming, thereby negating stereotypical notions of female sexual passivity and easy gratification: "Our lovemaking is rock and sand and water, he sucks and bites my breasts until I am half-dead from delight and fear of what will happen next, such is love, such should be love forever. When he enters me the first day he is as large as trees and forests, and I shake so much he has to stop – it has been a long time. His largeness gives me rain and stars, the strength in his leg muscles, his waist, rivet me to a place I never want to come back from. . . . I reach for more, and more" (46). Associating lovemaking with the natural poetry of stars, sand, trees and forests, the narrator's sexual experiences demonstrate the "natural" need for sentiments of love and sexual equality in a relationship so that both partners can reach a stage of healthy climactic transcendence.

"Safe Sex?" reveals the narrator's sexual assertiveness when she has a one-night stand with a corporate executive. By initiating the sexual advances, she creates an imbalance in the sexual power play whereby the man is feminized into a position of weakness – "Him saying weakly, God how you've got my adrenalin going" (46) – whereas she remains detached and "ironical for no good reason" (46). Sexual experimentation furnishes the script for the narrator's sexual education, whereby she can affirm her sexual freedom in an anonymous setting, "a house in the country" (46), without worrying about the implications of a soiled reputation. Moreover, the lover's request to leave his back unscathed during their lovemaking provides the narrator with another opportunity to reverse a traditional power imbalance:

> Yet in bed adventurously crawling all over my body, fingers, arms, toes, tongue, his cock on my forehead, in my ear, my cunt tracing stars everywhere on his body from nose to the knobbly fronts of beautiful knees, he finds the time to whisper just before he makes me come for the first of a dozen times, it seems, don't, don't scratch my back.
>
> My nails are slightly long, defensively, I guess. Did I think of scratching his back before he issued this condition? I don't know. But he says this and my hands curl of their own accord. I don't do it right away. . . . But sometime in the night my nails move on their own and rake his back, the insides of his wonderful legs, down across his neck and chest. He leaves me unmarked. (47)

It could be stated that the lover's request for an untarnished back expresses his desire for a clean slate that testifies to the invisibility of male sexual promiscuity. A scratched back that leaves the imprint of a woman's presence devalues the man in further sexual interactions because he has already been marked by the female other. He has been identified and branded as a perpetrator of female sexual victimization in the sex market and elsewhere, thereby minimizing his scope to continue these violations in the future. In this instance, the narrator uses the erotic as a powerful tool to learn vital techniques of survival and protection in the face of future male aggression.

Ramabai Espinet's use of the erotic is multifaceted and energizing in its articulation. By highlighting the potential for female libidinal release through unrepressed sexuality, her politics of the erotic have also advocated the right for female autonomy through a creative un-censoring of the body and spirit to reach "an internal sense of satisfaction to which, once we have experienced it, we know we can aspire".[41]

—·—

In "Callaloo Woman", Lelawattee Manoo-Rahming compares the preparation of callaloo to the art of lovemaking.[42] At the same time, the poem calls for an insertion of female sexuality in the national imaginary through culinary associations and the widespread acceptance of callaloo as a national dish. "Callaloo Woman" is the very personification of femaleness, a fiery salt and pepper combination mixed with the creamy smoothness of coconut milk. Manoo-Rahming's recipe for the preparation of callaloo provides the script for the inclusion of female pleasure in national discourses on sexuality through an inclusive, participatory model of sex to be enjoyed by men and women. This recipe is well thought out and deliberate in its articulation. Based on a six-step instructional model, it offers a graphically and meticulously elaborated process of action that guarantees a successful result. Like the graphic illustrations of the *Kama Sutra*, which have served as an effective sex manual for the initiated and debutants alike, "Callaloo Woman" provides a sexual documentation that inscribes itself within the annals of Indo-Caribbean sexual history:

> You must have crab.
> How else to tongue out the flesh
> From between hardened membranes?
> How else to make it crabby? (68)

The poem begins with a suggestion of oral sex, through the explicit reference to the vagina-shaped structure of the crab. The association of crab juice with feminine bodily secretions indicates that these fluids provide the basic preparatory sauce for callaloo/sex through their crabbiness and strong aftertaste. The tonguing out of flesh evokes the sensual pleasure of sucking on tasty morsels of flesh, whose plump moistness guarantees the whetting of the appetite:

> Put your pickled pig tail
> To make it salt
> But add a little saltfish,
> The rankness does make saliva flow. (68)

The recommendation early in the recipe to combine "pickled pig tail" with "saltfish", whose "rankness does make saliva flow", hints at the initial stages of libidinal excitation when the body begins to lubricate itself in preparation for intercourse:

> Don't forget the ochroes.
> Plenty does make it slimy
> So it just slide around the palate
> And slip down nice in the throat. (68)

The reference to the phallically constructed okra indicates the reciprocity of oral pleasure whereby the okra's sliminess can be compared to the viscousness of semen after a pleasurable ejaculation:

> You need a pint of coconut milk:
> It must have a creaminess,
> A little rich smoothness,
> Sweet like breast milk. (68)

The sweetness of sex is likened to the virgin purity of breast milk, reminiscent of the primary oral contact with the mother through the ingestion of breast milk. Just as mother's milk provides vital sustenance for a baby's growth, so also healthy and safe sex nourishes the individual's sense of physical and spiritual well-being. The development of a well-balanced attitude towards sex can help to eliminate the perceived necessity of sexual aggression, as a form of sexual power play, in favour of mutually agreeable foreplay and affectionate petting. The poem further stresses the importance of gentle explorations of the body through the power of touch by running one's fingers through "the silky greenness of dasheen leaves, / curly and coarse" (68). The body's stimulation by the sense of touch is reminiscent of the gentle caresses administered by the mother's care as an assurance of her physical presence and attempts to communicate with her child. Similarly, tactile explorations of a lover's body provide an intimate sense of its physical geography that leads to first-hand knowledge of its pleasure points. Tactile re-memberings help the lovers to develop their private body language as a sign of secret communication. Intimate gestures function as unspoken words, furtive glances and other forms of seduction that enhance foreplay. At the same time, the poem calls for a certain spontaneity of expression to fire the flames of passion through the element of surprise like the "ripe goat pepper" whose maturity provides the right balance of spicy flavouring ("not too much heat") to titillate the senses "so they always come again for more callaloo" (68).

"Callaloo Woman" raises the practice of lovemaking to the level of an erotic art of seduction. By focusing our attention on foreplay, seduction and intimate communication between partners, the poem underscores the primacy of vaginal penetration as the only acceptable form of sex. Callaloo sex broadens the scope of physical pleasure by rescuing sex from its narrow definition as a performative act whose success is measured in quantitative terms (successful or unsuccessful procreation). By including a plurality of sexual experiences and sensations, sex becomes a philosophy of intimacy as well as an appetizingly communicative exchange between partners, thereby confirming Michelle Mohabeer's claim that "the spirit of the erotic lingers like ether in our everyday existence. . . . It is through our engagement with erotic rituals that we have the potential to transform and reinvest the material into the realm of fantasy, sexual play and the spiritual."[43] By transforming the materiality of sex into the spiritual and fantastical ritual of erotic seduction, "Callaloo Woman" offers women, in particular, renewed possibilities for sexual enhancement through the depoliticizing of patriarchal sex and the affirmation of deterritorialized/decolonized sexual pluralisms.

Indo-Caribbean women writers have the onerous task of claiming and sustaining decolonized sexual subjectivities through the rupturing of classically defined male and female sexuality. The stronghold of cultural propriety continues to impose its inhibiting presence on the articulation of female sexuality in the form of taboos, cultural silencing and a strong predilection on the part of traditional Hindu men and women for maintaining images of mythical womanhood. In the face of severe opposition from within their respective communities and from external forces that would prefer to see Indo-Caribbean women in a secondary position, these writers have nevertheless accepted the challenge of redefining sexual prerogatives for women through their denunciation of public and private violence against women, their articulation of woman-identified sexuality and their engagement with the erotics of sexual pleasure. Their sustained and collective effort will help to create a new sexual order for Indo-Caribbean women in the future.

Conclusion

It seems unrealistic to propose a conclusion for a body of work that is hesitantly, although positively, emerging from the darkness of oblivion and exclusion. Rather than making any sweeping or definitive cultural generalizations about the Indo-Caribbean female experience in Trinidad and Guyana, when there is still so much more research to be done in this field, *Diasporic (Dis)locations* has attempted to provide a preliminary framework of investigation for future analyses of Indo-Caribbean women's writing and cultural representation through the grid of *kala pani* hybridity. An important factor to consider in such future deliberations is the basic premise that Indo-Caribbean women have never presented themselves as fatalistic victims of their history, despite the hardships of indentureship, gender bias and accommodation to new lands. Narratives of female agency have, in fact, been grounded in culturally specific contexts that have immortalized the primary initiatives of the first indentured women to contest otherness and marginalization in environments that proved to be hostile to female empowerment. However, as the chapters in this book have shown, restrictions within the family by overbearing males and inhibitions that resulted from the specifics of plantation life provided these women with the necessary motivation to denounce patterns of racism and sexism in their communities. These women recreated more favourable alternatives for themselves through a renegotiation of history in their individual circumstances. Although these re-creations of intent were often achieved at a tremendous price, resulting in death or severe abuse, this did not stop the cycle of female regeneration that had already been set in motion for successive families of women. The literary granddaughters were thus able to concretize their grandmothers' rural activism in the canefields on sheets of paper by transforming the obdurate cane stalk into the mighty pen that would establish a legacy of scripted knowledge of Indo-Caribbean women's dynamic and complicated histories.

It is hoped that these histories will be read within their specific cultural, social and political contexts to avoid unnecessary essentialisms or blanket impositions of Western-formulated strategies of victimhood on models of female affirmation that do not conform to academically defined notions of feminist agency. The meeting of the rural woman with her more urbanized counterpart constitutes an important focal point of influence in Indo-Caribbean women's writing, which identifies the rural with ancestral memory in the country of origin and the lands of adoption. The inscription of rural Indian memory on the Caribbean landscape provides concrete and lasting evidence of the Indian indentured experience as an integral part of a larger Caribbean historical experience, sharing a common language of both disinheritance and self-determination with the Afro-Caribbean majority and other ethnic and mixed-race minorities.

Indo-Caribbean women writers highlight and take pride in the cultural distinctiveness of their Indian heritage while exposing the perniciousness of Hindu racial, class and gender prejudice. At the same time, they call for their own insertion in the general corpus of Caribbean literature as Caribbean women writers and as Caribbean citizens to avoid the traditional ghettoization of their experiences and influence. They demand the unlearning of conventionally defined paradigms of Caribbeanness, which have negated a more inclusive and reflective model of citizenship. Collaborative efforts between different constituencies of Caribbean men and women in the fields of literature, feminist studies, cultural studies and the social sciences, together with transnational feminist alliances, will provide the much-needed impetus to guarantee these literatures their rightful place within the canon of twenty-first-century English literature by destabilizing outmoded Eurocentric expectations of literariness, racial prejudice and the literary and cultural hegemony of English literature. As Felix Mnthali reminds us once again in his poem "The Stranglehold of English Literature", "English Literature was more than a cruel joke; / it was the heart of alien conquest."[1]

Mnthali's statement should be taken to heart as it shows us the nefarious impact of intellectual colonizing through alien systems of influence that created neatly ordered categories of "acceptable" and "unacceptable" literature. Manipulating colonized populations into assimilating these very same patterns of discrimination against each other, English bourgeois literariness maintained its uncontested power through this literary divide. Indo-Caribbean women writers have exposed the negative consequences of such a divide, which has robbed Caribbean literature of its literary and cultural wholeness by excluding their voices. In this way, the subaltern has fought back, creating additional spaces of affirmation through spatial fractures that have outlined these newly formulated channels of articulation. The breaking of new ground through the rupture of structural permanence will undoubtedly lead to energized dialogues that rethink Caribbeanness according to a more transnational perspective. Indo-Caribbean women writers have taken the initiative to introduce these revised discourses on the Caribbean by converting invisibility into literary pioneering, thereby valorizing a rich Indian heritage in which women have always functioned as daring pathfinders.

Notes

Introduction

1. Ramabai Espinet, ed., *Creation Fire: A CAFRA Anthology of Caribbean Women's Poetry* (Toronto: Sister Vision; Tunapuna, Trinidad and Tobago: CAFRA, 1990); Joel Benjamin, Ian McDonald, Lakshmi Kallicharan and Lloyd Searwar, eds., *They Came in Ships: An Anthology of Indo-Guyanese Prose and Poetry* (Leeds, UK: Peepal Tree; Georgetown, Guyana: Indian Commemoration Trust, 1998); Rosanne Kanhai, ed., *Matikor: The Politics of Identity for Indo-Caribbean Women* (St Augustine, Trinidad and Tobago: School of Continuing Studies, University of the West Indies, 1999).

2. See Carole Boyce Davies, *Black Women, Writing and Identity: Migrations of the Subject* (London: Routledge, 1994).

3. Nesha Haniff, "My Grandmother Worked in the Field: Honorable Mention: Stereotypes Regarding Indian Women in the Caribbean", in *Matikor*, ed. Kanhai, 22–23.

4. Ibid., 26.

5. Kanhai, introduction to *Matikor*, xiv.

6. "Ramabai Espinet Talks to Elaine Savory: A Sense of Constant Dialogue: Writing, Woman and Indo-Caribbean Culture", in *The Other Woman: Women of Colour in Contemporary Canadian Literature*, ed. Makeda Silvera (Toronto: Sister Vision, 1995), 106.

7. Rhoda Reddock, "Contestations over National Culture in Trinidad and Tobago: Considerations of Ethnicity, Class and Gender", in *Caribbean Portraits: Essays on Gender Ideologies and Identities*, ed. Christine Barrow (Kingston: Ian Randle, 1998), 417.

8. Rosanne Kanhai, "The Masala Stone Sings: Poetry, Performance and Film by Indo-Caribbean Women", in *Matikor*, ed. Kanhai, 209–37.

9. Jeremy Poynting, "East Indian Women in the Caribbean: Experience and Voice", in *India in the Caribbean*, ed. David Dabydeen and Brinsley Samaroo (London: Hansib, 1989), 244.

10. Boyce Davies, *Black Women, Writing and Identity*, 4.

11. Benedict Anderson, *Imagined Communities: Reflections on the Origin and Spread of Nationalism* (New York: Verso, 1983).

12. Gloria Anzaldua, *Borderlands/La Frontera: The New Mestiza* (San Francisco: Aunt Lute Books, 1987); Merle Hodge, *For the Life of Laetitia* (New York: Farrar, Straus and Giroux, 1993).

13. Chandra Mohanty, *Feminism without Borders: Decolonizing Theory, Practicing Solidarity* (Durham, NC: Duke University Press, 2003), 46.

14. Anzaldua, *Borderlands/La Frontera*, 79.

15. Kamala Kempadoo, "Negotiating Cultures: A 'Dogla' Perspective", in *Matikor*, ed. Kanhai, 109.

16. Ibid., 103.

17. "Interview with Ramabai Espinet", in *From Pillar to Post: The Indo-Caribbean Diaspora*, ed. Frank Birbalsingh (Toronto: TSAR, 1997), 166–67.

18. Boyce Davies, *Black Women, Writing and Identity*, 4.

19. Rhoda Reddock, "Women, Labour and Struggle in Twentieth-Century Trinidad and Tobago" (PhD dissertation, University of Amsterdam, 1984).

20. Rawwida Baksh-Sooden, "Personal Grapplings with Race/Ethnicity, Class and Gender in the Caribbean" (paper presented at the Fourth World Conference on Women, Huairou, China, September 1995).

21. Rosanne Kanhai, "From Matikor to a Caribbean Dougla Feminism" (lecture given at the Centre for Gender and Development Studies, University of the West Indies, St Augustine, Trinidad, February 10, 1999).

22. Shalini Puri, "Race, Rape and Representation: Indo-Caribbean Women and Cultural Nationalism", in *Matikor*, ed. Kanhai, 272.

23. See Kempadoo, "Negotiating Cultures", 104.

24. "Dougla Woman" and "The Ganges and the Nile, Part Two" can be found on Rudder's release for Carnival 1999, *International Chantuelle.*

25. Rhoda Reddock, "Jahaji Bhai: The Emergence of a Dougla Poetics in Contemporary Trinidad and Tobago", in *Identity, Ethnicity and Culture in the Caribbean*, ed. Ralph Premdas (St Augustine, Trinidad and Tobago: School of Continuing Studies, University of the West Indies, 1999), 188.

26. See Kempadoo, "Negotiating Cultures", 107–8.

27. Michelle Mohabeer, "Dialogue with a Film Director: Framing Caribbeanness through a Self-Reflexive Look at Art, Cultural Identity, Diaspora and the Creative Process in the Films *Coconut/Cane and Cutlass* and *Child-Play*" (paper presented at the Sixth International Conference of Caribbean Women Writers and Scholars, Grand-Anse, Grenada, May 1998).

28. "Interview with Janice Shinebourne", in *From Pillar to Post*, ed. Birbalsingh, 153.

29. Ibid., 156.

30. "Ramabai Espinet Talks to Elaine Savory", 102.

31. "Interview with Ramabai Espinet", 176–77.

32. "Ramabai Espinet Talks to Elaine Savory", 100.

33. Lakshmi Persaud, *Sastra* (Leeds, UK: Peepal Tree, 1993); Persaud, *Butterfly in the Wind* (Leeds, UK: Peepal Tree, 1990).

34. "Ramabai Espinet Talks to Elaine Savory", 112–13.

35. Frank Birbalsingh, review of *The East Indian Diaspora*, ed. Tilokie Depoo and Prem Misir, in *From Pillar to Post*, ed. Birbalsingh, 209.

36. Arun Mukherjee, "Canadian Nationalism, Canadian Literature and Racial Minority Women", in *The Other Woman*, ed. Silvera, 431–32.

37. Ramabai Espinet, "The Absent Voice: Unearthing the Female Epistemology of CANE" (paper presented at the conference Sugarcane and Society, Toronto, July 1989).

38. Kanhai, "The Masala Stone Sings", 41.

Chapter 1

1. Ramabai Espinet, "The Invisible Woman in West Indian Fiction", *World Literature Written in English* 29, no. 2 (1989): 116.

2. Ibid., 117.

3. Lakshmi Persaud, *Sastra* (Leeds, UK: Peepal Tree, 1993); text references are to this edition.

4. Anita Sheth and Amita Handa, "A Jewel in the Frown: Striking Accord between India/n Feminists", in *Returning the Gaze: Essays on Racism, Feminism and Politics*, ed. Himani Banerjee (Toronto: Sister Vision, 1993), 51.

5. Gayatri Spivak, "Can the Subaltern Speak?" in *Marxism and Interpretation of Culture*, ed. Cary Nelson and Lawrence Grossberg (Urbana: University of Illinois Press, 1988), 271–313.

6. Sheth and Handa, "A Jewel in the Frown", 85.

7. Ramashraya Sharma, "The Ramakatha from Valmiki to Tulsidasa with Special Reference to Women", in *Women and Culture*, ed. Kumkum Sangari and Sudesh Vaid (Bombay: SNDT, 1994), 25.

8. Uma Chakravarti, "Whatever Happened to the Vedic Dasi? Orientalism, Nationalism, and a Script for the Past", in *Recasting Women: Essays in Indian Colonial History*, ed. Kumkum Sangari and Sudesh Vaid (Piscataway, NJ: Rutgers University Press, 1990), 60.

9. This is a reference to Tulsidasa's *Geetavali*, in which Rama's brother Laxman draws a protective magic line around his sister-in-law Sita to protect her when she is by herself. Once she is fenced in by this line, she "cannot be penetrated by an outsider" (quoted in Uma Chakravarti, "The Development of the Sita Myth: A Case Study of Women in Myth and Literature", in *Women and Culture*, ed. Sangari and Vaid, 43).

10. Haimanti Banerjee, "Portrayal of Women in Popular Hindi Cinema", in *Women and Culture*, ed. Sangari and Vaid, 143.

11. Koylaschander Bose, "On the Education of Hindu Females" (1846), quoted in Kumkum Sangari and Sudesh Vaid, "Recasting Women: An Introduction", *Recasting Women*, i.

12. Keya Ganguly, "Migrant Identities: Personal Memories and the Construction of Selfhood", *Cultural Studies* 6 (1992): 28.

13. Ibid., 29.

14. Ramabai Espinet, "Representation and the Indo-Caribbean Woman in Trinidad and Tobago", in *Indo-Caribbean Resistance*, ed. Frank Birbalsingh (Toronto: TSAR, 1993), 43.

15. Susie Tharu, "Tracing Savitri's Pedigree: Victorian Racism and the Image of Women in Indo-Anglian Literature", in *Recasting Women*, ed. Sangari and Vaid, 263.

16. Kumkum Sangari and Sudesh Vaid, introduction to *Women and Culture*, 21.

17. Ganguly, "Migrant Identities", 32.

18. Quoted in Chakravarti, "Whatever Happened to the Vedic Dasi?", 75–76.

19. Elleke Boehmer, "Stories of Women and Mothers: Gender and Nationalism in the Early Fiction of Flora Nwapa", in *Motherlands: Black Women's Writing from Africa, the Caribbean and South Asia*, ed. Susheila Nasta (Piscataway, NJ: Rutgers University Press, 1992), 5.

20. "Interview with Ramabai Espinet", in *From Pillar to Post: The Indo-Caribbean Diaspora*, ed. Frank Birbalsingh (Toronto: TSAR, 1997), 162–79.

21. Ibid., 164–65.

22. Persaud's Sastra (*Sastra*) and Kamla (*Butterfly in the Wind*) are Hindu by ethnicity. Shinebourne's June (*The Last English Plantation*) is of mixed race, with a Chinese father (Cyrus) and a mother (June) who is of Hindu origin but who has adopted Christianity as a way of camouflaging her Hinduness.

23. V. S. Naipaul, *A House for Mr Biswas* (London: Fontana, 1961), 78. See also Jeremy Poynting, "You Want to Be a Coolie Woman? Gender and Ethnic Identity in Indo-Caribbean Women's Writing", in *Caribbean Women Writers*, ed. Selwyn Cudjoe (Wellesley, Mass.: Calaloux Publications, 1990), 98–105.

24. Jan Shinebourne, *The Last English Plantation* (Leeds, UK: Peepal Tree, 1988); text references are to this edition.

25. The idea of cooliehood will be developed in detail in the third part of the analysis.

26. Gauri Vishwanathan, *Masks of Conquest: Literary Study and British Rule in India* (New York: Columbia University Press, 1989).

27. Homi Bhabha, *The Location of Culture* (London: Routledge, 1994), 70.

28. Simon Gikandi, *Writing in Limbo: Modernism and Caribbean Literature* (Ithaca, NY: Cornell University Press, 1992), 10.

29. Ibid., 6.

30. Frantz Fanon, *The Wretched of the Earth*, trans. Constance Farrington (New York: Grove, 1963), 152; see also Fanon, *Black Skin, White Masks*, trans. Charles Lam Markmann (New York: Grove, 1967).

31. The term *mimic men* is borrowed from V. S. Naipaul, *The Mimic Men* (London: Penguin, 1967).

32. Albert Memmi, *The Colonizer and the Colonized* (New York: Orion, 1965).

33. Clem Seecharan, *India and the Shaping of the Indo-Guyanese Imagination 1890s–1920s* (Leeds, UK: Peepal Tree, 1993).

34. Dorothy Norman, ed., *Nehru: The First Sixty Years*, vol. 1 (London: Bodley Head, 1965), 353.

35. Tapan Raychaudhuri, *Europe Reconsidered: Perceptions of the West in Nineteenth Century Bengal* (New Delhi: Oxford University Press, 1988), 8.

36. Seecharan, *India and the Shaping of the Indo-Guyanese Imagination*, 17.

37. Max Mueller (1823–1900) was an eminent Sanskrit scholar who translated numerous works of Indian philosophy, religion, culture and literature.

38. Seecharan, *India and the Shaping of the Indo-Guyanese Imagination*, 11.

39. Khal Torabully, "Coolitude: Prémisses historiques d'une non-parole", *Notre Librairie* 128 (October–December 1996): 59–71.

40. Ibid., 64.

41. Rajkumari Singh, "I Am a Coolie", in *They Came in Ships: An Anthology of Indo-Guyanese Prose and Poetry*, ed. Joel Benjamin, Lakshmi Kallicharan, Ian McDonald, and Lloyd Searwar (Leeds, UK: Peepal Tree, 1998), 87.

42. Seecharan, *India and the Shaping of the Indo-Guyanese Imagination*, 10.

43. bell hooks, *Teaching to Transgress: Education as the Practice of Freedom* (New York: Routledge, 1994), 11.

44. Ibid., 7.

45. Gikandi, *Writing in Limbo*, 10.

Chapter 2

1. Bridget Brereton, "General Problems and Issues in Studying the History of Women", in *Gender in Caribbean Development: Papers Presented at the Inaugural Seminar of the University of the West Indies Women and Development Studies Project*, ed. Patricia Mohammed and Catherine Shepherd (St Augustine, Trinidad and Tobago: Women and Development Studies Project, University of the West Indies, 1988), 124.

2. Ibid., 124.

3. Rhoda Reddock, *Women, Labour and Politics in Trinidad and Tobago: A History* (London: Zed Books, 1994), 10.

4. The term *dougla poetics* has been credited to Shalini Puri, who positions this poetics "as a means for articulating potentially progressive cultural identities delegitimized by both the Afro-Creole dominant culture and the Indian mother culture. . . . [T]he figure of the dougla draws attention to the reality of interracial contact: it names a contact that already exists" ("Canonized Hybridities, Resistant Hybridities: Chutney Soca, Carnival, and the Politics of Nationalism", in *Caribbean Romances: The Politics of Regional Representation*, ed. Belinda Edmonson [Charlottesville: University Press of Virginia, 1999], 32). Dougla poetics is a strategy to elaborate new discourses on Caribbean literariness by providing the necessary language to enunciate hybridized in-betweenness through "the collision of classifications" (32) and the subversion of racialized binary alienations. See also Puri, "Race, Rape and Representation: Indo-Caribbean Women and Cultural Nationalism", *Cultural Critique* 36 (May 1997): 119–63.

5. Brereton, "General Problems and Issues", 134.

6. Gender negotiations undertaken by Indo-Caribbean women will be discussed later in the chapter.

7. Brereton, "General Problems and Issues", 134.

8. Reddock, *Women, Labour and Politics in Trinidad and Tobago*, 3.

9. Ibid.

10. Ibid., 5.

11. Ibid., 37.

12. Christine Barrow, "Introduction and Overview: Gender Ideologies", in *Caribbean Portraits: Essays on Gender Ideologies and Identities*, ed. Christine Barrow (Kingston: Ian Randle, 1998), xviii.

13. Ibid., xxii.

14. Rhoda Reddock, *Elma François: The NWCSA and the Worker's Struggle for Change in the Caribbean* (London: New Beacon, 1988), 4.

15. Ibid., 6.

16. Ibid., 14–15.

17. Ibid., 18.

18. Ibid., 53.

19. Kusha Haraksingh, "Structure, Process and Indian Culture in Trinidad", in *After the Crossing: Immigrants and Minorities in Caribbean Creole Society*, ed. Howard Johnson (London: Frank Cass, 1988), 114.

20. Ibid., 116.

21. Reddock, *Women, Labour and Politics in Trinidad and Tobago*, 30–31.

22. Ibid., 43.

23. Nesha Haniff, "My Grandmother Worked in the Field: Honorable Mention: Stereotypes Regarding East Indian Women in the Caribbean", in *Matikor: The Politics of Identity for Indo-Caribbean Women*, ed. Rosanne Kanhai (St Augustine, Trinidad and Tobago: School of Continuing Studies, University of the West Indies, 1999), 18–31.

24. Ibid., 28.

25. Ibid., 30.

26. Theresa Ann Rajack-Talley, "Burying the Myth: Indian Women in the Sugar Cane Industry in Trinidad", in *Matikor*, ed. Kanhai, 181–93.

27. Quoted ibid., 189.

28. Haniff, "My Grandmother Worked in the Field", 22.

29. Ibid.

30. Ibid., 26.

31. Rajack-Talley, "Burying the Myth", 191.

32. Haniff, "My Grandmother Worked in the Field", 20.

33. Ibid., 27.

34. Indrani Rampersad, "Becoming a Pandita", in *Matikor*, ed. Kanhai, 140.

35. Ibid., 142.

36. Ibid., 142–43.

37. Patricia Stephens, *The Spiritual Baptist Faith* (Trenton, NJ: Red Sea Press, 1999), 3.

38. Carole Boyce Davies, *Black Women, Writing and Identity: Migrations of the Subject* (London: Routledge, 1994), 34.

39. Ibid., 36.

40. Ibid., 4.

41. Merle Collins, "Writing Fiction, Writing Reality", in *Caribbean Women Writers: Fiction in English*, ed. Mary Condé and Thorunn Lonsdale (New York: St Martin's, 1999), 30.

42. Ibid., 25.

43. Boyce Davies, *Black Women, Writing and Identity*, 36.

44. Joan Anim-Addo, "Audacity and Outcome: Writing African-Caribbean Womanhood", in *Framing the Word: Gender and Genre in Caribbean Women's Writing*, ed. Joan Anim-Addo (London: Whiting and Birch, 1996), 214.

45. Ibid.

46. Ibid., 215.

47. Ramabai Espinet, ed., *Creation Fire: A CAFRA Anthology of Caribbean Women's Poetry* (Toronto: Sister Vision; Tunapuna, Trinidad and Tobago: CAFRA, 1990); Makeda Silvera, ed., *The Other Woman: Women of Colour in Contemporary Canadian Literature*, ed. Makeda Silvera (Toronto: Sister Vision, 1995).

48. Merle Hodge, *For the Life of Laetitia* (New York: Farrar, Straus and Giroux, 1993), 6; text references are to this edition.

49. Ameena Gafoor, "The Depiction of Indo-Caribbean Female Experience by the Regional Woman Writer: Jan Shinebourne's *The Last English Plantation*", in *The Woman, the Writer and Caribbean Society: Critical Analyses of the Writings of Caribbean Women: Proceedings of the Second International Conference*, ed. Helen Pyne-Timothy (Los Angeles: UCLA Center for African-American Studies, 1998), 134–35.

50. Grant Cornwall and Eve Stoddard, "Cosmopolitan or Mongrel? Reading Créolité and Hybridity via 'Douglarization' in Trinidad", in *Identity, Ethnicity and Culture in the Caribbean*, ed. Ralph Premdas (St Augustine, Trinidad and Tobago: School of Continuing Studies, University of the West Indies, 1999), 213.

51. Ralph Premdas, introduction to *Identity, Ethnicity and Culture in the Caribbean*, ed. Premdas, 3.

52. *Tomorrow Is Another Day* is a scathing indictment of the postcolonial disorder instigated by a repressive, authoritarian state that imports and sustains colonial patterns of exploitation, coercion and divisive regimentation in its daily functioning. While making overt references to the dictatorial absolutism of Forbes Burnham's People's National Congress (PNC) regime, which decimated Guyana and its people from 1964 to 1985, the novel also makes a broader statement about the alienating impact of neocolonialism and its ensuing political dis-ease. The PNC's dubious ascent to power in 1968, after Guyanese independence in 1966, was a confirmation of the communally motivated and self-interested manipulations of the state and its intentions to maintain a race- and class-based autocracy through a violent programme of ethnic cleansing. Ethnic rivalries between Burnham's Afro-Guyanese PNC and Cheddi Jagan's Indian-dominated People's Progressive Party (PPP) resulted in the unilateral primacy of the PNC and the subsequent inauguration of a reign of terror that created an atmosphere of social and political anomie.

53. Narmala Shewcharan, *Tomorrow Is Another Day* (Leeds, UK: Peepal Tree, 1994), 43; text references are to this edition.

54. Filomena Steady, *The Black Woman Culturally* (Cambridge, Mass.: Schenkman, 1982), 31.

55. Premdas, introduction, 1–2.

56. Haniff, "My Grandmother Worked in the Field", 28.

57. Rosanne Kanhai-Brunton, "The Guyana Meeting", *CAFRA News* 7, no. 4 (1993), 1.

58. Rawwida Baksh-Sooden, "Personal Grapplings with Race/Ethnicity, Class and Gender in the Caribbean" (paper presented at the CAFRA panel on Caribbean Feminism: Past, Present and Future, NGO Forum, Fourth World Conference on Women, Huairou, China, September 1995).

59. Ramabai Espinet, "Barred: Trinidad 1987", in *Green Cane and Juicy Flotsam*, ed. Carmen Esteves and Lizabeth Paravisini-Gebert (New Brunswick, NJ: Rutgers University Press, 1991), 83.

60. Kanhai, introduction to *Matikor*, ed. Kanhai, xi–xii. See also Ramabai Espinet, "The Absent Voice: Unearthing the Female Epistemology of CANE" (paper presented at the conference Sugarcane and Society, Toronto, July 1989).

61. Kanhai, introduction, xiv.

62. Ibid.

63. Rhoda Reddock, "Contestations over National Culture in Trinidad and Tobago: Considerations of Ethnicity, Class and Gender", in *Caribbean Portraits*, ed. Barrow, 433.

64. Rawwida Baksh-Sooden, "Power, Gender and Chutney", in *Matikor*, ed. Kanhai, 196.

65. Ibid., 197–98.

66. Rosanne Kanhai, "The Masala Stone Sings: Poetry, Performance and Film by Indo-Caribbean Women", in *Matikor*, ed. Kanhai, 221.

67. Rajandaye Ramkissoon-Chen, *Ancestry* (London: Hansib Caribbean, 1997), 28–29.

68. Kanhai, "The Masala Stone Sings", 222–23.

69. Cecilia Babb, "Empowering Grass Roots Women", in *CAFRA News* 5, no. 1 (1991): 9; quoted in Rawwida Baksh-Sooden, "Issues of Difference in Contemporary Caribbean Feminism", *Feminist Review* 59 (Summer 1998): 81.

70. Sandra Chouthi, "Feminism in Need of a Stronger Voice", *Trinidad Express*, April 27, 2000, http://www.trinidadexpress.com

71. Ibid.

72. Brenda Gopeesingh, quoted ibid.

73. Virginia Harris and Trinity Ordona, "Developing Unity among Women of Color: Crossing the Barriers of Internalized Racism and Cross-Racial Hostility", in *Making Face, Making Soul: Creative and Critical Perspectives by Women of Color*, ed. Gloria Anzaldua (San Francisco: Aunt Lute Books, 1990), 304.

74. Andaiye, "The Red Thread Story: Resisting the Narrow Interests of a Broader Political Struggle", in *Spitting in the Wind: Lessons in Empowerment from the Caribbean*, ed. Suzanne Francis Brown (Kingston: Ian Randle, 2000), 62.

75. Ibid., 75.

76. Ibid.

77. Ibid., 78.

78. Ibid., 83.

79. Ibid.

80. Ibid.

Chapter 3

1. Christine Mackie, *Life and Food in the Caribbean* (New York: New Amsterdam Books, 1991), 152.

2. Ibid., 154.

3. See Uma Narayan, "Eating Cultures: Incorporation, Identity and Indian Food", *Social Identities* 1 (1995): 63–82.

4. Lakshmi Persaud, *Sastra* (Leeds, UK: Peepal Tree, 1993), 59; text references are to this edition.

5. Lakshmi Persaud, *Butterfly in the Wind* (Leeds, UK: Peepal Tree, 1990), 86; text references are to this edition.

6. Anne Goldman, "I Yam What I Yam: Cooking, Culture and Colonialism", in *De/Colonizing the Subject: The Politics of Gender in Women and Autobiography*, ed. Sidonie Smith and Julia Watson (Minneapolis: University of Minnesota Press, 1992), 191. This is an idea shared in Indo-Caribbean and Afro-Caribbean women's fiction.

7. Ibid., 172.

8. Paule Marshall, "The Making of a Writer: From the Poets in the Kitchen", in *Reena and Other Stories* (New York: Feminist Press, 1983), 7.

9. Ibid., 6.

10. Ibid., 7–8.

11. This term is borrowed from Chitra Banerjee Divakaruni's novel *The Mistress of Spices* (New York: Anchor, 1997).

12. Linda Brown and Kay Mussell, introduction to *Ethnic and Regional Foodways in the United States: The Performance of Group Identity*, ed. Linda Brown and Kay Mussell (Knoxville: University of Tennessee Press, 1984), 12.

13. Claude Lévi-Strauss, "The Culinary Triangle", *Partisan Review* 33 (1996): 595.

14. Eliot Singer, "Conversion through Foodways Enculturation: The Meaning of Eating in an American Hindu Sect", in *Ethnic and Regional Foodways in the United States*, ed. Brown and Mussell, 210.

15. Narayan, "Eating Cultures", 76.

16. Margot Badran and Miriam Cooke, introduction to *Opening the Gates: A Century of Arab Feminist Writing*, ed. Margot Badran and Miriam Cooke (Bloomington: Indiana University Press, 1991), xv.

17. Ibid., xiv.

18. Patricia Mohammed, "The Creolization of Indian Women in Trinidad", in *Trinidad and Tobago: The Independence Experience 1962–1982*, ed. Selwyn Ryan (St Augustine, Trinidad and Tobago: Institute of Social and Economic Research, University of the West Indies, 1988), 381.

19. Paula Morgan, "East/West/Indian/Woman/Other: At the Crossroads of Gender and Ethnicity" (paper presented at the Sixteenth Annual Conference on West Indian Literature, University of Miami, April 1997).

20. Brown and Mussell, introduction, 5.

21. See Stephen Mennell, Anne Murcott and Anneke Otterloo, eds., *The Sociology of Food: Eating, Diet and Culture* (London: Sage, 1992).

22. Aisha Khan, "Juthaa in Trinidad: Food, Pollution, and Hierarchy in a Caribbean Diaspora Community", *American Ethnologist* 21 (1994): 249.

23. Ibid., 246.

24. Ibid., 262.

25. "Ramabai Espinet Talks to Elaine Savory: A Sense of Constant Dialogue: Writing, Woman and Indo-Caribbean Culture", in *The Other Woman: Women of Colour in Contemporary Canadian Literature*, ed. Makeda Silvera (Toronto: Sister Vision, 1995), 110.

26. Edward Brathwaite, *The Development of Creole Society in Jamaica 1770–1820* (Oxford: Clarendon, 1971), 298.

27. Simon Gikandi, *Writing in Limbo: Modernism and Caribbean Literature* (Ithaca, NY: Cornell University Press, 1992).

28. Samuel Selvon, "Three into One Can't Go: East Indian, Trinidadian, West Indian", in *India in the Caribbean*, ed. David Dabydeen and Brinsley Samaroo (London: Hansib, 1987), 18.

29. Mohammed, "The Creolization of Indian Women in Trinidad", 381–413; Rhoda Reddock, "Contestations over National Culture in Trinidad and Tobago: Considerations of Ethnicity, Class and Gender", in *Caribbean Portraits: Essays on Gender Ideologies and Identities*, ed. Christine Barrow (Kingston: Ian Randle, 1998), 414–35.

30. Mohammed, "The Creolization of Indian Women in Trinidad", 31.

31. Yannick Lahens, afterword to *Caribbean Creolization: Reflections on the Cultural Dynamics of Language, Literature and Identity*, ed. Kathleen M. Balutansky and Marie-Agnès Sourieau (Gainesville: University Press of Florida; Kingston: University Press of the West Indies, 1998), 162.

32. Wilson Harris, *The Womb of Space: The Cross-Cultural Imagination* (Westport, Conn.: Greenwood, 1983).

33. Ramabai Espinet, "Indian Cuisine", *Massachusetts Review* (Autumn–Winter 1994) 563; text references are to this edition.

34. Mikhail Bakhtin, *The Dialogic Imagination: Four Essays*, trans. Caryl Emerson and Michael Holquist (Austin: University of Texas Press, 1981), 304. See also Robert Young, *Colonial Desire: Hybridity in Theory, Culture and Race* (London: Routledge, 1995).

35. Ibid, 304–5.

36. Homi Bhabha, *The Location of Culture* (London: Routledge, 1994), 115.

37. Veronica Gregg, "The Caribbean as a Certain Kind of Woman" (typescript, n.d.). Gregg's article has been published as " 'You Know Bout Coo-Coo? Where Yuh Know Bout Coo-Coo?' Language and Representation, Creolisation and Confusion in Ramabai Espinet's 'Indian Cuisine' ", in *Questioning Creole*, ed. Verene Shepherd and Glen Richards (Kingston: Ian Randle, 2002), 148–64. Quotations here are taken from the unpublished typescript.

38. Reddock, "Contestations over National Culture in Trinidad and Tobago", 418.

39. Mohammed, "The Creolization of Indian Women in Trinidad", 392.

40. Ibid., 394.

41. Kelvin Singh, "East Indians and the Larger Society", in *Calcutta to Caroni: The East Indians of Trinidad*, ed. John La Guerre (London: Longman, 1974), 60.

42. Quoted in Stefano Harney, *Nationalism and Identity: Culture and the Imagination in a Caribbean Diaspora* (London: Zed Books, 1996), 1.

43. C. L. R. James, *The Artist in the Caribbean* (Mona, Jamaica: Open Lecture Series, University of the West Indies, 1965), 6.

44. Gregg, "The Caribbean as a Certain Kind of Woman", 15.

45. Ibid., 15.

Chapter 4

1. See Partha Chatterjee, *The Nation and Its Fragments: Colonial and Postcolonial Histories* (Princeton, NJ: Princeton University Press, 1993), for a detailed analysis of nationalist constructions of space and their repercussions on female subjectivity. See also Inderpal Grewal, *Home and Harem: Nation, Gender, Empire, and the Cultures of Travel* (Durham, NC: Duke Unviersity Press, 1996).

2. Meena Alexander, *Fault Lines: A Memoir* (New York: Feminist Press, 1993), 202.

3. Homi Bhabha, "The World and the Home", *Social Text* 10 (1992): 141.

4. Homi Bhabha, *The Location of Culture* (London: Routledge, 1994), 13. See also Anindyo Roy's article "Postcoloniality and the Politics of Identity in the Diaspora: Figuring 'Home', Locating Histories", in *Postcolonial Discourse and Changing Cultural Contexts*, ed. Gita Rajan and Radhika Mohanram (Westport, Conn.: Greenwood, 1995), 101–15; and R. Radhakrishnan, *Diasporic Mediations: Between Home and Location* (Minneapolis: University of Minnesota Press, 1996).

5. Patricia Mohammed, "Towards Indigenous Feminist Theorizing in the Caribbean", *Feminist Review* 59 (Summer 1998): 9, 12.

6. R. T. Smith, "Kinship and Class in the West Indies" (1988), quoted in Lydia Pulsipher, "Changing Roles in the Life Cycles of Women in Traditional West

Indian Households", in *Women and Change in the Caribbean*, ed. Janet Momsen (Bloomington: Indiana University Press, 1993), 138.

7.	Bhabha, *The Location of Culture*, 17.

8.	Trinh T. Minh-ha, *Woman, Native, Other: Writing Postcoloniality and Feminism* (Bloomington: Indiana University Press, 1989), 121.

9.	Lakshmi Holmström, ed., *The Inner Courtyard: Stories by Indian Women* (London: Virago, 1990), ix.

10.	Kenneth Parmasad, *Salt and Roti: Indian Folk Tales of the Caribbean: A First Collection* (Charlieville, Trinidad and Tobago: Sankh Productions, 1984).

11.	Chandra Mohanty and Satya Mohanty, introduction to *The Slate of Life: Contemporary Short Stories by Indian Women Writers*, ed. Kali for Women (New York: Feminist Press, 1994), 3.

12.	This term was coined by Beverly Stoeltje of University of Texas and quoted by Gay Wilentz in her introduction to *Binding Cultures: Black Women Writers in Africa and the Diaspora* (Bloomington: Indiana University Press, 1992), xii.

13.	Ramabai Espinet, "Singing *Ramayana:* The Text of Sita's Fidelity" (paper presented at the Sixth International Conference of Caribbean Women Writers and Scholars, Grenada, May 1998).

14.	Wilson Harris, *Tradition, the Writer and Society: Critical Essays* (London: New Beacon, 1973), 64.

15.	Raphaël Confiant and Ernest Pépin, "The Stakes of Créolité", in *Caribbean Creolization: Reflections on the Cultural Dynamics of Language, Literature and Identity*, ed. Kathleen M. Balutansky and Marie-Agnès Sourieau (Gainesville: University Press of Florida; Kingston: University of the West Indies Press, 1998), 98.

16.	Evelyn O'Callaghan, *Woman Version: Theoretical Approaches to West Indian Fiction by Women* (New York: St Martin's, 1993).

17.	Carolyn Cooper, "Something Ancestral Recaptured: Spirit Possession as Trope in Selected Feminist Fictions of the African Diaspora", in *Motherlands: Black Women's Writing from Africa, the Caribbean and South Asia*, ed. Susheila Nasta (London: Women's Press, 1991), 65.

18.	Quoted in Jeremy Poynting, "East Indian Women in the Caribbean: Experience and Voice", in *India in the Caribbean*, ed. David Dabydeen and Brinsley Samaroo (London: Hansib, 1987), 251.

19.	Alice Walker, *In Search of Our Mothers' Gardens* (New York: Harcourt Brace Jovanovich, 1983), xi–xii.

20.	See Stanlie James, "Mothering: A Possible Black Feminist Link to Social Transformation", in *Theorizing Black Feminisms*, ed. Stanlie James and Abena Busia (New York: Routledge, 1993), 144–54.

21.	Valerie Lee, *Granny Midwives and Black Women Writers: Double-Dutched Readings* (New York: Routledge, 1996).

22. Ibid., 14.

23. Ramabai Espinet, "The Absent Voice: Unearthing the Female Epistemology of CANE" (paper presented at the conference Sugarcane and Society, University of Toronto, July 1989).

24. Narmala Shewcharan, *Tomorrow Is Another Day* (Leeds, UK: Peepal Tree, 1994), 23; text references are to this edition.

25. Jan Shinebourne, *The Last English Plantation* (Leeds, UK: Peepal Tree, 1988), 127; text references are to this edition.

26. Khal Torabully, "Coolitude: Prémisses historiques d'une non-parole", *Notre Librairie* 128 (October–December 1996): 59–71.

27. Mary Chamberlain, "Gender and Memory: Oral History and Women's History", in *Engendering History: Caribbean Women in Historical Perspective*, ed. Verene Shepherd, Bridget Brereton, and Barbara Bailey (New York: St Martin's, 1995), 108–9.

28. Simone Schwarz-Bart, *The Bridge of Beyond*, trans. Barbara Bray (New York: Atheneum, 1974).

29. Houston Baker, *Workings of the Spirit: The Poetics of Afro-American Women's Writing* (Chicago: University of Chicago Press, 1991), 77.

30. Ibid., 44.

31. Derek Walcott, "What the Twilight Said: An Overture", in *Dream on Monkey Mountain and Other Plays* (New York: Farrar, Straus and Giroux, 1970), 17.

32. Helen Pyne-Timothy, "Language as Subversion in Postcolonial Literature: The Case of Two Caribbean Women Writers", *Macomère* 1 (1998): 110.

33. Ibid.

34. *Bacchcha* = child, *madarsa* = school, *aray bapray* = "Oh my God", *bap* = father, *bahin* = sister, *chitthi* = letter.

35. Pyne-Timothy, "Language as Subversion in Postcolonial Literature", 113.

36. Lakshmi Persaud, *Butterfly in the Wind* (Leeds, UK: Peepal Tree, 1990), 31; text references are to this edition.

Chapter 5

1. Quoted in Rob Nixon, "London Calling: V. S. Naipaul and the License of Exile", *South Atlantic Quarterly* 87 (Winter 1988): 9.

2. V. S. Naipaul, *Finding the Center: Two Narratives* (New York: Random House 1986), 46.

3. V. S. Naipaul, *The Enigma of Arrival* (New York: Random House, 1987), 157.

4. Huma Ibrahim, *Bessie Head: Subversive Identities in Exile* (Charlottesville: University Press of Virginia, 1996), 2.

5.   Edward Saïd, "Reflections on Exile", in *Out There: Marginalization and Contemporary Cultures*, ed. Russell Ferguson, Martha Gever, Trinh T. Minh-ha and Cornel West (Cambridge, Mass.: MIT Press, 1990), 357.

6.   Ibid., 359.

7.   Edward Saïd, *The World, the Text and the Critic* (London: Faber, 1984), 7.

8.   Myriam Chancy, *Searching for Safe Spaces: Afro-Caribbean Women Writers in Exile* (Philadelphia: Temple University Press, 1997).

9.   Cited in Rhonda Cobham, "Revisioning Our Kumblas: Transformation of Feminist and Nationalist Agendas in Three Caribbean Women's Texts", *Callaloo* 16, no. 1 (1993): 44–64.

10. Ibid., 45.

11. Quoted in Marie-Denise Shelton, "Condé: The Politics of Gender and Identity", *World Literature Today* 67, no. 4 (1993): 718–22.

12. Edouard Glissant, *Caribbean Discourse: Selected Essays*, trans. J. Michael Dash (Charlottesville: University Press of Virginia, 1989), 122–23.

13. Françoise Lionnet, "Inscriptions of Exile: The Body's Knowledge and the Myth of Authenticity", trans. Joseph Heath, *Callaloo* 15, no. 1 (1992): 30–40.

14. Mahadai Das, *Bones* (Leeds, UK: Peepal Tree, 1988), 12; text references are to this edition.

15. Elaine Scarry, *The Body in Pain: The Making and Unmaking of the World* (New York: Oxford University Press, 1985), 19.

16. Lionnet, "Inscriptions of Exile", 34.

17. Ernest Pépin, "La femme antillaise et son corps", *Présence Africaine* 14, no. 1 (1987): 182, in Lionnet, "Inscriptions of Exile", 34.

18. Hortense Spillers, "Mama's Baby, Papa's Maybe: An American Grammar Book", *Diacritics* 17 (Summer 1987): 67.

19. Edward Saïd, *Orientalism* (London: Routledge and Kegan Paul, 1978).

20. John Berger, *Ways of Seeing* (Harmondsworth, UK: Penguin, 1972), 10.

21. Lionnet, "Inscriptions of Exile", 35.

22. Phyllis Chesler, *Women and Madness* (New York: Doubleday, 1972), 15.

23. Ibid., 31.

24. Lelawattee Manoo-Rahming, *Curry Flavour* (Leeds, UK: Peepal Tree, 2000), 19; text references are to this edition.

25. Chesler, *Women and Madness*, 31.

26. See Mahadai Das, "They Came in Ships", in *India in the Caribbean*, ed. David Dabydeen and Brinsley Samaroo (London: Hansib, 1989), 288.

27. Carmen Esteves and Lizabeth Paravisini-Gebert, introduction to *Green Cane and Juicy Flotsam*, ed. Carmen Esteves and Lizabeth Paravisini-Gebert (New Brunswick, NJ: Rutgers University Press, 1991), xv.

28. Ramabai Espinet, "Barred: Trinidad 1987", in *Green Cane and Juicy Flotsam*, ed. Esteves and Paravisini-Gebert, 83; text references are to this edition.

29. In her seminal essay "Can the Subaltern Speak?", postcolonial critic Gayatri Spivak argues that the subaltern status engenders a loss of subjectivity and the consequent inability to position oneself as a speaking subject. See Spivak, "Can the Subaltern Speak?" in *Marxism and Interpretation of Culture*, ed. Cary Nelson and Lawrence Grossberg (Urbana: University of Illinois Press, 1998), 271–313.

30. Quoted in Soheila Ghaussy, "A Stepmother Tongue: Feminine Writing in Assia Dejbar's *Fantasia: An Algerian Cavalcade*", *World Literature Today* 68 (1994): 458.

31. Ibid.

32. V. S. Naipaul, *The Overcrowded Barracoon* (New York: Vintage, 1983), 254; Renu Juneja, *Caribbean Transactions: West Indian Culture in Literature* (London: Macmillan, 1996), 7.

33. J. Michael Dash, introduction to Glissant, *Caribbean Discourse*, xxxii.

34. Michelle Cliff, "Caliban's Daughter: The Tempest and the Teapot", *Frontiers* 12, no. 2 (1991): 40.

35. Glissant, *Caribbean Discourse*, 240.

36. Ralph Premdas, "Ethnic Identity in the Caribbean: Decentring a Myth" (keynote address to the Association for the Study of Ethnicity and Nationalism, London School of Economics and Political Science, March 1995).

37. Simon Gikandi, *Writing in Limbo: Modernism and Caribbean Literature* (Ithaca, NY: Cornell University Press, 1992), 57.

38. See Salman Rushdie, *Imaginary Homelands* (Harmondsworth, UK: Penguin, 1992); see also Jan Carew, "The Caribbean Writer and Exile", in *Fulcrums of Change: Origins of Racism in the Americas and Other Essays* (Trenton, NJ: Africa World Press, 1988), 91.

39. Betty Wilson, "History and Memory in *Un Plat de porc aux bananes vertes* and *Pluie et vent sur Télumée Miracle*", *Callaloo* 15, no. 1 (1992): 185.

40. Rajandaye Ramkissoon-Chen, *Ancestry* (London: Hansib, 1997), 10; text references are to this edition.

41. Chancy, *Searching for Safe Spaces*, 210.

42. Ibid., 209–10.

43. Ibrahim, *Bessie Head*, 21.

44. Edward Saïd, *Representations of the Intellectual* (New York: Vintage, 1996), 49.

45. Juneja, *Caribbean Transactions*, 132.

46. Glissant, *Caribbean Discourse*, 153–54.

47. Simon Gikandi, "The Politics and Poetics of National Formation: Recent African Writing" (paper presented at the annual conference of the Association

for Commonwealth Literature and Language Studies, Canterbury, UK, August 1989).

48. Trinh T. Minh-ha, *When the Moon Waxes Red* (New York: Routledge, 1991), 135–36.

49. Juneja, *Caribbean Transactions*, 162.

50. Lionnet, "Inscriptions of Exile", 30–31.

51. Trinh Minh-ha, *Woman, Native, Other: Writing Postcoloniality and Feminism* (Bloomington: Indiana University Press, 1989), 36.

52. Ibid., 38.

53. Minh-ha, *When the Moon Waxes Red*, 144.

54. Glissant, *Caribbean Discourse*, 11.

55. Ramabai Espinet, *Nuclear Seasons* (Toronto: Sister Vision, 1991), 27; text references are to this edition.

56. Hélène Cixous, "Sorties", in *La Jeune Née* (Paris: UGE, 1975), 172.

57. Minh-ha, *When the Moon Waxes Red*, 141.

58. Dennis Bassier, "Kali Mai Worship in Guyana: A Quest for a New Identity", in *Indians in the Caribbean*, ed. Bahadur Singh (New Delhi: Sterling, 1987), 269.

59. David Kinsley, *The Goddesses' Mirror* (Albany: State University of New York Press, 1987), 4.

Chapter 6

1. Evelyn O'Callaghan, " 'Compulsory Heterosexuality' and Textual/Sexual Alternatives in Selected Texts by West Indian Women Writers", *Caribbean Portraits: Essays on Gender Ideologies and Identities*, ed. Christine Barrow (Kingston: Ian Randle, 1998), 297.

2. V. S. Naipaul, *The Mimic Men* (London: Penguin, 1967), 28.

3. Kavita Sharma, "Ginu Kamani's *Junglee Girl*", *India Star: A Literary Art Magazine* (1997): 1–9.

4. Patricia Mohammed, "The Creolization of Indian Women in Trinidad", in *Trinidad and Tobago: The Independence Experience 1962–1982*, ed. Selwyn Ryan (St Augustine, Trinidad and Tobago: Institute of Social and Economic Research, University of the West Indies, 1988), 381–98.

5. Ibid., 396.

6. Bridget Brereton, *Race Relations in Colonial Trinidad 1870–1900* (Cambridge: Cambridge University Press, 1979), 182–83.

7. Mohammed, "The Creolization of Indian Women in Trinidad", 398.

8. Ibid., 395.

9. Paula Duncker, *Sisters and Strangers: An Introduction to Contemporary Feminist Fiction* (Oxford: Blackwell, 1992), 132.

10. Kim Johnson, "Considerations on Indian Sexuality" (paper presented at the Third Conference on East Indians, St Augustine, Trinidad, August–September 1984).

11. Mohammed, "The Creolization of Indian Women in Trinidad", 397.

12. "Interview with Ramabai Espinet", in *From Pillar to Post: The Indo-Caribbean Diaspora*, ed. Frank Birbalsingh (Toronto: TSAR, 1997), 175–76.

13. Rhoda Reddock, "Indian Women and Indentureship in Trinidad and Tobago: 1845–1917", *Economic and Political Weekly* 20 (1985): 80, 84.

14. For more details, consult M. Jacqui Alexander, "Redrafting Morality: The Postcolonial State and the Sexual Offences Bills of Trinidad and Tobago", in *Third World Women and the Politics of Feminism*, ed. Chandra Talpade Mohanty, Ann Russo, and Lourdes Torres (Bloomington: Indiana University Press, 1991), 133–52.

15. Mohammed, "The Creolization of Indian Women in Trinidad", 409.

16. "Interview with Ramabai Espinet", in *From Pillar to Post: The Indo-Caribbean Diaspora*, ed. Frank Birbalsingh (Toronto: TSAR, 1997), 174.

17. Ramabai Espinet, "The Absent Voice: Unearthing the Female Epistemology of CANE" (paper presented at the conference Sugarcane and Society, University of Toronto, July 1989).

18. Shani Mootoo, *Cereus Blooms at Night* (New York: Grove, 1996), 8; text references are to this edition.

19. Monique Wittig, "The Straight Mind", *Feminist Issues* 1, no. 1 (Summer 1980): 103–10.

20. Alexander, "Redrafting Morality", 140.

21. Ibid., 148.

22. Brereton, *Race Relations in Colonial Trinidad*, 183.

23. Adrienne Rich, "Compulsory Heterosexuality and Lesbian Existence", in *The Lesbian and Gay Studies Reader*, ed. Henry Abelove, Michèle Aina Barale and David M. Halperin (New York: Routledge, 1993), 227.

24. Kathleen Barry, *Female Sexual Slavery* (Englewood Cliffs, NJ: Prentice-Hall, 1979), 100.

25. Audre Lorde, *Sister Outsider* (Trumansburg, NY: The Crossing Press, 1984), 44.

26. Shoshana Felman, "Women and Madness: The Critical Phallacy", *Diacritics* 5 (1975): 7.

27. Wittig, "The Straight Mind", 105.

28. Shani Mootoo, *Out on Main Street and Other Stories* (Vancouver: Press Gang, 1993), 11; text references are to this edition.

29. Kavita Sharma, "Ginu Kamani's *Junglee Girl*", 1.

30. Marianne Hirsch, "Clytemnestra's Children: Writing (Out) the Mother's Anger", in *Alice Walker: Modern Critical Views*, ed. Harold Bloom (New York: Chelsea House, 1989), 195–213.

31. Teresa de Lauretis, *Technologies of Gender: Feminism, Film and Fiction* (Bloomington: Indiana University Press, 1987), 276–77.

32. M. Jacqui Alexander, "Not Just (Any) Body Can Be a Citizen: The Politics of Law, Sexuality and Postcoloniality in Trinidad and Tobago and the Bahamas", *Feminist Review* 48 (Autumn 1994): 6.

33. Ibid., 22.

34. Michelle Mohabeer, "A Brief Filmic Take on the Erotic as an Act of Defiance and Transformation in 'Two/Doh' and 'Coconut, Cane and Cutlass' " (typescript, n.d.).

35. Espinet, "The Absent Voice".

36. Ramabai Espinet, "Erotic Fragments", in *The Girl Wants To: Women's Representations of Sex and Body*, 2d ed., ed. Lynn Crosbie (Toronto: Wolsak Wynn, 1997), 45–48; text references are to this edition.

37. Marjorie Agosin, preface to *Pleasure in the Word: Erotic Writings by Latin American Women*, ed. Margarite Fernández Olmos and Lizabeth Paravisini-Gebert (New York: White Pine, 1993), 15.

38. Lorde, *Sister Outsider*, 53.

39. Ibid., 47.

40. *La mala palabra* means "a language of dirty words" and is a term coined by Luisa Valenzuela, "Dirty Words", in *Pleasure in the Word: Erotic Writings by Latin American Women*, ed. Margarite Fernandez Olmos and Lizabeth Paravisini-Gebert; trans. Cynthia Ventura (New York: White Pines Press, 1993), 127.

41. Lorde, *Sister Outsider*, 1–2.

42. Lelawattee Manoo-Rahming, "Callaloo Woman", in *Curry Flavour* (Leeds, UK: Peepal Tree, 2000), 78; text references are to this edition.

43. Mohabeer, "A Brief Filmic Take on the Erotic", 1.

Conclusion

1. Felix Mnthali, "The Stranglehold of English Literature", in *Penguin Book of Modern African Poetry*, ed. Gerald Moore and Ulli Beier (New York: Penguin Books, 1984), 139–40.

Bibliography

Agosin, Marjorie. Preface. *Pleasure in the Word: Erotic Writings by Latin American Women*, edited by Margarite Fernández Olmos and Lizabeth Paravisini-Gebert, 15–16. New York: White Pine, 1993.

Alexander, M. Jacqui. "Not Just (Any) Body Can Be a Citizen: The Politics of Law, Sexuality and Postcoloniality in Trinidad and Tobago and the Bahamas". *Feminist Review* 48 (Autumn 1994): 5–23.

———. "Redrafting Morality: The Postcolonial State and the Sexual Offences Bills of Trinidad and Tobago". In *Third World Women and the Politics of Feminism*, edited by Chandra Talpade Mohanty, Ann Russo, and Lourdes Torres, 133–52. Bloomington: Indiana University Press, 1991.

Alexander, Meena. *Fault Lines: A Memoir.* New York: Feminist Press, 1993.

Andaiye. "The Red Thread Story: Resisting the Narrow Interests of a Broader Political Struggle". In *Spitting in the Wind: Lessons in Empowerment from the Caribbean*, edited by Suzanne Francis Brown, 53–98. Kingston: Ian Randle, 2000.

Anderson, Benedict. *Imagined Communities: Reflections on the Origin and Spread of Nationalism.* New York: Verso, 1983.

Anim-Adoo, Joan. "Audacity and Outcome: Writing African-Caribbean Womanhood". In *Framing the Word: Gender and Genre in Caribbean Women's Writing*, edited by Joan Anim-Adoo, 210–24. London: Whiting and Birch, 1996.

Anzaldua, Gloria. *Borderlands/La Frontera: The New Mestiza.* San Francisco: Aunt Lute Books, 1987.

Badran, Margot, and Miriam Cooke, eds. *Opening the Gates: A Century of Arab Feminist Writing.* Bloomington: Indiana University Press, 1991.

Baker, Houston. *Workings of the Spirit: The Poetics of Afro-American Women's Writing.* Chicago: University of Chicago Press, 1991.

Bakhtin, Mikhail. *The Dialogic Imagination: Four Essays.* Translated by Caryl Emerson and Michael Holquist. Austin: University of Texas Press, 1981.

Baksh-Sooden, Rawwida. "Issues of Difference in Contemporary Caribbean Feminism". *Feminist Review* 59 (Summer 1998): 77–85.

———. "Personal Grapplings with Race/Ethnicity, Class and Gender in the Caribbean". Paper presented at the CAFRA panel on Caribbean Feminism: Past, Present and Future, NGO Forum, Fourth World Conference on Women, Huairou, China, September 1995.

————. "Power, Gender and Chutney". In Kanhai, *Matikor*, 194–98.

Balutansky, Kathleen M., and Marie-Agnès Sourieau, eds. *Caribbean Creolization: Reflections on the Cultural Dynamics of Language, Literature and Identity*. Gainesville: University Press of Florida; Kingston: University of the West Indies Press, 1998.

Banerjee, Haimanti. "Portrayal of Women in Popular Hindi Cinema". In Sangari and Vaid, *Women and Culture*, 129–45.

Barrow, Christine, ed. *Caribbean Portraits: Essays on Gender Ideologies and Identities*. Kingston: Ian Randle, 1998.

Barry, Kathleen. *Female Sexual Slavery*. Englewood Cliffs, NJ: Prentice-Hall, 1979.

Bassier, Dennis. "Kali Mai Worship in Guyana: A Quest for a New Identity". In *Indians in the Caribbean*, edited by Bahadur Singh, 269–93. New Delhi: Sterling, 1987.

Benjamin, Joel, Ian McDonald, Lakshmi Kallicharan and Lloyd Searwar, eds. *They Came in Ships: An Anthology of Indo-Guyanese Prose and Poetry*. Leeds, UK: Peepal Tree; Georgetown, Guyana: Indian Commemoration Trust, 1998.

Berger, John. *Ways of Seeing*. Harmondsworth, UK: Penguin, 1972.

Bhabha, Homi. *The Location of Culture*. London: Routledge, 1994.

————. "The World and the Home". *Social Text* 10 (1992): 145–53.

Birbalsingh, Frank, ed. *From Pillar to Post: The Indo-Caribbean Diaspora*. Toronto: TSAR, 1997.

Boehmer, Elleke. "Stories of Women and Mothers: Gender and Nationalism in the Early Fiction of Flora Nwapa". In *Motherlands: Black Women's Writing from Africa, the Caribbean and South Asia*, edited by Susheila Nasta, 3–23. Piscataway, NJ: Rutgers University Press, 1992.

Boyce Davies, Carole. *Black Women, Writing and Identity: Migrations of the Subject*. London: Routledge, 1994.

Brathwaite, Edward. *The Development of Creole Society in Jamaica 1770–1820*. Oxford: Clarendon, 1971.

Brereton, Bridget. "General Problems and Issues in Studying the History of Women". In *Gender in Caribbean Development: Papers Presented at the Inaugural Seminar of the University of the West Indies Women and Development Studies Project*, edited by Patricia Mohammed and Catherine Shepherd, 123–41. St Augustine, Trinidad and Tobago: Women and Development Studies Project, University of the West Indies, 1988.

————. *Race Relations in Colonial Trinidad 1870–1900*. Cambridge: Cambridge University Press, 1979.

Brown, Linda, and Kay Mussell. *Ethnic and Regional Foodways in the United States: The Performance of Group Identity*. Knoxville: University of Tennessee Press, 1984.

Carew, Jan. *Fulcrums of Change: Origins of Racism in the Americas and Other Essays*. Trenton, NJ: Africa World Press, 1988.

Chakravarti, Uma. "The Development of the Sita Myth: A Case Study of Women in Myth and Literature". In Sangari and Vaid, *Women and Culture*, 35–45.

———. "Whatever Happened to the Vedic Dasi? Orientalism, Nationalism, and a Script for the Past". In Sangari and Vaid, *Recasting Women*, 27–87.

Chamberlain, Mary. "Gender and Memory: Oral History and Women's History". In *Engendering History: Caribbean Women in Historical Perspective*, edited by Verene Shepherd, Bridget Brereton, and Barbara Bailey, 94–110. New York: St Martin's, 1995.

Chancy, Myriam. *Searching for Safe Spaces: Afro-Caribbean Women Writers in Exile*. Philadelphia: Temple University Press, 1997.

Chatterjee, Partha. *The Nation and Its Fragments: Colonial and Postcolonial Histories*. Princeton, NJ: Princeton University Press, 1993.

Chesler, Phyllis. *Women and Madness*. New York: Doubleday, 1972.

Cixous, Hélène. *La Jeune Née*. Paris: UGE, 1975.

Cliff, Michelle. "Caliban's Daughter: The Tempest and the Teapot". *Frontiers* 12, no. 2 (1991): 36–52.

Cobham, Rhonda. "Revisioning Our Kumblas: Transformation of Feminist and Nationalist Agendas in Three Caribbean Women's Texts". *Callaloo* 16, no. 1 (1993): 44–64.

Collins, Merle. "Writing Fiction, Writing Reality". In *Caribbean Women Writers: Fiction in English*, edited Mary Condé and Thorunn Lonsdale, 23–31. New York: St Martin's, 1999.

Confiant, Raphaël, and Ernest Pépin. "The Stakes of Créolité". In Balutansky and Sourieau, *Caribbean Creolization*, 96–100.

Cooper, Carolyn. "Something Ancestral Recaptured: Spirit Possession as Trope in Selected Feminist Fictions of the African Diaspora". In *Motherlands: Black Women's Writing from Africa, the Caribbean and South Asia*, edited by Susheila Nasta, 64–87. London: Women's Press, 1991.

Cornwall, Grant, and Eve Stoddard. "Cosmopolitan or Mongrel? Reading Créolité and Hybridity via 'Douglarization' in Trinidad". In Premdas, *Identity, Ethnicity and Culture in the Caribbean*, 211–40.

Dabydeen, David, and Brinsley Samaroo, eds. *India in the Caribbean*. London: Hansib, 1989.

Das, Mahadai. *Bones*. Leeds, UK: Peepal Tree, 1988.

———. "They Came in Ships". In Dabydeen and Samaroo, *India in the Caribbean*, 288–90.

Dash, J. Michael. Introduction. In Glissant, *Caribbean Discourse*, xi–xlvii.

de Lauretis, Teresa. *Technologies of Gender: Feminism, Film and Fiction*. Bloomington: Indiana University Press, 1987.

Divakaruni, Chitra Banerjee. *The Mistress of Spices*. New York: Anchor, 1997.

Duncker, Paula. *Sisters and Strangers: An Introduction to Contemporary Feminist Fiction.*
    Oxford: Blackwell, 1992.

Espinet, Ramabai. "The Absent Voice: Unearthing the Female Epistemology of
    CANE". Paper presented at the conference Sugarcane and Society, Toronto,
    July 1989.

———. "Barred: Trinidad 1987". In Esteves and Paravisini-Gebert, *Green Cane and
    Juicy Flotsam,* 80–85.

———, ed., *Creation Fire: A CAFRA Anthology of Caribbean Women's Poetry.* Toronto:
    Sister Vision; Tunapuna, Trinidad and Tobago: CAFRA, 1990.

———. "Erotic Fragments". In *The Girl Wants To: Women's Representations of Sex and
    Body,* 2d ed., edited by Lynn Crosbie, 45–48. Toronto: Wolsak Wynn,
    1997.

———. "Indian Cuisine". *Massachusetts Review* (Autumn–Winter 1994): 563–73.

———. "The Invisible Woman in West Indian Fiction". *World Literature Written in
    English* 29, no. 2 (1989): 116–26.

———. *Nuclear Seasons.* Toronto: Sister Vision, 1991.

———. "Representation and the Indo-Caribbean Woman in Trinidad and
    Tobago". In *Indo-Caribbean Resistance,* edited by Frank Birbalsingh, 42–61.
    Toronto: TSAR, 1993.

———. "Singing *Ramayana:* The Text of Sita's Fidelity". Paper presented at the
    Sixth International Conference of Caribbean Women Writers and Scholars,
    Grenada, May 1998.

Esteves, Carmen, and Lizabeth Paravisini-Gebert, eds. *Green Cane and Juicy Flotsam.*
    New Brunswick, NJ: Rutgers University Press, 1991.

Fanon, Frantz. *Black Skin, White Masks.* Translated by Charles Lam Markmann.
    New York: Grove, 1967.

———. *The Wretched of the Earth.* Translated by Constance Farrington. New York:
    Grove, 1963.

Felman, Shoshana. "Women and Madness: The Critical Phallacy". *Diacritics* 5
    (1975): 2–10.

Gafoor, Ameena. "The Depiction of Indo-Caribbean Female Experience by the
    Regional Woman Writer: Jan Shinebourne's *The Last English Plantation*". In *The
    Woman, the Writer and Caribbean Society: Critical Analyses of the Writings of Caribbean
    Women: Proceedings of the Second International Conference,* edited by Helen Pyne-
    Timothy, 128–39. Los Angeles: UCLA Center for African-American Studies,
    1998.

Ganguly, Keya. "Migrant Identities: Personal Memories and the Construction of
    Selfhood". *Cultural Studies* 6 (1992): 27–50.

Ghaussy, Soheila. "A Stepmother Tongue: Feminine Writing in Assia Dejbar's
    Fantasia: An Algerian Cavalcade". *World Literature Today* 68 (1994): 457–62.

Gikandi, Simon. "The Politics and Poetics of National Formation: Recent African Writing". Paper presented at the annual conference of the Association for Commonwealth Literature and Language Studies, Canterbury, UK, August 1989.

————. *Writing in Limbo: Modernism and Caribbean Literature.* Ithaca, NY: Cornell University Press, 1992.

Glissant, Edouard. *Caribbean Discourse: Selected Essays.* Translated by J. Michael Dash. Charlottesville: University Press of Virginia, 1989.

Goldman, Anne. "I Yam What I Yam: Cooking, Culture and Colonialism". In *De/Colonizing the Subject: The Politics of Gender in Women and Autobiography,* edited by Sidonie Smith and Julia Watson, 169–95. Minneapolis: University of Minnesota Press, 1992.

Gregg, Veronica. "The Caribbean as a Certain Kind of Woman". Typescript. N.d.

Grewal, Inderpal. *Home and Harem: Nation, Gender, Empire, and the Cultures of Travel.* Durham, NC: Duke University Press, 1996.

Haniff, Nesha. "My Grandmother Worked in the Field: Honorable Mention: Stereotypes Regarding Indian Women in the Caribbean". In Kanhai, *Matikor,* 18–31.

Haraksingh, Kusha. "Structure, Process and Indian Culture in Trinidad". In *After the Crossing: Immigrants and Minorities in Caribbean Creole Society,* edited by Howard Johnson, 113–22. London: Frank Cass, 1988.

Harney, Stefano. *Nationalism and Identity: Culture and the Imagination in a Caribbean Diaspora.* London: Zed Books, 1996.

Harris, Virginia, and Trinity Ordona. "Developing Unity among Women of Color: Crossing the Barriers of Internalized Racism and Cross-Racial Hostility". In *Making Face, Making Soul: Creative and Critical Perspectives by Women of Color,* edited by Gloria Anzaldua, 304–16. San Francisco: Aunt Lute Books, 1990.

Harris, Wilson. *Tradition, the Writer and Society: Critical Essays.* London: New Beacon, 1973.

————. *The Womb of Space: The Cross-Cultural Imagination.* Westport, Conn.: Greenwood, 1983.

Hirsch, Marianne. "Clytemnestra's Children: Writing (Out) the Mother's Anger". In *Alice Walker: Modern Critical Views,* edited by Harold Bloom, 195–213. New York: Chelsea House, 1989.

Hodge, Merle. *For the Life of Laetitia.* New York: Farrar, Straus and Giroux, 1993.

Holmström, Lakshmi, ed. *The Inner Courtyard: Stories by Indian Women.* London: Virago, 1990.

hooks, bell. *Teaching to Transgress: Education as the Practice of Freedom.* New York: Routledge, 1994.

Ibrahim, Huma. *Bessie Head: Subversive Identities in Exile.* Charlottesville: University Press of Virginia, 1996.

James, C. L. R. *The Artist in the Caribbean*. Mona, Jamaica: Open Lecture Series, University of the West Indies, 1965.

James, Stanlie. "Mothering: A Possible Black Feminist Link to Social Transformation". In *Theorizing Black Feminisms*, edited by Stanlie James and Abena Busia, 144–54. New York: Routledge, 1993.

Johnson, Kim. "Considerations on Indian Sexuality". Paper presented at the Third Conference on East Indians, St Augustine, Trinidad, August–September 1984.

Juneja, Renu. *Caribbean Transactions: West Indian Culture in Literature*. London: Macmillan, 1996.

Kanhai, Rosanne. "From Matikor to a Caribbean Dougla Feminism". Lecture given at the Centre for Gender and Development Studies, University of the West Indies, St Augustine, Trinidad, February 1999.

———. "The Masala Stone Sings: Poetry, Performance and Film by Indo-Caribbean Women". In Kanhai, *Matikor*, 209–37.

———, ed. *Matikor: The Politics of Identity for Indo-Caribbean Women*. St Augustine, Trinidad and Tobago: University of the West Indies, School of Continuing Studies, 1999.

Kanhai-Brunton, Rosanne. "The Guyana Meeting". *CAFRA News* 7, no. 4 (1993): 1.

Kempadoo, Kamala. "Negotiating Cultures: A 'Dogla' Perspective". In Kanhai, *Matikor*, 103–13.

Khan, Aisha. "Juthaa in Trinidad: Food, Pollution, and Hierarchy in a Caribbean Diaspora Community". *American Ethnologist* 21 (1994): 245–69.

Kinsley, David. *The Goddesses' Mirror*. Albany: State University of New York Press, 1987.

Lahens, Yannick. Afterword. *Caribbean Creolization*, edited by Balutansky and Sourieau, 155–64.

Lee, Valerie. *Granny Midwives and Black Women Writers: Double-Dutched Readings*. New York: Routledge, 1996.

Lévi-Strauss, Claude. "The Culinary Triangle". *Partisan Review* 33 (1966): 586–95.

Lionnet, Françoise. "Inscriptions of Exile: The Body's Knowledge and the Myth of Authenticity". Translated by Joseph Heath. *Callaloo* 15, no. 1 (1992): 30–40.

Lorde, Audre. *Sister Outsider*. Trumansburg, NY: The Crossing Press, 1984.

Mackie, Christine. *Life and Food in the Caribbean*. New York: New Amsterdam Books, 1991.

Manoo-Rahming, Lelawattee. *Curry Flavour*. Leeds, UK: Peepal Tree, 2000.

Marshall, Paule. *Reena and Other Stories*. New York: Feminist Press, 1983.

Memmi, Albert. *The Colonizer and the Colonized*. New York: Orion, 1965.

Mennell, Stephen, Anne Murcott and Anneke Otterloo, eds. *The Sociology of Food: Eating, Diet and Culture*. London: Sage, 1992.

Minh-ha, Trinh T. *When the Moon Waxes Red*. New York: Routledge, 1991.

———. *Woman, Native, Other: Writing Postcoloniality and Feminism.* Bloomington: Indiana University Press, 1989.

Mnthali, Felix. "The Stranglehold of English Literature". In *Penguin Book of Modern African Poetry*, edited by Gerald Moore and Ulli Beier, 139–40. New York: Penguin Books, 1984.

Mohabeer, Michelle. "A Brief Filmic Take on the Erotic as an Act of Defiance and Transformation in 'Two/Doh' and 'Coconut, Cane and Cutlass' ". Typescript. N.d.

———. "Dialogue with a Film Director: Framing Caribbeanness through a Self-Reflexive Look at Art, Cultural Identity, Diaspora and the Creative Process in the Films *Coconut/Cane and Cutlass* and *Child-Play*". Paper presented at the Sixth International Conference of Caribbean Women Writers and Scholars, Grand-Anse, Grenada, May 1998.

Mohammed, Patricia. "The Creolization of Indian Women in Trinidad". In *Trinidad and Tobago: The Independence Experience 1962–1982*, edited by Selwyn Ryan, 381–413. St Augustine, Trinidad and Tobago: Institute of Social and Economic Research, University of the West Indies, 1988.

———. "Towards Indigenous Feminist Theorizing in the Caribbean". *Feminist Review* 59 (Summer 1998): 6–33.

Mohanty, Chandra. *Feminism without Borders: Decolonizing Theory, Practicing Solidarity.* Durham, NC: Duke University Press, 2003.

Mohanty, Chandra, and Satya Mohanty. "Lives of Their Own". In *The Slate of Life: Contemporary Short Stories by Indian Women Writers*, edited by Kali for Women, 1–25. New York: Feminist Press, 1994.

Mootoo, Shani. *Cereus Blooms at Night.* New York: Grove, 1996.

———. *Out on Main Street and Other Stories.* Vancouver: Press Gang, 1993.

Morgan, Paula. "East/West/Indian/Woman/Other: At the Crossroads of Gender and Ethnicity". Paper presented at the Sixteenth Annual Conference on West Indian Literature, University of Miami, April 1997.

Mukherjee, Arun. "Canadian Nationalism, Canadian Literature and Racial Minority Women". In Silvera, *The Other Woman*, 421–44.

Naipaul, V. S. *The Enigma of Arrival.* New York: Random House, 1987.

———. *Finding the Center: Two Narratives.* New York: Random House, 1986.

———. *A House for Mr Biswas.* London: Fontana, 1961.

———. *The Mimic Men.* London: Penguin, 1967.

———. *The Overcrowded Barracoon.* New York: Vintage, 1983.

Narayan, Uma. "Eating Cultures: Incorporation, Identity and Indian Food". *Social Identities* 1 (1995): 63–82.

Nixon, Rob. "London Calling: V. S. Naipaul and the License of Exile". *South Atlantic Quarterly* 87 (Winter 1988): 1–37.

Norman, Dorothy, ed. *Nehru: The First Sixty Years*. Vol. 1. London: Bodley Head, 1965.

O'Callaghan, Evelyn. " 'Compulsory Heterosexuality' and Textual/Sexual Alternatives in Selected Texts by West Indian Women Writers". In Barrow, *Caribbean Portraits*, 294–319.

————. *Woman Version: Theoretical Approaches to West Indian Fiction by Women*. New York: St Martin's, 1993.

Parmasad, Kenneth. *Salt and Roti: Indian Folk Tales of the Caribbean: A First Collection*. Charlieville, Trinidad and Tobago: Sankh Productions, 1984.

Pépin, Ernest. "La femme antillaise et son corps". *Présence Africaine* 14, no. 1 (1987): 181–93.

Persaud, Lakshmi. *Butterfly in the Wind*. Leeds, UK: Peepal Tree, 1990.

————. *Sastra*. Leeds, UK: Peepal Tree, 1993.

Poynting, Jeremy. "East Indian Women in the Caribbean: Experience and Voice". In Dabydeen and Samaroo, *India in the Caribbean*, 231–63.

————. "You Want to Be a Coolie Woman? Gender and Ethnic Identity in Indo-Caribbean Women's Writing". In *Caribbean Women Writers*, edited by Selwyn Cudjoe, 98–105. Wellesley, Mass.: Calaloux Publications, 1990.

Premdas, Ralph. "Ethnic Identity in the Caribbean: Decentring a Myth". Keynote address to the Association for the Study of Ethnicity and Nationalism, London School of Economics and Political Science, March 1995.

————, ed. *Identity, Ethnicity and Culture in the Caribbean*. St Augustine, Trinidad and Tobago: University of the West Indies, School of Continuing Studies, 1999.

Pulsipher, Lydia. "Changing Roles in the Life Cycles of Women in Traditional West Indian Households". In *Women and Change in the Caribbean*, edited by Janet Momsen, 50–63. Bloomington: Indiana University Press, 1993.

Puri, Shalini. "Canonized Hybridities, Resistant Hybridities: Chutney Soca, Carnival, and the Politics of Nationalism". In *Caribbean Romances: The Politics of Regional Representation*, edited by Belinda Edmonson, 12–38. Charlottesville: University Press of Virginia, 1999.

————. "Race, Rape and Representation: Indo-Caribbean Women and Cultural Nationalism". *Cultural Critique* 36 (May 1997): 119–63. Reprinted in Kanhai, *Matikor*, 238–82.

Pyne-Timothy, Helen. "Language as Subversion in Postcolonial Literature: The Case of Two Caribbean Women Writers". *Macomère* 1 (1998): 101–14.

Radhakrishnan, R. *Diasporic Mediations: Between Home and Location*. Minneapolis: University of Minnesota Press, 1996.

Rajack-Talley, Theresa Ann. "Burying the Myth: Indian Women in the Sugar Cane Industry in Trinidad". In Kanhai, *Matikor*, 181–93.

Ramkissoon-Chen, Rajandaye. *Ancestry*. London: Hansib Caribbean, 1997.

Rampersad, Indrani. "Becoming a Pandita". In Kanhai, *Matikor*, 140–43.

Raychaudhuri, Tapan. *Europe Reconsidered: Perceptions of the West in Nineteenth Century Bengal.* New Delhi: Oxford University Press, 1988.

Reddock, Rhoda. "Contestations over National Culture in Trinidad and Tobago: Considerations of Ethnicity, Class and Gender". In *Caribbean Portraits,* 414–35.

———. *Elma François: The NWCSA and the Worker's Struggle for Change in the Caribbean.* London: New Beacon, 1988.

———. "Indian Women and Indentureship in Trinidad and Tobago: 1845–1917". *Economic and Political Weekly* 20 (1985): 80–84.

———. "Jahaji Bhai: The Emergence of a Dougla Poetics in Contemporary Trinidad and Tobago". In Premdas, *Identity, Ethnicity and Culture in the Caribbean,* 185–210.

———. *Women, Labour and Politics in Trinidad and Tobago: A History.* London: Zed Books, 1994.

———. "Women, Labour and Struggle in Twentieth Century Trinidad and Tobago". PhD dissertation, University of Amsterdam, 1984.

Rich, Adrienne. "Compulsory Heterosexuality and Lesbian Existence". In *The Lesbian and Gay Studies Reader,* edited by Henry Abelove, Michèle Aina Barale and David M. Halperin, 227–54. New York: Routledge, 1993.

Roy, Anindyo. "Postcoloniality and the Politics of Identity in the Diaspora: Figuring 'Home', Locating Histories". In *Postcolonial Discourse and Changing Cultural Contexts,* edited by Gita Rajan and Radhika Mohanram, 101–15. Westport, Conn.: Greenwood, 1995.

Rushdie, Salman. *Imaginary Homelands.* Harmondsworth, UK: Penguin, 1992.

Saïd, Edward. *Orientalism.* London: Routledge and Kegan Paul, 1978.

———. "Reflections on Exile". In *Out There: Marginalization and Contemporary Cultures,* edited by Russell Ferguson, Martha Gever, Trinh T. Minh-ha and Cornel West, 357–66. Cambridge, Mass.: MIT Press, 1990.

———. *Representations of the Intellectual.* New York: Vintage, 1996.

———. *The World, the Text and the Critic.* London: Faber, 1984.

Sangari, Kumkum, and Sudesh Vaid, eds. *Recasting Women: Essays in Indian Colonial History.* Piscataway, NJ: Rutgers University Press, 1990.

———, eds. *Women and Culture.* Bombay: SNDT, 1994.

Savory, Elaine. "Ramabai Espinet Talks to Elaine Savory: A Sense of Constant Dialogue: Writing, Woman and Indo-Caribbean Culture". In Silvera, *The Other Woman,* 94–115.

Scarry, Elaine. *The Body in Pain: The Making and Unmaking of the World.* New York: Oxford University Press, 1985.

Schwarz-Bart, Simone. *The Bridge of Beyond.* Translated by Barbara Bray. New York: Atheneum, 1974.

Seecharan, Clem. *India and the Shaping of the Indo-Guyanese Imagination 1890s–1920s.* Leeds, UK: Peepal Tree, 1993.

Selvon, Samuel. "Three into One Can't Go: East Indian, Trinidadian, West Indian". In Dabydeen and Samaroo, *India in the Caribbean*, 13–24.

Sharma, Kavita. "Ginu Kamani's *Junglee Girl*". *India Star: A Literary Art Magazine* (1997): 1–9.

Sharma, Ramashraya. "The Ramakatha from Valmiki to Tulsidasa with Special Reference to Women". In Sangari and Vaid, *Women and Culture*, 45–99.

Shelton, Marie-Denise. "Condé: The Politics of Gender and Identity". *World Literature Today* 67, no. 4 (1993): 717–22.

Sheth, Anita, and Amita Handa. "A Jewel in the Frown: Striking Accord between India/n Feminists". In *Returning the Gaze: Essays on Racism, Feminism and Politics*, edited by Himani Banerjee, 45–99. Toronto: Sister Vision, 1993.

Shewcharan, Narmala. *Tomorrow Is Another Day.* Leeds, UK: Peepal Tree, 1994.

Shinebourne, Jan. *The Last English Plantation.* Leeds, UK: Peepal Tree, 1988.

Silvera, Makeda, ed. *The Other Woman: Women of Colour in Canadian Literature.* Toronto: Sister Vision, 1993.

Singer, Eliot. "Conversion through Foodways Enculturation: The Meaning of Eating in an American Hindu Sect". In Brown and Mussell, *Ethnic and Regional Foodways in the United States*, 195–214.

Singh, Kelvin. "East Indians and the Larger Society". In *Calcutta to Caroni: The East Indians of Trinidad*, edited by John La Guerre, 39–68. London: Longman, 1974.

Singh, Rajkumari. "I Am a Coolie". In Benjamin, McDonald, Kallicharan and Searwar, *They Came in Ships*, 85–87.

———. "Per-Ajie: A Tribute to the First Immigrant Women". In Benjamin, McDonald, Kallicharan and Searwar, *They Came in Ships*, 189–91.

Spillers, Hortense. "Mama's Baby, Papa's Maybe: An American Grammar Book". *Diacritics* 17 (Summer 1987): 65–81.

Spivak, Gayatri. "Can the Subaltern Speak?" In *Marxism and Interpretation of Culture*, edited by Cary Nelson and Lawrence Grossberg, 271–313. Urbana: University of Illinois Press, 1988.

Steady, Filomena. *The Black Woman Culturally.* Cambridge, Mass.: Schenkman, 1982.

Stephens, Patricia. *The Spiritual Baptist Faith.* Trenton, NJ: Red Sea Press, 1999.

Tharu, Susie. "Tracing Savitri's Pedigree: Victorian Racism and the Image of Women in Indo-Anglian Literature". In Sangari and Vaid, *Recasting Women*, 254–68.

Torabully, Khal. "Coolitude: Prémisses historiques d'une non-parole". *Notre Librairie* 128 (October–December 1996): 59–71.

Valenzuela, Luisa. "Dirty Words". In *Pleasure in the Word: Erotic Writings by Latin American Women*, edited by Margarite Fernandez Olmos and Lizabeth Paravisini-

Gebert; translated by Cynthia Ventura, 126–29. New York: White Pines Press, 1993.

Vishwanathan, Gauri. *Masks of Conquest: Literary Study and British Rule in India.* New York: Columbia University Press, 1989.

Walcott, Derek. *Dream on Monkey Mountain and Other Plays.* New York: Farrar, Straus and Giroux, 1970.

Walker, Alice. *In Search of Our Mothers' Gardens.* New York: Harcourt Brace Jovanovich, 1983.

Wilentz, Gay. *Binding Cultures: Black Women Writers in Africa and the Diaspora.* Bloomington: Indiana University Press, 1992.

Wilson, Betty. "History and Memory in *Un Plat de porc aux bananes vertes* and *Pluie et vent sur Télumée Miracle*". *Callaloo* 15, no. 1 (1992): 179–89.

Wittig, Monique. "The Straight Mind". *Feminist Issues* 1, no. 1 (Summer 1980): 103–10.

Young, Robert. *Colonial Desire: Hybridity in Theory, Culture and Race.* London: Routledge, 1995.

Index